The Asylum as Utopia

What Asylums Were, Are, and Ought to Be, first published in 1837, was of considerable significance in the history of lunacy reform in Britain. It contains perhaps the single most influential portrait by a medical author of the horrors of the traditional madhouse system. Its powerful and ideologically resonant description of the contrasting virtues of the reformed asylum, a hive of therapeutic activity under the benevolent but autocratic guidance and control of its medical superintendent, provided within a brief compass a strikingly attractive alternative vision of an apparently attainable utopia. Browne's book thus provided important impetus to the efforts then under way to make the provision of county asylums compulsory, and towards the institution of a national system of asylum inspection and supervision.

This edition, originally published in 1991 as part of the *Tavistock Classics in the History of Psychiatry* series, contains a lengthy introductory essay by Andrew Scull. Scull discusses the social context within which *What Asylums Were, Are, and Ought to Be* came to be written, examines the impact of the book on the progress of lunacy reform, and places its author's career in the larger framework of the development of Victorian psychiatry as an organised profession. Through an examination of Browne's tenure as superintendent of the Crichton Royal Asylum in Dumfries, Scull compares the theory and practice of asylum care in the moral treatment era, revealing the remorseless processes through which such philanthropic foundations degenerated into more or less well-tended cemeteries for the still-breathing – institutions almost startlingly remote from Browne's earlier visions of what they ought to be.

The Asylum as Utopia

W.A.F. Browne and the mid-nineteenth century consolidation of psychiatry

Edited with an introduction by
Andrew Scull

Routledge
Taylor & Francis Group
LONDON AND NEW YORK

First published in 1991
by Routledge

This edition first published in 2014 by Routledge
27 Church Road, Hove, BN3 2FA

Simultaneously published in the USA and Canada
by Routledge
711 Third Avenue, New York, NY 10017

Routledge is an imprint of the Taylor & Francis Group, an informa business

Publisher's Note
The publisher has gone to great lengths to ensure the quality of this reprint but
points out that some imperfections in the original copies may be apparent.

Disclaimer
The publisher has made every effort to trace copyright holders and welcomes
correspondence from those they have been unable to contact.

A Library of Congress record exists under ISBN: 0415017262

ISBN: 978-0-415-73060-0 (hbk)
ISBN: 978-1-315-85012-2 (ebk)
ISBN: 978-0-415-73063-1 (pbk)

THE ASYLUM
AS UTOPIA

W. A. F. Browne and the Mid-Nineteenth
Century Consolidation of Psychiatry

Edited with an Introduction by
Andrew Scull

TAVISTOCK/ROUTLEDGE
London and New York

First published in 1991
by Routledge
11 New Fetter Lane, London EC4P 4EE

Simultaneously published in the USA and Canada
by Routledge
a division of Routledge, Chapman and Hall Inc.
29 West 35th Street, New York, NY 10001

Printed in Great Britain by Antony Rowe Ltd

British Library Cataloguing in Publication Data

Browne, William Alexander Francis
[What asylums were, are, and ought to be] The Asylum as
Utopia: W. A. F. Browne and the mid-nineteenth century
consolidation of psychiatry. – (Tavistock classics
in the history of psychiatry)
1. Great Britain. Psychiatric hospitals
[What asylums were, are, and ought to be] I. Title II.
Scull, Andrew *1947*– III. Series
362.210941

Library of Congress Cataloging in Publication Data

Browne, W. A. F. (William Alexander Francis), 1806–1885.
[What asylums were, are, and ought to be]
The asylum as Utopia: W. A. F. Browne and the mid-nineteenth
century consolidation of psychiatry / edited by Andrew Scull.
p.   cm. — (Tavistock classics in the history of psychiatry)
Reprint. Originally published: What asylums were, are, and ought
to be. Edinburgh: A. & C. Black, 1837.
Includes bibliographical references.
1. Psychiatric hospitals. 2. Psychiatry—Early works to 1900.
I. Scull, Andrew T. II. Title. III. Series.
RC439.B88   1991   90–8448
362.2'1—dc20   CIP

ISBN 0–415–01726–2

CONTENTS

v

INTRODUCTION

Andrew Scull

The education of an alienist

The public reception of *What Asylums Were, Are, and Ought to Be*, and the extraordinarily successful career of its author, a previously obscure if ambitious provincial surgeon and mad-doctor, are intimately bound up with the progress of the nineteenth century lunacy reform movement and consolidation of the newly emerging profession of alienism in Scotland and England. Book and author made notable contributions to both these developments, and the importance of the text which follows can only be understood when it is placed in this larger context.[1] For Browne's literary style, as critics at the time noted, is sentimental, overblown, and bombastic[2] even by the standards of Victorian philanthropists; and his clinical observations and therapeutic suggestions, as he himself concedes, have 'no claim to originality', being 'as scrupulously as was practicable collected and collated from the writings and opinions of others'.[3]

Between the publication of his first and only book in 1837, and his retirement as the first Scottish Lunacy Commissioner in 1870, William Alexander Francis Browne occupied a position among Scottish alienists that was every bit as dominant as that of his English counterpart, John Conolly,[4] and the parallels between the two men's lives and careers present some intriguing points of comparison. In the middle years of the nineteenth century, Browne's reputation extended south of the border, to the Continent, and even to North America, and derived principally, though not exclusively, from the text reprinted here – a course of lectures he delivered when only thirty-two years of age to the managers of the obscure provincial asylum at Montrose. Much of Conolly's fame and influence may be traced to his successful adoption of Robert Gardiner Hill's policy of running an asylum without any resort to what was termed 'mechanical restraint' – straight-jackets, muffs, and the like – an innovation for which he managed to appropriate almost all the credit and to make the ruling orthodoxy of British asylumdom. More broadly, however, Conolly's stature derived from his role as the foremost English spokesman on behalf of the new system of reformed asylums and the most eloquent and effective exponent of the expropriation of the new system of moral treatment by medical men.[5] It is his contributions in precisely these directions that account for Browne's prominence among Scottish alienists, and for the extension of his fame and influence beyond his native land.

We should not be surprised by this state of affairs. Notwithstanding the long history of medical speculations about the causes and cure of insanity, and the involvement of some segments of the medical profession in the eighteenth century 'trade in lunacy',[6] it was only in the first half of the nineteenth century, concomitant with the emergence of state regulation of the mad business and the rise of a publicly funded asylum system, that medicine sought a cognitive and practical monopoly of the treatment of insanity. In this project, the reformed asylum, its image distanced as far as possible from the stereotyped portrait of the eighteenth century madhouse, was pictured as the indispensable apparatus for the remanufacture of sanity from madness. Equally important, it constituted the built form whose replication and control would give medical men an unchallengeable physical and institutional foundation on which to erect exclusive and exclusionary claims to jurisdiction over insanity. In parallel fashion, moral treatment, while in its origins a lay discovery that threatened to undermine medical claims to special expertise or competence in the therapeutics of madness,[7] was inescapably linked in the public mind with the new humane system of treatment for insanity, and provided the essential technical means for administering the reformed asylum. Thus, those who most effectively persuaded the public of the virtues of an asylum-based response to madness, and who simultaneously managed to secure the unambiguous assimilation of moral treatment into the medical armamentarium, had richly earned the gratitude of their alienist contemporaries; and quite properly are accorded a central place of honour by those historians who equate the rise of psychiatry with the advance of science and humanity.

The striking similarities in the underlying sources of the prominence achieved by Browne and Conolly in their mature years find a curious echo in the circumstances of their early biographies. Browne was born into a precariously genteel family in Stirling, central Scotland, on June 24, 1805. Within a few weeks of his birth, his father, an army officer en route to join Wellington's troops in fighting the Peninsular War, was drowned when his troop transport was wrecked and sank on the Goodwin Sands. William was thus left to be brought up in his maternal grandparents' house, receiving a meagre education at the local high school and facing uncertain prospects for retaining his middle-class status. Conolly, some eleven years his senior, came from a not dissimilar social background (his father being the younger son of an impecunious minor branch of the Irish gentry), and he, too, was orphaned at a very early age. In Conolly's case, it was his mother's remarriage[8] which led to his being farmed out at the age of five to live with relatives in the provincial backwater of Hedon in the East Riding, where, as he remarked bitterly later in life, he received a 'dull, mechanical' and hopelessly inadequate education at the local grammar school. After dabbling in a military career and finding his prospects in this direction foreclosed by Napoleon's defeat, Conolly's own fecklessness, and his possession of a small inheritance, allowed him to contract an unwise marriage and to spend two years in idleness, before the frittering away of his capital forced him to seek some stable source of income.

For those clinging precariously to gentlemanly status in early nineteenth century Britain, the choice of acceptable careers was remarkably narrow. To engage in 'trade' was to face an irrevocable loss of caste, and of the remaining options, both the Church and the military remained heavily dependent on the possession of quantities of social connections and capital which both Browne and Conolly conspicuously lacked. The 'choice' both made of a career in medicine was thus scarcely a choice at all, though their prospects of making a decent living at their chosen profession were inevitably clouded by the large numbers of middle-class boys who had reached identical conclusions. The remarkable expansion and reconstitution of the traditional professions in the nineteenth century may have comprised, as Magali Larson has argued,[9] an attempt at collective social mobility on the part of an expanding middle class, but the market for professionals' services failed to expand (early in the century, at least), as fast as the supply of eager recruits. The consequence, as Irvine Loudon's meticulous study of general practice has shown,[10] was that the 1820s were an extraordinarily inhospitable period in which to attempt to launch a medical career, a time of unparalleled intraprofessional rivalry in a grossly over-crowded professional marketplace.

Nonetheless, such was the prospect facing Browne and Conolly, both of whom elected to seek their training at Edinburgh University. For the provincial Englishman as for the provincial Scot, this decision must have seemed an equally obvious one. Medical training was then at its nadir at Oxford and Cambridge, the only sources of university credentials south of the border. Besides, a career as a physician to the upper classes, the only prospect for which the desultory classical instruction at Oxbridge might prove suitable, demanded social capital, connections, and advantages neither man possessed. Edinburgh, by contrast, was in a flourishing state, providing unquestionably the finest clinical training in the English-speaking world, even if the snobbery and reactionary politics of the English Royal College of Physicians still largely barred its graduates from the richest rewards open to a medical man, which were confined to elite practice in London.[11]

Conolly's arrival at Edinburgh in 1819 just antedated Browne's. The former proceeded to acquire the MD degree, the prerequisite to practice in the elite branch of the profession as a physician, rather than the surgical licentiate leading to general practice, with which Browne was forced to content himself. In other respects, their student careers were almost carbon copies of one another's: both served a term as President of the Royal Medical Society; and both acquired an interest in insanity that was to prefigure their later specialization. Conolly's MD dissertation of 1821 was devoted to a brief discussion of *De statu mentis in insania et melancholia*; and as Browne boasted some years later, when applying for the vacant superintendency of the Montrose Lunatic Asylum, he too, through-out his undergraduate training and even after his qualification as

LRCSE in 1826, 'made the human mind, both in its healthy and diseased condition, an especial subject of investigation'.[12] Both men also acquired an acquaintance with the doctrines of phrenology – something they could scarcely avoid, given its prominent presence on the Edinburgh intellectual scene;[13] adopted its major tenets;[14] and, in common with most other prominent alienists of their generation,[15] incorporated the new 'science of mind' into their understanding of the roots of insanity.

The two men's embrace of phrenological doctrine, and Browne's subsequent dedication of *What Asylums Were, Are, and Ought to Be* to Andrew Combe MD[16] (with his brother George[17] the most prominent figure in British phrenological circles), may strike the modern reader as somewhat odd. After all, phrenology was for many years 'an approved object of laughter for ... intellectual historians'.[18] One had simply to recall its association with carnival sideshows offering character readings to the credulous and could safely dismiss it as a pseudo-science of the lumps and bumps on the cranium, a doctrine whose proper place in the scheme of things was neatly encapsulated in the name of one of its most successful itinerant practitioners, J. Q. Rumball. Recent historiography, however, has demonstrated the foolishness of such judgements.[19] Phrenology, in Ackerknecht's words, was 'at least as influential in the first half of the nineteenth century as psychoanalysis in the first half of the twentieth'.[20] Gall and Spurzheim's researches into the anatomical structure of the brain were anything but the work of charlatans; and socially, phrenological ideas were of the utmost significance, linked closely to campaigns 'for penal reform, more enlightened treatment of the insane, the provision of scientific education for the working classes, the education of women, the modification of capital punishment laws, and the re-thinking of British colonial policy'.[21]

In the local Edinburgh context, the conversion of Browne and Conolly is still more readily understandable. Among the established Edinburgh cultural elite – the traditional upper estates of law, landed property, and established learning – phrenology was always viewed with hostility and disdain.[22] From the appearance of John Gordon's critical article on phrenology in its July 1815 issue, the *Edinburgh Review* never passed up an opportunity to pour scorn on the science's adherents or to treat its doctrines with contempt, and throughout the 1820s, phrenology remained 'under almost continuous seige from Edinburgh intellectuals'.[23] But the obverse of this fierce rejection in elite circles was an equally passionate attachment to the new science on the part of the bourgeois and petit-bourgeois elements, particularly the commercial and mercantile classes and those ambitious younger professionals with weak or deficient kinship ties or other social linkages to traditional landed interests – precisely the social background from which Browne and Conolly came.[24] Phrenology's association with 'a far-reaching programme of social and cultural reform'[25] and its intellectual challenge to the Scottish Common-Sense philosophy that was the ruling orthodoxy in traditional elite circles, brought it a steady stream of adherents from amongst those 'young middle-class liberals who resented the political, social, and cultural restrictions still imposed upon them by the ancien regime'.[26]

As a medical student, Browne struck up a close personal friendship with both Combes,[27] assisting George with his phrenological studies and soon establishing himself as one of the more popular phrenological lecturers in the city. But in 1828, he left Edinburgh for the Continent, having been entrusted with the care of a well-to-do lunatic who was to be treated through travel and changes of scene. During the two years that followed, as he travelled through Belgium, France, and Italy, Browne 'attentively examined the arrangements and mode of treatment in some of the most celebrated asylums in the different countries through which I passed'.[28] Having been particularly impressed by the Parisian asylums, he returned to Paris during the summer and autumn of 1832, studying under Esquirol at Charenton and Pariset at the Salpêtrière before returning to Stirling in early 1833 to try to establish himself as a general practitioner.

Conolly had moved more directly into general practice in southern England, experiencing failure in both Lewes and Chichester before he secured a modest livelihood in Stratford-on-Avon. He, too, turned his interest in insanity to some modest account, supplementing his income with an appointment as 'inspecting physician to the Lunatic Houses of the County of Warwick', an impressive title that disguised the minor task of accompanying two local magistrates on their annual inspection of the county's half dozen madhouses. Briefly, his Edinburgh connections promised to rescue him from provincial obscurity, when his ties to Lord Brougham and George Birkbeck secured him a position on the medical faculty of the new University College in London, and a platform from which to launch some decidedly heterodox ideas about the deficiencies of asylums as sites for the treatment of mental disturbance.[29] But Conolly's lack of business sense, his inability to build up a private practice, and the fiscal difficulties of the struggling new medical school proved too much for him, and he was soon forced to retreat back to the provinces. Almost a decade was to pass before the expanding English county asylum system offered him a last chance to escape a hand-to-mouth existence principally characterized by debt and despair. His appointment as superintendent of the Middlesex County Asylum at Hanwell and his successful introduction there of Robert Gardiner Hill's strategy of treating the insane wholly without resort to 'mechanical restraint' (manacles, muffs, straightjackets, and the like), brought him fame, greatly improved financial prospects, and the status of one of the founding fathers of English alienism.

Browne had secured his position as one of the first of the newly consolidating group of alienists much more quickly, and with far less trouble. Barely a year after his return to Stirling, the March 22, 1834 issue of the *North British Advertiser* carried a notice of an opening as superintendent of the Royal Lunatic Asylum at Montrose (the oldest charity asylum in Scotland), with what was promised to be 'a liberal salary' attached. Andrew Combe himself was tempted to apply, writing to his brother George that 'I have a hankering after some such charge, as better suited to my present condition of body and mind than general practice, for which I do not feel I have adequate stamina'.[30] The next post, however, brought a letter from Browne, soliciting the support of both brothers for *his* application, at which Andrew 'immediately gave up all idea of himself applying for the situation, and cordially supported the pretensions of his young friend' (support that proved weighty because of the Combes' high 'standing with the Sheriff and some of the resident gentry of Forfarshire').[31]

As Browne and Conolly's biographies remind us, in the early part of the nineteenth century, recruitment into the ranks of asylum superintendents was largely – and necessarily – an unstructured process. Even among the medical men entering the field, few could claim to have had any formal training or practical experience in the care and cure of the insane. Indeed, with jurisdiction over the treatment of madness anything but the monopoly of any particular group, the issue of what kind of background, personal and intellectual qualities, and experience qualified an individual to run an asylum was unavoidably uncertain and potentially contentious. Stable and formalized patterns of recruitment and training would only emerge once doctors had acquired sole jurisdiction over the rapidly burgeoning network of institutions that were to make up Victorian asylumdom, for until this task was accomplished, it was 'always possible that people outside the [proto] occupation [could] claim equal or greater skill'[32] in the management of the mad.

Browne's application for the vacancy at Montrose sought to put the best possible face on his qualifications. He stressed his long-standing interest in insanity, dating back to his student days, and pointed to his extensive acquaintance with some of the best European institutions. Together with his powerful outside support, this sufficed to gain him the position by a majority vote[33] – though he was to confess, some thirty years after the fact, that 'so exclusive and mysterious were these abodes, that the first time I entered, or could enter, an asylum in this country, was to take possession as a superintendent ...'.[34] In consequence, once installed as head of the asylum, it was 'with fear and trembling' that he advanced 'the simplest and most innocent innovations – such as that airing yards should be planted with shrubs, that Divine service should be performed on Sunday, – I saw expressive looks, and shrank from significant whispers, that the doctor was as wild and visionary as his charges ...'.[35] But Browne persisted, even insisting upon 'the first lighting [of] the Montrose Asylum with gas in 1836', an event which prompted the assembly of a crowd 'at the gate to witness and perhaps to enjoy the conflagration, which was expected inevitably to follow so daring and desperate an experiment'.[36]

The asylum did not burn down. On the contrary, it flourished in Browne's hands as never before. The principles of the new moral treatment, which he had observed at first hand in Paris, were imported for the first time into a Scottish establishment, and made the foundation of its institutional routines. What the asylum had been was increasingly overtaken by Browne's vision of what it could and ought to be: an ideal environment in which to provide for the moral and physical management of the insane, and to work towards their restoration to sanity.

In the autumn of 1836, emboldened by his success, Browne sought a wider audience, announcing a course of public lectures to be given before the managers of the asylum and assorted local notables. Intending in these talks 'to condense, in a plain, practical, and still popular form, the results of observation in the treatment of insanity, for the specific and avowed purpose of demanding from the public an amelioration of the condition of the insane',[37] Browne succeeded in producing an extraordinarily effective piece of propaganda. Published in May 1837, *What Asylums Were, Are, and Ought to Be* contains perhaps the single most influential portrait by a medical writer of the horrors of the traditional madhouse system; and its powerful and ideologically resonant description of the contrasting virtues of the reformed asylum, a hive of therapeutic activity under the benevolent autocratic guidance and control of its medical superintendent, provided within a brief compass a strikingly attractive alternative vision of an apparently attainable Utopia. Small wonder, then, that Browne's modest volume rapidly received a string of favourable notices in the medical press,[38] propelled its author to the forefront of the newly consolidating profession of alienism, and secured for him a new job as head of the most richly endowed new asylum in the British Isles. For almost twenty years, Browne was to serve as superintendent of the new Crichton Royal Asylum in Dumfries, turning down lucrative offers to head the Edinburgh Royal Asylum and even Bethlem itself before resigning in 1857 to become the first Scottish Commissioner in Lunacy. And despite his long self-imposed exile in the provinces, he remained during all this time among the four or five most prominent British alienists of his generation.

The movement for lunacy reform

One does not have to search very far afield to discern some of the more important factors that prompted Browne's (and Conolly's) initial interest in insanity. By the late eighteenth century, general medical interest in the subject was clearly on the upswing,[39] a development given further impetus by George III's recurrent bouts of 'mania'.[40] The Hellenic tradition of a humoural physiology, pathology, and therapeutics provided a recognizably medical account of mental disorder; and though such traditional claims to jurisdiction over the insane had hitherto been neglected by the bulk of the profession, within an increasingly naturalistic and secularized cultural universe, they provided perhaps the most intellectually coherent available explanation to the etiology of insanity – an explanation which possessed the not inconsiderable advantage of offering ready-made the means 'to classify [insanity], to reason about it, and to take action on it: in more formal terms, to diagnose, to infer, and to treat'.[41] In the context of a growing interest in madness, and an expanding market for those 'trading in lunacy', William Cullen had begun offering lectures on the subject at Edinburgh as early as the 1770s. Most of the prominent mad-doctors of the late eighteenth and nineteenth century – such figures as Thomas Arnold, Alexander Crichton, William Hallaran, John Ferriar, Thomas Trotter and John Haslam – had preceded Browne and Conolly at the University, and contemporaneously with the latter's matriculation, Alexander Morison was busily (if unsuccessfully) lobbying for the establishment at the medical school of a chair for the study and treatment of mental diseases, with himself as its first occupant.[42]

More immediately, the English parliamentary inquiries of 1807 and 1815–16, had served to alert a larger public to the issue of the treatment of the insane. The generalized portrait of inhumanity and neglect, and the lurid revelations of medical malfeasance, maltreatment, and even murder which had punctuated the latter inquiry had placed lunacy reform at the centre of philanthropic attention – with the *Edinburgh Review* taking a major role in retailing the Select Committee's findings to a wider audience, and in endorsing the conclusion that 'they were the offspring of circumstances that, without a radical change of system in the control of madhouses, cannot fail to produce again the same deplorable effects'.[43] Moreover, unlike the situation in 1807, when the absence of a clear alternative conception of how to cope with madness had served to check reformers' ambitions and to limit the scope of the legislation they proposed, the new-found prominence of the York Retreat in the following decade,[44] with its practical demonstration of a therapeutic regime founded on the principles of what William Tuke called 'moral treatment', provoked the introduction of far more ambitious and wide-ranging legislative proposals.

For medical men, neither the founding of the York Retreat nor the findings of the House of Commons investigation constituted an unmixed blessing. Though even in an English context moral treatment was not solely Tuke's invention,[45] it had now been firmly identified in the collective consciousness with him and with his institution. In sharp contrast with more traditional practices, Tuke had insisted upon 'the superior efficacy ... of a mild system of treatment'. External, physical coercion was minimized and, in its most blatant forms – 'gyves, chains, and manacles' – done away with entirely. In its place came an emphasis on 'treating the patient as much in the manner of a rational being as the state of mind will possibly allow' and on carefully designed measures to induce inmates to collaborate in their own recapture by the forces of reason.[46] From the reformers' perspective, Tuke had successfully established that the supposedly continuous danger and frenzy to be anticipated by maniacs were the *consequence* of, rather than the occasion for, harsh and misguided methods of management and restraint – indeed, that this reputation was in great measure the self-serving creation of the madhouse keepers. More promisingly still, he had apparently demonstrated that the asylum could provide a comfortable and forgiving environment which not only spared the insane the neglect which would otherwise have been their lot, but also could play a vital role in restoring a substantial proportion of them to sanity. At the same time, however, as Samuel Tuke had boldly announced, 'the experience of the Retreat ... will not add much to the honour or extent of medical science. I regret ... to relate the pharmaceutical means which have failed, rather than record those which have succeeded'. All the enthusiastic efforts of the medical men working at the Retreat had led to failure, demonstrating only, as one of them conceded 'that medicine, as yet, possesses very inadequate means to relieve the most grievous of human diseases', and prompting a rueful acknowledgement of 'how much was to be done by moral, and how little by any known medical means'.[47]

To make matters worse, many of the most serious abuses exposed by the 1815–16 Committee had occurred at medically-run institutions and medical men were deeply implicated in the beatings and maltreatment of patients, even in their deaths. Nor was the performance of the medical witnesses called before the Committee – whether of those implicated in the scandals or those representing and trying to rescue the interests of the profession at large – such as to salvage their collective reputation;[48] or to quell what taken together amounted to 'a rather damning attack on the medical profession's capacity to deal with mental illness'.[49] If madness was now the subject of potential legislative intervention, and of ever greater public interest and concern, it was by no means clear that the outcome of such interventions would prove favourable to medical interests.

The 1815–16 inquiry had been almost entirely the product of lay initiative – the investigations of provincial figures like the Yorkshire magistrate Godfrey Higgins[50] and his allies, Jonathan Gray[51] and Samuel Nicoll;[52] and of their metropolitan counterparts, Henry Alexander, and the prominent Quaker philanthropists, Edward Wakefield[53] and Thomas Hancock.[54] Higgins and Wakefield, the most active in the cause, had developed a thorough-going scepticism, even a hostility to medical claims to jurisdiction over insanity, and did not hesitate to make their feelings known. Wakefield denounced doctors as 'the most unfit of any class of persons' to serve as 'Inspectors and Controllers of Madhouses', since 'medicine has little or no effect on the disease' and medical men had shown themselves amply inclined to engage in ruthless profiteering at the expense of the mad.[55] And Higgins, his pen dripping sarcasm, noted that,

> Among much medical nonsense, published by physicians interested to conceal their neglect, and the abuses of their establishments, it has been said, that persons afflicted with insanity are more liable than others to mortification of their extremities. . . . If members of the royal and learned College of Physicians were chained, or shut up naked, on straw saturated with urine and excrement, with a scanty allowance of food – exposed to the indecency of a northern climate, in cells having windows unglazed – I have no doubt that they would soon exhibit as strong a tendency to mortified extremities, as any of their patients.

He had found, he confidently proclaimed, a 'medicine' far superior to the bleedings, purges, and powders prescribed by these mountebanks, a rigorous system of inspection and supervision by lay 'visitors and committees'.[56] Echoing these sentiments, the reformers' parliamentary allies endorsed schemes which not only gave no recognition to medicine's claims to a privileged position in the treatment of the insane, but even threatened to subordinate those medical men already engaged in the madhouse trade to supervision and direction from outside committees of laymen.

The 1815–16 inquiry had been wholly confined to an examination of the treatment of the insane in England, with not even passing attention to conditions north of the border. This was significant since, even after the Union in 1707, Scotland had remained legislatively separate from the remainder of the united kingdoms, with its poor law arrangements, in particular, differing quite markedly from those operating south of the border. The Scots, indeed, recoiled with horror from the English use of the compulsory poor rate, retaining a Calvinist distrust of relief for the able-bodied unemployed, viewing the effects of Speenhamland as confirmation of the evils of the English approach, and continuing to rely on a parish-based system of 'voluntary contributions ... [as] the prime method of financing poor relief expenditure'.[57] No legislation to alter this religiously-based system was passed until 1845,[58] with the legal basis of the system continuing to rest on an act of 1574 designed to secure 'the punishment of strong and idle beggars and provision for the sustenation of the Poor and Impotent'.

The upshot of the 1815–16 reports of the Select Committee on Madhouses was nonetheless separate legislative proposals for both England and Scotland which shared a number of common features: the compulsory provision of systems of asylums built at public expense and designed to accommodate at least all pauper lunatics (so as to eliminate the inducements to maltreatment which the reformers were convinced were inherent in allowing lunatics to be kept for profit); and the introduction of a vigorous national system of inspection by outsiders with no ties to the asylum administration (designed to provide a check against the tendency of all institutions to fall away from their initial ideals and the temptations for the madhouse keepers to neglect and maltreat their helpless charges, the mad).

Even for the English, these proposals were too much to swallow. The essential difficulty was that such measures threatened a transformation in political relationships whose importance extended far beyond the narrow sphere of lunacy reform. If enacted, they would have set the precedent for a notable expansion of the central coercive machinery at the disposal of the state. Opposition to such a concentration of power at the national level remained extraordinarily widespread and well entrenched at both the structural and ideological levels,[59] and it was to be some thirty years before the lunacy reformers were to secure legislative enactment of their plans in England and Wales (and it took even longer for Scotland to fall into line). Only after the obstacles to central administration had been confronted and dealt a decisive defeat, not over the marginal issue of the treatment of lunatics, but over the critically important issue of Poor Law reform, was there a serious possibility of passing such far-reaching legislation.

For the Scots, the proposals were, if anything, still more pernicious, for they constituted a serious and threatening attempt to breach the foundational principles of their own poor law system (and system of governance more generally), replacing voluntary, religiously motivated charity by state-financed relief and the compulsory levying of taxes. The precedent was too awful to contemplate, and the 1818 Scottish Lunacy Bill, introduced in February by Lord Binning, was rapidly and decisively sent down to defeat.[60] Till the arrival in 1855 of the formidable American lunacy reformer, Dorothea Dix,[61] the Scots were to continue to insist that a combination of family care, the boarding of harmless lunatics with strangers, and the limited accommodation provided by a handful of charity asylums (the so-called 'Royal Asylums')[62] was superior to English asylumdom, compromised and contaminated as that system inevitably was by the morally corrupting effects of compulsory taxation.

Lunacy reform was thus an extremely protracted affair, on both sides of the border. To resistance founded on opposition to increased political centralization were superadded worries about the exposure of shameful and stigmatizing family secrets if asylums were efficiently inspected and regulated; and apathy and parsimony which blocked the expenditure of the capital sums a system of reformed public asylums would require. Necessarily, therefore, those committed to the restructuring of existing arrangements found themselves embarked upon a complex task of political persuasion, one which required that they develop a convincing ideological account of the superiority of their chosen solution.

Much of the reformers' moral fervour came from their acquaintance with the worst features of the 'trade in lunacy' and one of their most effective weapons in the thirty-year struggle to implement their plans was the periodic exposure of 'the crimes and horrors' endemic in existing madhouses.[63] The difficulty with this tactic, of course, was that it threatened to undermine their simultaneous attempt to persuade the public of the virtues of a reformed 'madhouse' or asylum as the preferred solution to the problem of managing the mad.[64] Thus, quite central to their efforts was an attempt to develop an elaborate account of the *differences* between the places they planned to erect and institutions of a more traditional sort, and a vision of the asylum as the place of the first rather than last resort, preferable to even the best and most solicitous domestic arrangements.

The task was the more difficult since institutional responses to all forms of dependence and debility still lacked social legitimacy. Even the poorest families among the working classes made strenuous efforts to avoid the disgrace of confinement in a workhouse. Similarly, hospitals for the physically sick, their enormous mortality rates uncompensated for by greatly improved chances of recovery, enjoyed a public reputation of being little better than charnel houses, vectors of disease and death to be avoided by all who had the means to do so. As for the deranged, an audience periodically regaled with evidence which appeared to confirm their worst gothic nightmares about what transpired behind the high walls and barred windows of the madhouse[65] had somehow to be brought to embrace the need for a network of purpose-built asylums; and to be convinced, should the occasion arise, that they should send their own loved ones into the institution for treatment.[66]

For the reformers sought not merely to transform existing asylums for the benefit of those already immured in them, but to expand the system greatly, to embrace many more of the insane than had hitherto been thought to require institutionalization. On the one hand, the burgeoning literature on insanity in the 1820s and 1830s contended that madness was an ever more prevalent and deeply threatening problem, the dark side – indeed the product – of the growth of civilization, and an expanding threat to the social order and to civil and domestic peace. At the same time, those laying claim to jurisdiction over the insane insisted that with proper treatment (which necessitated early removal to a properly constituted asylum), this disorder was one of the most readily cured of the afflictions to which human flesh was heir. Expenditures on asylums were thus justified by an increasingly elaborate claim that there existed an 'economics of compassion'[67] – that the higher initial costs of a properly constituted asylum system would be rapidly offset by the high proportion of cures that would result, with the return of the dependent to the ranks of the productive citizenry.

The defence of medical prerogatives

Thus, the construction of a more benign and salubrious image for the asylum, and the insistence on the potential curability of insanity when properly treated were vital components of the reformers' efforts to reshape attitudes towards madness and the mad. The contrast between what asylums were, and what they ought to be, lay at the heart of their attempts to overcome the political and economic obstacles to lunacy reform.[68] Perhaps unsurprisingly, however, those medical men who interested themselves in the subject exhibited an equally central concern with the question of how to establish an exclusively *medical* jurisdiction over the treatment of insanity.

In the aftermath of the 1815–16 inquiry, medical men clearly found themselves on the defensive, their claims to jurisdiction (as one of them fearfully, if exaggeratedly, noted) 'almost ... wrestled by the philosopher out of the hands of the physician'.[69] Francis Willis, grandson of the Lincolnshire physician-cum-divine who had treated George III's madness, complained that 'derangement has been considered by some to be merely and exclusively a mental disease, curable without the aid of medicine, by what are termed moral remedies; such as travelling and various kinds of amusements'.[70] His insistence on the value of medical treatment was reiterated in more truculent form by William Lawrence, the newly appointed surgeon at Bethlem: 'Arguments, syllogisms, discourses, sermons, have never yet restored any patient; the moral pharmacopoeia is quite inefficient, and no real benefit can be conferred without vigorous medical treatment, which is as efficacious in these affections, as in the disease of any other organ.'[71] Others, however, while insisting that medical men remained the most qualified to administer asylums, drew a rather different picture, conceding that,

> the powers of medicine, merely upon mental hallucinations are exceedingly circumscribed and feeble ... we want principles on which to form any satisfactory indications of treatment. ... Almost the whole of ... what may be called the strict medical treatment of madness must be regarded, at present, at least, as empirical, and the most extensive experience proves that very little is to be done.[72]

As we have seen, outside the ranks of the medical profession, and especially among those writing the first bills to implement the reformers' plans, an even more sceptical position appeared to hold sway. Hence the introduction of legislation in which, as an alarmed John Haslam noted,

> it has been seriously proposed, in a great deal to remove both the medical treatment and the moral treatment of insane persons from the care of physicians, and to transfer this important and responsible department of medicine into the hands of magistrates and senators. For the welfare of these afflicted persons, and for the security of the public,

he insisted, 'it is to be hoped that such a transfer may never be established; but that the medical and moral treatment of the insane may continue to be directed by the medical practitioner ...'.[73]

Haslam's alarm was widely shared, and the medical men interested in insanity mobilized to help defeat the reformers' initial proposals. George Man Burrows, having recently played a major role in securing the passage of the Apothecaries Act of 1815, led the lobbying,[74] and other prominent mad-doctors engaged in a similar campaign in 1828, when a renewed attempt was made to legislate some control of the mad business.[75] Despite some temporary successes, however, the attempt 'to vindicate the rights of [the medical] profession over Insanity'[76] clearly required a less reactive strategy, one which offered a realistic prospect of pushing the reform movement in directions more congenial to medical interests. Crucial to any long-term success in these respects was the development of a firmer and more fully-articulated intellectual rationale for granting exclusive jurisdiction over insanity to the medically qualified, a task to which much effort was devoted over the course of the next two decades.[77]

On all these fronts – persuading those with power in the political arena of the horrors of the traditional and still flourishing madhouse system and thus of the urgency of reform; establishing asylums run on the new system of moral treatment as the solution to the problem of providing care and treatment for the insane; and reasserting and establishing on a more secure foundation medicine's threatened jurisdiction over madness, *What Asylums Were, Are, and Ought to Be* was to prove enormously influential. Browne's genius did not lie in his diligence in investigating and exposing the realities of the trade in lunacy (an area where he depended almost wholly on the labours of others); in the novelty of the ideas he put forward (for it is difficult to discern wherein this might consist); or in his own special talents in the treatment and cure of the mad (though it must be said that his years at the Crichton Royal were subsequently to demonstrate that he was a devoted and skilful asylum administrator). His recognition that 'I have no claim to originality, either in the design or the execution of the present production'[78] represents, from these points of view, no false or feigned modesty. But if his lectures comprise, from this limited perspective, no more than a combination of the findings of investigations conducted and reported by others, together with an expropriation of Tuke's and Pinel's ideas about the moral treatment of insanity and a derivative defence of medicine's claims to exclusive jurisdiction over the mad, one must simultaneously recognize that they also constitute, in a wider view, the single most skilled and forceful synthesis of these various elements produced between 1815 and 1840 – a powerful piece of propaganda that proved to be of major value in advancing the plans put forth by the lunacy reform movement, and in securing medical men's prerogatives in the administration of the emerging Victorian empire of asylumdom.

In Browne's own words, he sought to use his lectures to launch 'a crusade'.[79] Endeavouring to secure an audience among the politically influential, he aimed 'to condense, in a plain, practical, and still popular form, the results of observation in the treatment of insanity, for the specific and avowed purpose of demanding from the public an amelioration of the condition of the insane'. The consequence, he hoped, would be to raise 'the cry for improvement ... where hitherto the silence of indifference has reigned'.[80]

For several weighty reasons, one might have expected that this 'cry for improvement' would be couched in the rhetoric of phrenology. Among George Combe's earliest arguments for 'the utility of ... phrenology' had been the claim that 'it is peculiarly fitted to throw a powerful light [on] Education, Genius, the Philosophy of Criticism, Criminal Legislation, and Insanity',[81] and a number of scholars have noted the doctrine's 'pronounced association with movements for social reform'.[82] Of even more direct and immediate relevance to those concerned with reforming the treatment of the insane, the appearance in 1831 of Andrew Combe's *Observations on Mental Derangement*[83] had (briefly and temporarily) reinforced the sense among medical men that phrenology had taken a decisive step towards resolving the enigma of mind, an advance the younger Combe had insisted was of direct and immediate *practical* significance. After all, 'If Phrenology is any thing, it is an exposition of the functions of the brain; and if insanity is any thing, it is disease of the brain, which implicates the integrity of the mental functions.'[84] And from the insights it provided into the structure and functioning of the brain, 'Phrenology gives us a power of acting, and of adapting external circumstances to the exigencies of the case, with a precision, confidence, and consistency, which it is impossible to obtain in any other way.'[85]

Given their role in affording a clear physiological explanation of the operations of the brain, one that permitted a parsimonious account of abnormal as well as normal mental functioning while advancing a coherent rationale for the application of *both* medical and moral treatment in cases of insanity, one would be astonished if phrenological ideas had failed to exert a considerable fascination for the emerging profession of alienism. In fact, a large proportion of the most prominent figures among this generation of asylum superintendents – John Connolly, Sir William Ellis, Disney Alexander, Richard Poole, David Uwins, and Forbes Winslow, to name but a few – professed themselves converts to the doctrine during the 1820s and 1830s.[86] And at this crucial period in medical men's efforts to monopolize the treatment of madness, phrenology clearly played a vital role in physicians' attempts to assimilate moral treatment into the medical armamentarium.[87]

If there appear at first glance to be strong general grounds for expecting that phrenological ideas would occupy a prominent place in Browne's text, his own experience and allegiances seem to make this still more likely. As we have seen, as a student Browne was an early convert to phrenology, and developed close ties to both George and Andrew Combe. In the early 1830s, he had established himself as 'one of the most popular lecturers on phrenology to middle- and working-class audiences throughout Scotland',[88] and his earliest published writings on insanity appeared in the *Phrenological Journal,* and exhibited a close embrace of phreno-logical thinking.[89] Moreover, the sponsorship of the Combe brothers had played a vital role in his obtaining the superintendency of the Montrose Asylum. Intellectually and personally, few were more firmly a part of the phrenological camp.

Yet in late January 1837, when Browne forwarded the page proofs of his lectures to Andrew Combe for comment, they contained not a single reference to phrenology. This apostasy prompted a swift response from Combe:

> I am not aware whether you intend to introduce Phrenology openly as your guide in the investigation and treatment of insanity. In the first sheet there is no allusion to it, and it therefore seems *possible* that you do not mean to notice it. If you really do not, I would strongly advise a contrary course, as due both to the cause of truth and to yourself. ... It is true, present popularity is gained; but my conviction is, that truth is retarded in the long run ...[90]

Somewhat shame-faced, Brown proceeded to dedicate the published text to his mentor, 'as an acknowledgement of the benefits con-ferred on society, by his exposition of the application of phrenology in the treatment of insanity and nervous diseases';[91] and to add a preface acknowledging that 'Insanity can neither be understood, nor described, nor treated by the aid of any other philosophy.'[92] With these exceptions, however, his private convictions about phrenology's value were set to one side, and lacked any discernible influence on his discussion of insanity and its treatment.

As Combe acknowledged,[93] Browne was scarcely the only

alienist who by this time exhibited considerable circumspec-
tion about publicly owning up to his phrenological convictions.
However useful phrenological accounts of insanity had previously proved to be, and notwithstanding Browne's still powerful
private conviction that 'whatever success may have attended my
efforts to ameliorate the condition of those confided to my charge,
... I am inclined to attribute ... to [phrenology]',[94] the fact was
that by the late 1830s, Gall's system had lost credibility among
serious intellectuals and had been 'effectively rejected as a scientific
system'.[95] Increasingly the province of itinerant head-readers
and mountebanks, at whose hands it was being transformed into
'a form of entertainment',[96] phrenology had become far too
dangerous a doctrine to be openly embraced by a profession as
marginal as alienism. In 1837, notwithstanding his tactical silence,
Browne and his alienist colleagues may yet have hoped for a re-
versal of phrenology's fortunes, for its doctrines were of potentially great utility in anchoring the treatment of madness in
medicine. Instead, however, its reputation declined further still,
until it was little more than 'the object of popular ridicule' –
prompting him to confess to George Combe some two decades later
'that if he were to state his views on the dependence of mental
disorder in explicitly phrenological language, he would provoke
incredulity'.[97]

Subsequent events thus vindicated Browne's tactical choice to
'avoid ... the phraseology of the science', and to pursue 'the noble
cause which I have undertaken' by different means.[98] His discussion
opens with two chapters only tangentially related either to his
avowed goal of transforming the treatment of the insane, or to the
subject matter announced in his title: a lengthy examination of the
definition and classification of the varieties of madness; and another
concerned with what epidemiologists would now call its incidence
and prevalence. In many respects, these are the most tedious, least
successful portions of his polemic, lacking in much interest for the
lay audience he claims to be courting, and functioning quite poorly
as a call to action, particularly in comparison with the vivid
contrast he subsequently draws between the gothic horrors of the
traditional madhouse and the Utopian idyll of the asylum as it ought
to be. John Conolly saw this as symptomatic of 'a defective
arrangement very prevalent in his lectures', and suggested that 'the

real commencement of the book' was its third chapter on 'What Asylums Were'.[99]

Understandable as this view is, to accede to the suggestion that one can safely ignore these first two chapters would be to commit a serious historiographic error. Retrospectively, of course, they are of considerable interest to those attempting to reconstruct and understand the beliefs held about the nature and incidence of madness by early Victorian alienists. But, more than this, embedded in these passages are arguments and assumptions that were of great contemporary significance.

Of utmost importance, the definition and aetiology of insanity were obviously subjects of enormous moment when it came to deciding who should have jurisdiction over the treatment of the insane. Recognizing 'how momentous the interests are which hinge upon a clear comprehension of what insanity is',[100] this was the first topic on which Browne focused attention. Here there was no room for argument or ambiguity: insanity, in his view,

> is inordinate or irregular, or impaired action of the mind, of the instincts, sentiments, intellectual or perceptive powers, depending upon and produced by an organic change in the brain. ... In all cases where disorder of the mind is detectable, from the faintest peculiarity to the widest deviation from health, it must and can only be traced directly or indirectly to the brain.[101]

As a phenomenon that was 'strictly a bodily disease'[102] it was therefore a condition medical men were uniquely qualified to treat.[103]

Moreover, provided only that relatives, '[f]rom mistaken kindness or an erroneous estimate of the soothing and curative powers of friendship and affection',[104] did not attempt to treat the case at home, but promptly forwarded the patient for treatment in a properly conducted asylum, Browne insisted that the happiest results could be anticipated. 'Medical men [themselves had] long acted as if nothing could be done with any chance of success in insanity',[105] but recent experience had demonstrated how misplaced such pessimism was. An array of British and American mad-doctors – Monro, Burrows, Ellis, Todd – utilizing the combined resources of medical and moral treatment, had been able to 'cure ninety out of every hundred cases. Such a result', Browne commented, 'proves . . . that instead of being the most intractable it is the most curable of all diseases.'[106]

In making claims for the somatic origins of all cases of mental disorder and for the medical profession's ability to cure an extraordinarily high proportion of the mad, Browne is echoing the consensus of his professional colleagues. Indeed, he relies heavily on their assertions to lend authority to his own statements.[107] It was, he scornfully commented, 'A want of power or inclination to discriminate between the inutility of medicine from its being inapplicable, and from its being injudiciously applied, [which] has led to the adoption of the absurd opinion that the insane ought not to be committed to the charge of a medical man.'[108] Likewise, talk of 'functional' cases of mental disorder was simply a reflection of ignorance or incompetence. In all cases of insanity where a careful post-mortem examination could be conducted, 'In, or around the brain will be detected some obvious alteration of structure, with the existence of which health was incompatible.'[109]

Notwithstanding his recital of medical authorities, Browne's claims that the theoretical commitment to physicalism had an unimpeachable empirical basis were simply false, and hence vulnerable to contradiction. The many assertions he cites that death made the physical basis of the disease transparent were not matched by any consensus about 'just what was visible'[110] and many medical men confessed that, though they were convinced that insanity was brain disease, they could not detect any form of pathology however hard they looked. As Nisbet summarized the evidence, 'In three fourths of the cases of insanity, where they have been subjected to dissection after death, the knife of the anatomist has not been able, with the most scrutinizing care, to trace any organic change to which the cause of the disease could be traced.'[111]

Nor did Browne provide any satisfactory resolution to a related problem, 'the connection of the faculties of the mind with the brain . . .'.[112] Like Burrows (for whom, 'to discuss the validity of this or that hypothesis would be plunging into an inextricable labyrinth'),[113] Browne simply dismissed the issue: 'In what manner this connexion between mind and matter is effected, is not here inquired into. The link will, perhaps, ever escape human research.' It was, quite simply, a divine mystery, and as such, beyond man's power to solve. The physical basis of insanity remained, however, 'the foundation of all inquiries into the nature of mental alienation, and of all attempts to improve the condition of the insane'[114] (to say nothing of medicine's jurisdictional claims).

And yet, if, in Roger Smith's words, 'Medical aetiology was strikingly incoherent in its language of mind and body',[115] and rested on a distinctly murky empirical foundation, it nevertheless was tied to metaphysical underpinnings of great weight and power. Overwhelmingly, in the 1820s and 1830s, medical men writing on insanity had pictured the mind as immaterial, an entity correspond-ing to the immortal soul of the human organism,[116] forced in this world to operate through the medium of a material instrument, the brain.[117] Disease, debility, and death, therefore, could not afflict the mind itself, on pain of calling into question the very foundation of Christian belief.[118] By contrast, a physicalist account created no such dilemma: 'From the admission of this principle, derangement is no longer considered a disease of the understanding, but of the centre of the nervous system, upon the unimpaired condition of which the exercise of the understanding depends. The brain is at fault and not the mind.'[119] The brain, as a material organ, was liable to irritation and inflammation, and it was this which produced insanity.[120] Consequently, '[b]ut let this oppression [of the brain] be relieved, this irritation removed, and the mind rises in its native strength, clear and calm, uninjured, immutable, immortal'[121] – a conclusion which made it abundantly clear why the treatment of madness necessarily involved attention to the body, and un-ambiguously belonged within medicine's recognized sphere of competence.[122]

Madness and civilization

Establishing that insanity was a physical disorder settled one crucial issue, but left a number of related questions unresolved: how much insanity existed in the community; what caused people to go mad; and the differential social incidence of mental alienation. These were all matters of the most significant import. The more extensive the legions of the mad, the more urgent the question of lunacy reform became. The more closely insanity was bound up with the conditions of modern civilized existence, the more threatening the future prospects for society at large and the more crucial the necessity for expert and effective intervention to mitigate the problem. And the more susceptible the rich and powerful to the ravages of mental disorder, the more urgently their own self-interest commanded them to adopt the reformers' prescriptions, lest they wake some morning to find themselves incarcerated in one of those 'wild and secluded abodes of human misery' to which the mad were traditionally consigned.

Browne's conclusions on all these points were scarcely reassuring. Conceding the defects of existing statistics, he nonetheless concurred with Halliday and Esquirol, 'that a much greater number of cases is known to exist, and to require treatment, than formerly', and that the numbers of the insane appeared to be increasing at a far more rapid rate than the population in general.[123] Nor should one be surprised to find 'the poisoned stream larger, and wider, and deeper' given 'the too palpable multiplication of the causes which produce mania'.[124] Wherever 'the sources of moral agitation and excitement are most abundant', there, he confidently asserted, 'will the proportion of insanity be the highest'[125] – grim news indeed for a social order characterized by wrenching social change and up-heaval, and for the commercial, manufacturing and professional elites who so relentlessly sought to exploit the resulting opportunities for social and material advancement.

The Rousseauist myth that the noble savage was somehow immune from the ravages of insanity was quite widely canvassed by Regency and early Victorian writers on the subject.[126] In Browne's formulation, 'as we recede, step by step, from the simple, that is, the savage manners of our ancestors, and advance in industry and knowledge and happiness, this malignant persecutor strides on-ward, signalizing every era in the social progress by an increase, a new hecatomb of victims'.[127] Here was a paradox, particularly for an audience which as a matter of course equated a 'higher' civiliza-tion with progress in almost all spheres of existence. Moreover, if the connection were to prove an inseparable and inevitable one, it was a peculiarly discomforting paradox, for it implied that one could look forward to a rapid and persistent rise in the numbers of mad folk. In the face of this troubling prospect, Browne offered both warning and consolation: it was true that 'the barbarian

xxxi

escapes this scourge . . .;' while 'the members of civilized communities are subjected to it . . .'. Yet this occurs, not inevitably, but,

> because the enjoyments and blessings of augmented power are abused; because the mind is roused to exertion without being disciplined, it is stimulated without being strengthened; because our selfish propensities are cultivated while our moral nature is left barren, our pleasures becoming poisonous; and because in the midst of a blaze of scientific light, and in the presence of a thousand temptations to multiply our immediate by sacrifice of our ultimate gratifications, we remain in the darkest ignorance of our own mind. . . . With civilization then come sudden and agitating changes and vicissitudes of fortune; vicious effeminacy of manners; complicated transactions; misdirected views of the objects of life; ambition, and hopes, and fears, which man in his primitive state does not and cannot know. But these neither constitute, nor are they necessarily connected with, civilization. They are defects, obstacles which retard the advancement of that amelioration of condition towards which every discovery in art, or ethics, must ultimately tend.[128]

If society could but be brought to listen to those who were lifting the veil of 'ignorance of our own mind' (and who were simultaneously developing expertise in restoring the mad to sanity), the worst might be averted. But, unavoidably, insanity would remain a major social issue, since,

> The occupations, amusements, follies, and above all, the vices of the present race, are infinitely more favourable for the development of the disease than at any previous period. We live under the dominion of the propensities and we must pay the penalty for so doing: and madness is one of these.[129]

Nor could wealth or social position provide any security against its inroads.[130] While he conceded that 'We do not possess sufficient data to determine the relative proportions of the insane rich and the insane poor [nonetheless, t]he information which has been obtained tends to show that the former are most numerous.'[131] Such was the opinion of no less an authority than Esquirol, and Browne found further confirmation in the growth of the trade in lunacy, the 'very great number of Retreats, etc., in this country, which are mere speculations, and have been intended for the reception of those who can afford to pay for such an investment of capital ...'.[132] Circular reasoning from the postulated causes of insanity provided the final 'proof' that not only do 'Rank, riches, and education, afford no protection against this disease as they do against others'; but they give 'rise to hopes and fears, and exertions and vicissitudes which the humble and illiterate escape'. While the agricultural population, and particularly the rural poor, 'is to a great degree exempt from insanity', the bourgeoisie and the plutocracy remain especially susceptible to its ravages, exposed as they are 'to excitement ... and ... to the formation of habits of thought and action inimical to the preservation of mental serenity and health'.[133]

To the extent that such assertions secured a measure of public credibility and acceptance, they provided a powerful motive among the well-to-do to embrace Browne's suggested reforms.[134] Once a network of reformed asylums was constructed, it was from the ranks of the poor and disenfranchised that the overwhelming bulk of the patient population was to be drawn;[135] and within a generation or so, alienists would respond with a very different portrait of the aetiology and social distribution of insanity – one which emphasized the role of physical degeneration and hereditary taint, and portrayed the insane as 'morbid varieties or degenerates of the human kind',[136] a horde of anti-social beings who 'will, if not rendered innocuous by sequestration . . ., or if not extruded violently from [society], give rise to disorder incompatible with its stability'.[137] With pauper asylums bulging at the seams, the notion of who was susceptible to madness would undergo rapid revision, and in place of assertions that the rich were at least as liable to mental disturbance as the poor, alienists would proclaim the mad 'an infirm type of humanity largely met with in the lower classes', a pauper residuum which bore plainly visible stigmata of its moral and mental depravity.[138]

In the 1830s, however, the asylum was still far from constituting a legitimate feature of the social landscape and the question of who would constitute the inhabitants of an enlarged and reformed madhouse system remained the subject of speculation and uncertainty. For those in a position to exercise some choice in the matter, institutionalization remained very much a last resort. As Browne's

first professional employment had ironically confirmed, 'So indifferent is even now the repute of public asylums, that the physician
in many instances recommends change of scene or of occupation,
travelling, anything in fact rather than mere incarceration.'[139] And
in the light of recent developments, no informed observer could
doubt that,

> it will long be difficult to convince the rich, who can purchase
> other, and, as they imagine, better modes of isolation, that the
> vicious condition brought home to certain asylums no longer
> continues, or to allay the horror inspired by the prospect of
> being exposed to the system supposed to be prevalent in all,
> because certainly prevailing in many.[140]

The madhouse and the asylum: dystopia and Utopia

Browne's own description of what asylums 'were and are' is drawn
directly from the findings of the Parliamentary inquiries of 1815–16
and 1827–28 (supplemented by some European materials). A carefully orchestrated denunciation of the evils of the *ancien regime* and
the defects that characterized the traditional 'trade in lunacy', his
account simultaneously makes plain what 'everyone knew' about
asylums, and just why the informed public should have learned to
view them with 'horror'. Sex, madness, maltreatment, and murder
are repeatedly linked in a series of exemplary tales designed at once
to titillate and to repel, while illustrating 'the errors, absurdities, and
atrocities of the old system', a system pictured as little more than a
protracted 'reign of terror'.[141]

The audience is invited to contemplate, for instance, the effects of
the indiscriminate mingling of male and female, flung together
without the pretence of classification or supervision. The 'decorum
and purity of the intercourse which ensued' can be imagined,
bearing in mind 'that the beings thus having uninterrupted access to
each other were irrational, acting under the impulse of ungovernable passions, and unrestrained, perhaps by the sacred obligations of
religion, and certainly unmindful of the conventional check of
public opinion'.[142] Meanwhile, even those madwomen who retained
some remnants of innate feminine purity and modesty were not

xxxiv

safe, their bodies being at the disposal of the ruthless and lascivious ruffians who served as madhouse attendants. The lurid conse-quences of a system in which the mad were '[r]egarded as wild beasts, [and] all maniacs were indiscriminately treated as such'[143] extended in every direction: public inquiries provided graphic descriptions of patients dying in the act of force-feeding; the indiscriminate bleeding and drugging of patients into insensibility; the array of 'bolts, bars, chains, muffs, collars, and strait-jackets' employed to coerce a measure of order; the public display of inmates, like 'the animals in a menagerie'; the corrupt confinement of the sane, 'guiltless, not even guilty of being diseased' amidst the shrieks and ravings of the mad; the mysterious deaths and disappearance of more than a hundred and forty inmates at the York Asylum; the notorious case of William Norris, confined in Bedlam with a purpose-built iron cage round his body for some fourteen years. All these and more were 'but a fraction of the evils which have been brought home to asylums as they were', giving asylums the reputation 'rather as places for the concentration and aggrava-tion, than for the relief of disease'.[144]

Having portrayed the past in the bleakest of hues, Browne now hastens to offer a vivid contrast. From Pinel's liberation of the insane, at the height of the bloodiest excesses of the French Revolution, 'may be dated a total revolution in the opinions of medical men and legislators, respecting the insane, and in the principles upon which houses of detention are professed to be conducted'.[145] Henceforth, '[f]rom darkness [the mad] passed into light – from savage ferocity into Christian benevolence'.[146] But not completely: more precisely, the 'promised land was [merely] in sight; it was not reached ... it has succeeded at certain points only, in shaking the strongholds of prejudice and ignorance'.[147] The principles of a rational, humane, and curative treatment of the insane were to hand: it remained only to implement them to transform asylums as they are into asylums as they ought to be.

The most striking images in Browne's book occur in its final chapter, where he sketches for his audience the characteristics of an ideal asylum, the moral qualities of its physician-superintendent, and the therapeutic regime which promises to restore the vast majority of the mad to sanity and back to society. As other scholars have noted, there is a strong Utopian strand running through early nineteenth century discussions of the asylum, and this is nowhere more manifest than in Browne's discussion of what asylums ought to be. Indeed, he begins his concluding lecture by acknowledging that 'A perfect asylum may appear to be a Utopia; "a sight to dream of, not to see".'[148]

The contrast with the images of the traditional madhouse – the shit, straw, and stench, the beatings, intimidation, and rapes – could scarcely be more marked. So far from being 'a moral lazar house' wherein the deranged were hidden and hope and humanity abandoned, the asylum is now transmuted into the 'moral machinery' through which the mind is strengthened, and reason is restored. Indeed, properly organized and managed, like the Invisible Hand now regulating civil society, 'the system is at once beautiful and self-operating. [The] presence [of keepers] is required to regulate the machine, but its motions are spontaneous . . .',[149] serving all but imperceptibly to secure 'the regulation and tranquillization of the unhealthy mind'.[150]

How is such a miraculous transformation to be accomplished? By careful attention to the location and construction of the asylum buildings; by insisting upon the moral and intellectual character of the medical superintendent who serves as the autocratic guiding spirit of the whole apparatus; and by the introduction of active moral treatment, requiring a constant insistence on kindness and the steady occupation of the inmates. Physically, the reformed asylum could scarcely be more remote from the old madhouse. Designed from the outset to facilitate 'the comfort and the cure of the inmates . . .',[151] and providing spacious and aesthetically pleasing accommodations, it made its own vital contributions to their 'moral training' and to replacing 'their morbid feelings . . . [with] healthy trains of thought'.[152] Browne emphasized how even its siting could influence both patients' thoughts and behaviour; its architecture, the possibility of classification and separation (both central to the implementation of moral treatment); its grounds, the availability of exercise and the possibility of employment in farming and similar healthy activities.

Organizationally, Browne acknowledged, the 'association of lunatics requires to be skilfully managed'.[153] Here, he touched on dangerous ground, for many people, including some of his medical brethren,[154] questioned the logic of gathering the insane together under one roof, fearing emulation and imitation, to say nothing of isolation from sane influences, would only serve to deepen their alienation. Classification was in any event a vital component of moral treatment, but it here acquired a double significance, allowing Browne to stress the careful separation of the tranquil and the raving, the convalescent and the incurable, while emphasizing the advantages to be derived from interaction among inmates in carefully constructed communities of the mad.[155] Such segregation was also vital to allow treatment to be individualized, adapted to 'the idiosyncracies of the patients, ... the symptoms, the duration and the complications of the disease'[156] – an implicit and telling contrast with the indiscriminate mass-medication of the *ancien regime*.

Classification also allowed asylum keepers to offer another kind of reassurance: that no improper mingling of the social classes would be permitted. One might well imagine the 'unhappiness which would flow from bringing the ignorant and brutal into constant and compulsory contact with the enlightened and refined'.[157] Besides,

> The pauper could not appreciate, nor prize, nor derive benefit from the refinement and delicacies essential to the comfort, and instrumental in the recovery of the affluent. Most fortunately, [therefore,] this arrangement, which is called for by the usages of society, is found to correspond with those higher and less artificial distinctions which are dictated by philosophy.[158]

Class distinctions finding support in Nature itself, the asylum superintendent could proceed with a clear conscience to make 'fitting preparations' with which to 'tempt the rich to have recourse to those measures from choice, which the poor have long pursued from necessity'.[159]

Internally, the structural differentiation of space corresponded not only to social boundaries, but to moral ones as well, providing the asylum's guiding spirit with the means to 'watch, analyze, grapple with insanity among the insane, and seek for his weapons of aggression in the constitution and dispositions of each individual, and not in general rules or universal specifics'.[160] In particular, linking classification to amenities and rewards allowed one 'to offer temptations to the lunatic to cooperate in his own restoration'[161] through active employment; and facilitated the use of every aspect of the environment as 'a more powerful lever in acting upon the intractable'.[162]

Crucial in this whole process, of course, were the abilities, character, and discrimination of the asylum's director, someone who must be able to exploit the 'slightest differences of disposition, and sympathies in pursuit or taste'[163] to induce his patients to exercise self-control and advance towards mastery over their madness. Previously, 'the care of the insane was monopolized by medical and other adventurers [creating] a ridiculous stigma [which] deterred regular and well-educated practitioners from attempting to compete, and even from qualifying to do so'.[164] Finally, however, the quack and 'mere drug exhibiter'[165] were giving way to the professional man of 'high integrity and honour', possessed of 'that moral and physical courage which confer calmness and decision in the midst of danger ... and imbues the whole character with that controlling influence, which ... governs the turbulent while it appears to guide, and commands the most wild and ferocious by the sternness and at the time time by the serenity of its orders ...'.[166] In such hands, humanity and cures were all but assured.

Browne's concluding paragraphs conjure up a quite extravagant portrait of ideal asylums as 'miniature worlds, whence all the disagreeable alloys of modern life are as much as possible excluded, and the more pleasing portions carefully cultivated'.[167] Here is a social universe that constitutes an organic, harmonious whole – a hierarchical order arrayed under its benevolent philosopher-king,[168] in which everyone knows and respects his or her place; where even the rage of madness is reigned in without whips, chains, or corporal chastisement, amidst the comforts of domesticity and the invisible yet infinitely potent fetters of the 'desire for esteem'; a community whose inhabitants 'literally work in order to please themselves', virtually without recompense, but so readily that 'a difficulty is found in restraining their eagerness, and moderating their exertions'; a setting in which, amongst the higher ranks, the most elevated cultural and intellectual pursuits find their place – a Utopia in which 'all are so busy as to overlook, or all are so contented as to forget their misery'. 'Such', he grandly concludes, 'is a faithful picture of what may be seen in many institutions, and of what might be seen in all, were asylums conducted as they ought to be.'[169]

Ideologically, of course, this was a vision of extraordinary resonance and attractiveness, particularly for a ruling class surrounded by alarming signs of increasing social friction and political discontent, and forced to confront the discord, disruptions and divisiveness that were so central a feature of the Great Transformation.[170] Browne's stress on social harmony and tranquility; his claim to replace violent repression, conflict, and strife by moral suasion, docility, and willing submission to authority, even among the depraved and unruly; his practical demonstration of the powers of 'reason and morality' when allied to a new kind of 'moral machinery' – these constituted a potent advertisement for the merits of reformed asylums run by practitioners initiated into the mysteries of moral treatment and medical psychology.[171] Accepting these claims as the 'description, ... not ... of a theorist, or of an enthusiast, but of a practical man long accustomed to the management of lunatics',[172] the Victorian governing classes were provided with powerful incentives to embrace the lunacy reformers' schemes and to construct the new realm of asylumdom. And in England and Wales, at least, there was rapid progress over the next few years towards making the provision of county asylums compulsory and towards instituting a national system of asylum inspection and supervision.

The asylum as it turned out to be

The publication of Browne's lectures had a dramatic effect on his own career, prompting a brief visit to Montrose by Elizabeth Crichton, during which she offered him the superintendency of the new Crichton Royal Asylum at Dumfries, at an annual salary of £350.[173] Doubtless attracted by the new institution's generous endowment, and by the prospect of implementing his ideas in a more favourable environment, Browne accepted the offer just as promptly. The next year was spent 'in fitting up and furnishing the building and in organizing the staff,' with the asylum finally opening to receive patients on June 3, 1839.[174] For almost twenty years, Browne remained its superintendent,[175] resigning reluctantly in 1857 to become the first Scottish lunacy commissioner, when the Scots finally succumbed to pressures to build a network of publicly funded asylums on the English model.

Browne's long tenure as superintendent of a richly endowed asylum designed as it 'ought to be', as a vehicle for implementing moral treatment, provides us with an almost irresistible temptation to compare the ideal and the real, the theory and the practice of asylum administration in the moral treatment era. It is a temptation worth succumbing to, though it is as well to note at the outset that the surviving source materials do not allow us to probe very deeply into these antimonies. Not the least of the drawbacks is that our primary data for investigating Browne's practice turn out to be his own annual reports, documents obviously written to put the best possible front on the asylum's achievements, to attract potential patrons and patients' families, to forward the cause of lunacy reform, and to persuade a broader public of the legitimacy of psychiatric expertise.[176]

With all their limitations and partiality, however, Browne's lengthy reports, viewed over the entire span of his superintendency, turn out to be remarkably revealing documents. Regardless of their propagandistic intent, they disclose someone who devoted enormous energy and ingenuity to the moral discipline and treatment of his charges, with little or no respite or relief from the strains this entailed.[177] Browne was unquestionably a very talented administrator, and he took advantage of the considerable resources at his disposal in a variety of imaginative ways. A wide range of activities was made available in an effort to restore the patients to sanity (and, as he later confessed, as ways of 'combatting monotony, the giant evil of even well regulated seclusion'):[178] within the asylum walls, 'concerts, public readings, evening parties, dances, games at bowls, billiards, summer ice, cards, chess, backgammon, have afforded means of diversifying the dull routine of discipline; although, perhaps, the exhibition of the magic lantern yielded the most unalloyed pleasure, and to the greatest number ...'; and, notwithstanding initial trepidation and complaints from the town-folk, escorted outside, 'the patients have participated in every public amusement which combined present gratification with prospective benefit, and in which they could mingle without excitement or injury to themselves, or offence or disturbance to others' – races, regattas, art and natural history exhibits, fishing, walks, concerts, the circus, outings to the theatre.[179]

In the face of considerable disapproval in some local Calvinist circles, the theatre was next brought within the walls, the patients themselves presenting (and forming the audience for) a performance 'on Twelfth Night, 1843, ... of James Kenney's farce, "Raising the Wind", all the parts in which being sustained by the patients, who also contributed musical selections.'[180] By the following year, Browne confidently announced that 'The attempt is no longer an experiment. It is a great fact of moral science, and must be accepted and acted upon.'[181] And in December 1844, the patients began publication of their own monthly journal, *The New Moon, or Crichton Royal Institution Literary Register*.[182] An omnibus was procured to make outside activities 'more agreeable and accessible to a greater number'.[183] Gymnastics, hymn-writing, instrumental music and singing, drawing and painting, language lessons in Arabic, Greek, Hebrew, French, and Latin, and the keeping of animals as pets, all were introduced to create 'a healthy tone and an invigorating moral climate'.[184] And (though not among the patients of the higher ranks, for whom labour was socially stigmatizing),[185] patients were routinely pressed to employ themselves in a variety of useful ways.[186]

All of these activities took place within a minutely organized, rigidly structured routine. Patients outside the highest classes were to rise at six in the summer, seven in the winter; to breakfast at eight; take dinner at one, after two and a half hours of walking and an hour of rest; tea came at four; exercise was resumed at six, and supper and bed followed by eight. As a general rule, 'The patients are left less to their own discretion ... the distribution of their time and occupations, and so far of their very thoughts, is taken into the hands of their governors. Every hour has its appropriate object and occupation, and they become more the creatures of a system, and less the sport of their own distempered inclinations.'[187]

Nor was the possible utility of medical treatment neglected. In keeping with his continued insistence on the 'incontrovertible proposition, that derangement never occurs in a healthy body ...'[188] Browne made sure that 'medical are associated with moral means in the efforts to re-establish health'.[189] From the outset, opiates were employed freely, as a narcotic and tranquillizer,

> to such an extent as would startle those who repose confidence in the time-honoured doses of days gone by. The quantities

even alarmed those who were accustomed to deal with the singular power of resistance to medicine, which is often a characteristic of insanity ... although triple, quadruple, in some cases six times, the amount of the ordinary doze [sic], neither drowsiness nor sleep have been observed.[190]

Convinced that 'the narcots used [must] have a special, and it may be unobserved effect on the nervous system, apart from, and altogether independent of the production of sleep', Browne nonetheless persisted with them, while acknowledging that 'further investigation and experiment are required as to the assistance to be derived from particular drugs'.[191] In later years, he displayed equally aggressive tendencies, trying inhalation of ether, perchloride of formyle, and chloroform, and even experimenting with animal and electro-magnetism – and justifying his behaviour with the argument that it was 'a duty that all new and powerful agents should be tried in the treatment of a disease which so often defies the ordinary resources of medicine'.[192]

The dismal clinical outcomes of these somatic interventions failed, even momentarily, to shake his confidence that only to a 'well-educated physician' was the 'sacred and momentous trust' of treating the insane to be consigned.[193] Still, they could not but confirm his conviction that 'moral means ... unquestionably constitute the most powerful class of remedies that has yet been discovered'[194] – and it was therefore to the various forms of moral treatment that he principally gave his attention. Through careful planning, he insisted that these various elements were to be brought to act in concert, so as to constitute an extraordinarily powerful mechanism for remoralizing the mad and restoring 'that respect for order and tranquility which is the basis of all sanity and serenity of mind'.[195]

Reflecting the professional consensus of his peers, Browne viewed the exercise of self-control and the ability to repress one's morbid propensities as the defining characteristics of sanity,[196] and saw the asylum regime and its 'curative discipline'[197] as contributing in multiple ways to the achievement of these ends:

> In order to obtain [various] gratifications [for instance], in anticipation of them, and from the conviction that propriety of demeanour will alone entitle to indulgence, the insane

exercise control over their minds; secondly, during enjoyment they control their minds, or rather their minds are controlled, as they become engrossed, as the happiness of others spreads to them, and as the memory of the past is shut out by the agreeable feelings of the present; and thirdly, they control their minds under the fear of compromising their right and expectation of a repetition of the indulgence. This power of control, or of concealment of predominating and morbid feelings is an indication of health, a beneficial exercise of the will, which may be trained, strengthened, and established.[198]

Browne insisted that it was towards accomplishing these ends that the asylum's 'moral governor' must devote his energies, presiding over the whole establishment, witnessing and regulating 'the most minute working of the great moral machine'[199] and making 'discriminate use of ordinary circumstances and trifles in depressing, elevating, tranquilizing, rousing, persuading, or governing the insane . . .'.[200] Within the tightly controlled asylum environment, he could thereby ensure that 'the impress of authority is never withdrawn, but is stamped upon every transaction'.[201]

Such passages make quite transparent, as Browne himself insisted, that '[t]here is a fallacy even in conceiving that Moral Treatment consists in being kind and humane to the insane'.[202] While marking a clear rupture with the more directly brutal coercion, fear, and constraint that characterized an older asylum regime, the new approach constituted a prodigiously effective set of techniques for imposing and inducing conformity, and incorporated a latent (and rapidly realized) potential for deterioration into a repressive form of moral management. And even in Browne's generously endowed and imaginatively run establishment, it was this darker side that soon came to dominate.

Within five years of receiving the first patients at the Crichton Royal, Browne begins to sound a distinctly more cautious note about the likely outcome of asylum treatment. His own statistics reveal that only a little more than a third of those admitted are being cured, and even this figure, he suggests, may give the wrong impression: 'It is a question of some importance', he informs his readers, 'whether the human mind be ever restored to its original health and strength after an attack of insanity.' Certainly, expert intervention can restore a measure of 'calmness and composure . . . and that self-possession and correctness of external deportment which are regarded as indices of health . . .'. Patients may even regain 'the capacity to engage in complicated matters of business or abstruse studies . . .; but is there not generally retained some peculiarity or perversity, some tendency to excitement or extravagance, some infirmity or unsteadiness which require shelter or sympathy?' Were one to ignore this difficulty, it would be 'easy to augment the apparent curability of derangement'; but to do so would be to 'usher . . . into the world persons of odd and eccentric dispositions, disturbers of families and of society, who are tolerated, but not trusted; who perpetrate crimes and outrages under the protection of their infirmity . . .'.[203] The asylum, he starts to hint, can fail to deliver on the extravagant promises of its early promoters, and yet continue to fulfil vital social functions, remaining therefore, in some larger sense, a successful enterprise.

A year later, in a letter to the Royal Commission investigating the Scottish Poor Laws, he more bluntly articulates this very different rationale for maintaining and expanding the asylum system. As one might expect, the prospects of curing a certain fraction of cases, and the potential savings this would represent, are still presented as one argument for preferring treatment to neglect. But Browne no longer urges the likelihood of curing eighty or ninety per cent of those afflicted, opting for the far more modest claim that 'if the recognized and approved medical and moral expedients be resorted to, there is almost a certainty that one-third of them will recover'.[204] There is still a nod, too, towards an earlier emphasis on the need to rescue the insane from the neglect and hardships too often their lot in the community. But the urgent necessity to ensure that 'the gaps, and gashes, and leprosy of the mind . . . be withdrawn from the public eye'[205] has a very different source, the threat their continued presence poses to morality and social order:

> It is not calculated to improve morals, that half-naked maniacs should haunt our paths, with the tendencies, as well as the aspect of satyrs. . . . They have appetites as well as we. Unchecked, uncontrolled, they obey the injunction to multiply; and, undoubtedly, multiply their *own kind*. They commit murder; they commit suicide . . . while they are inaccessible to

the shame, the sorrow, or the punishment; presenting the humiliating spectacle of drunken, ribald, rebellious maniacs. Reason or religion cannot reach them, and they are abandoned to the dominion of sin.[206]

The turn away from an emphasis on the asylum as a reliable mechanism for manufacturing sane citizens from mad raw materials appears to have had little discernible impact on its growing popularity with the families of potential patients. Certainly, Browne's own establishment suffered from no lack of recruits. Each year, his reports recorded a large excess of applications for admission, both private and pauper, over those for whom there was room, and the Crichton Royal attracted moneyed patients from considerable distances, many of them from England. But Browne was losing his illusions about why they were sent, and about what could be accomplished once they had been admitted:

> patients are constantly sent to asylums because they have become burdens; and not merely because they have exhausted the pecuniary resources, but the tender mercies, the sympathy, the love of their friends. They are exiled from the home of their youth, because their presence is incompatible with the interests or comforts of other members of the family. ... Patients are secluded as public nuisances; they are cast off from the community as offending members, and are consigned to the asylum on similar grounds to those that consign a robber or a rioter to a prison. Retained among their relatives so long as they are calm and manageable, so long as they are robust; whenever affected with bodily ailment or infirmity, they are sent to asylums to die.[207]

Clearly the campaign to persuade the public of the near-certain curability of insanity, with prompt treatment of recent cases in a properly run asylum, had been lost. Worse yet, the widespread refusal to accept the alienists' optimistic claims came to seem increasingly well-founded. As Browne himself was to concede before the decade was out,

> All men entrusted with the care of the insane must be conscious how infinitely inferior the actual benefit conferred is to the standard originally formed of the efficacy of

medicine, or of the powers of the calm and healthy over the agitated and perverted mind ... how intractable nervous disease is found to be and how indelible its ravages are even where reason appears to be restored.[208]

But from some points of view, it turned out not to matter. Cures might prove evanescent, but the asylum retained its utility as a convenient depository for inconvenient people, a valued and valuable way 'of secluding the insane, and of protecting the public from the evils which arise from contact with debased appetites, violent passions, and excited imaginations.'[209] Therapeutically successful or not, there remained ample demand for them as places 'to receive and reduce to subordination, and symmetry, and peace, all the degraded appetites, ungovernable passions, the wild and erratic imaginations, and blinded judgments, which have been cast out as inconsistent with the order and well being of society.'[210]

'Success', it now transpired, 'may be estimated in various ways.'[211] Every bit as important as the cures one promoted,

> is the development of sources of calm and contentment, where restoration cannot be effected ... the general amount of mental health and happiness secured to all residing in the Institution, and especially those whose calamities must render them permanent inhabitants ... [the creation of] a new and artificial modification of society adapted to the altered dispositions and circumstances of the insane. ... [212]

And fortunately, moral and medical treatment, though nowhere near as effective in producing cures as once advertised, remained rather more efficacious 'in establishing tranquillity, and in suggesting a deportment which closely resembles, if it do [sic] not entirely realize, that of sanity and serenity'.[213] The accumulation of chronic patients was of great assistance here, for a large fraction of this group could be exploited to form 'a permanent and stationary basis or stock which is of great utility in manipulating the details of classification. It forms a sort of conservative body, whose tendency is, on the whole, to support constituted authority and regular government.'[214] The goal of tranquillity and good order, at least, was thus within reach:

The effect of long-continued discipline is to remove all salient parts of the character, all obtrusive and irregular propensities and peculiarities ... the majority [of asylum inmates], enfeebled by monotony, by the absence of strong impulses and new impressions, tamed, and stilled, and frozen, by the very means to which they may owe life, and some remains of reason, exhibit a stolidity and torpor which are obviously superadded to their original malady[215]

– but which are equally obviously of great utility to those charged with managing and supervising such dead souls.

Self-evidently, such sharply diminished ambitions, acceptable though they may have proved to patients' families and to the public at large, carried highly damaging implications for alienists' social standing, and constituted a bitter pill for Browne to swallow. For all his attempts to reassure his audience (and himself) that 'the progress is in the right direction, and that the efforts and aspirations of so many ardent and powerful, and pure minds, as are now devoted to the amelioration of the insane, must ultimately and speedily elicit the truth and the whole truth ...',[216] reality on a daily basis remained recalcitrant and bleak. A note of quiet desperation about 'the intrinsic repulsiveness of the records of sorrow and suffering'[217] which he must constantly encounter now entered his reports, and he conceded that,

> There are no more painful convictions in the mind of those engaged in the care and cure of the insane than that so little can be done to restore health, to re-establish order and tranquillity, than that, after the best application of the most sagacious and ingenious measures, the results are so barren and incommensurate, that in defiance of sympathy and solicitude, misery and violence, and vindictiveness should predominate. . . . [218]

Astonishingly, given his own role in creating the image of the asylum as Utopia, he subsequently complained of those who foster

> the erroneous impression that alienation is scarcely a privation, and the restraints which it entails may be converted into golden bonds. It has become a fashion to paint Asylum interiors in brilliant and attractive colours. This error, as it is,

may be the natural tendency of generous and sanguine minds to describe that which is hoped and expected and might be, as objects already accomplished – to present a course which it may be a duty to tread as a goal which has been reached.[219]

His final report as superintendent at Dumfries was written in 1857. Producing it was, he acknowledged, 'a difficult and painful duty'[220] – partly because of his imminent departure from the scene of his lifetime's labours, but surely also because of the depressing contrast between the high hopes he had entertained on assuming his post, and the grim realities that now confronted him. The Crichton Royal was as popular as ever with its clientele: in the preceding twelve months, of one hundred applicants for admission from the affluent classes, he had been able to admit but twenty-six; and from the 122 pauper applicants, but fifty-one. Moral treatment was pursued as vigorously as before, and on an experimental basis, convalescent patients were now spending some time at a neighbouring country house. Still, in ministering to 'the waifs and strays, the weak and wayward of our race',[221] Browne could find many reasons for disquiet. The overcrowded state of the asylum could perhaps be a source of some pride, as a sign of people's confidence in the establishment. 'It may even be argued that the physical and moral evils created by the crowded state of a moral hospital are infinitely less than the miseries and misfortunes which follow refusal of admission.'[222] But such attempts to find consolation were in some larger sense misplaced. For, inescapably,

> The moral evils of a vast assemblage of incurable cases in one building, are greater still. The community becomes unwieldy; the cares are beyond the capacity of the medical officers; personal intimacy is impossible; recent cases are lost, and overlooked in the mass; and patients are treated in groups and classes. An unhealthy moral atmosphere is created; a mental epidemic arises, where delusion, and debility, and extravagance are propagated from individual to individual, and the intellect is dwarfed and enfeebled by monotony, routine, and subjection.[223]

His own asylum's cure rate compared favourably with its competitors, but even this could not be a source of pride, since 'it is incumbent to confess, that the nature of what there is a disposition to describe as cures, is not satisfactory'.[224] Nor could Browne find solace in the romanticized portraits of the amusements and attractions of asylum life that were so prominent a feature of his early reports. Alongside the usual recital of plays and concerts given, activities and occupations engaged in, a strikingly different picture now appears:

> It has been customary to draw a veil over the degradation of nature, which is so often a symptom of insanity. But it is right that the real difficulties of the management of large bodies of the insane should be disclosed; it is salutary that the involuntary debasement, the animalism, the horrors, which so many voluntary acts tend to, should be laid bare. No representation of blind frenzy, or of vindictive ferocity, so perfectly realizes, so apparently justifies, the ancient theory of metempsychosis, or the belief in demoniacal possession, as the manic glorying in obscenity and filth; devouring garbage or ordure, surpassing those brutalities which may to the savage be a heritage and a superstition. ... These practices are not engrafted upon disease by vulgar customs, by vicious or neglected training, or by original elements of character. They are encountered in victims from the refined and polished portions of society, of the purest life, the most exquisite sensibility. Females of birth drink their urine. ... Outlines of high artistic pretensions have been painted in excrement; poetry has been written in blood, or more revolting media. ... Patients are met with ... who daub and drench the walls as hideously as their disturbed fancy suggests; who wash or plaster their bodies, fill every crevice in the room, their ears, noses, hair, with ordure; who conceal these precious pigments in their mattresses, gloves, shoes, and who will wage battle to defend their property.[225]

In the face of these realities, the optimistic might still choose to speak (as some now did) of asylums as mental hospitals. But those who set aside their rose-tinted spectacles must face a grimmer truth: 'An Asylum is only in one sense an hospital. They both receive and relieve the suffering. But in an hospital the patients enter, depart, die. In an Asylum, the inmates, or about one-half of them, remain for life.'[226] Institutional care was still preferable, in Browne's view, to the alternatives – a position he would subsequently defend at greater length;[227] yet what asylums had become – reasonably well-tended cemeteries for the still breathing – constituted a system almost startlingly remote from his earlier visions of what they ought to be.

The elder statesman

Browne's departure from his position as superintendent of the Crichton Royal was the direct consequence of the passage of the 1857 Scottish Lunacy Act (20 and 21 Vict., cap. 71). The Act in its turn was the product of Dorothea Dix's brief visit to Scotland in 1855, and of her subsequent complaints to the British government about the neglected condition of Scottish lunatics. The new legislation established a General Board of Commissioners in Lunacy for Scotland, who were charged with the supervision of all asylums and lunatics in the country; and it required the construction of district asylums at taxpayers' expense throughout Scotland. The trustees of the Crichton Royal had consistently opposed compulsory, tax-financed asylums over the years, and when the Dix-inspired Royal Commission on the state of lunatics in Scotland had visited the asylum in 1856, Browne had reminded them 'that in Scotland hitherto the charity of the affluent has supplied spontaneously what in other countries is exacted by law from the whole community; and that he hopes that this peculiarity will continue to distinguish our national policy'.[228] Nonetheless, his standing as the most eminent Scottish alienist made him a natural choice as one of the first two medical commissioners, and to the approbation of his colleagues, he accepted the nomination.[229]

Browne spent a good portion of the next thirteen years on the official circuit, visiting the existing Royal Lunatic Asylums and workhouses, and advising on the construction and organization of the new district asylums. The task suited him less well than the day-to-day challenge of running an asylum, and he seized such opportunities as came his way to broaden the range of his responsibilities. He seems to have particularly enjoyed the opportunity of combining, from time to time, his official visit to a provincial asylum with a clinical lecture on some aspect of insanity

1

and its treatment, usually delivered by pre-arrangement to Thomas Laycock's Edinburgh students in medical psychology.[230]

Both in these lectures, and in his Presidential Address to the Medico-Psychological Association (delivered in 1866),[231] Browne devoted much of his attention to a further defence of medical prerogatives and jurisdiction over the insane, a choice perhaps prompted by the sobering realization of just how tenuous the foundations of alienism's privileged status still remained. The vaunted Utopia of asylums run as they ought to be had failed to produce results commensurate with the profession's promises. Indeed, in private moments, even Browne had come close to confessing therapeutic bankruptcy. Surely, one had to fear the consequences of this situation:

> If therapeutical agents are cast aside or degraded from their legitimate rank, it will become the duty of the physician to give place to the divine or moralist, whose chosen mission it is to minister to the mind diseased; and of the heads of an establishment like [the Crichton Royal] to depute their authority to the well-educated man of the world, who could, I feel assured, conduct an asylum fiscally, and as an intellectual boarding-house, a great deal better than any of us.[232]

Browne's response to the implicit threat, like that adopted by most of the rest of his colleagues,[233] was to insist on 'the absurdity of a pure metaphysician being entrusted with the study of the mind diseased'[234] since,

> We know it as a physiological truth that we cannot reach the mind even when employing purely *psychical* means, when bringing mind to act on mind, except through material organs. It may be that even moral means exercise *their* influence by stimulating or producing changes in organization. It is *certain* that all we know of mental disease is as a symptom, an *expression*, of morbid changes in our bodies. ...[235]

In language all-too-revelatory of the political issues at stake, he denounced '[h]e who refuses the aid of medicine [as being] as much a heretic to the truth faith as he who doubts the efficacy of moral agents'[236] – a conclusion which prompted a rueful retrospective

glance at the very book which had brought him fame and professional prominence:

> Benevolence and sympathy suggested and developed, and, in
> my opinion, unfortunately enhanced the employment of
> moral means, either to the exclusion, or to the undue dis-
> paragement of physical means, of cure and alleviation. I
> confess to have aided at one time in this revolution; which
> cannot be regarded in any better light than as treason to the
> principles of our profession.[237]

In the final analysis, one might abandon the millenarian expectations on which the edifice that was Victorian asylumdom had been
mistakenly constructed – but not betray one's commitment to the
medical monopolization of the treatment of the mad.

Browne's election as the first president of the newly-named
Medico-Psychological Association capped a long career as one of
the most prominent of British alienists. Soon thereafter, however,
an accident brought an abrupt and unexpected end to his service
as a Lunacy Commissioner, and to his active involvement in the
administration of Victorian asylumdom. While inspecting the
condition of lunatics in Haddingtonshire in the winter of 1870, he
was thrown from his carriage, suffering serious head injuries which
within six months left him blind. For the last fifteen years of his life
he was thus forced into an unwanted retirement, cared for by his
two unmarried daughters at his Dumfries home, till his sudden
death from a heart attack on March 2, 1885, just three months short
of his eightieth birthday.

Notes

1. For a comprehensive overview of these developments in England, see
   Andrew Scull (1979) *Museums of Madness: The Social Organization
   of Insanity in Nineteenth Century England*, London: Allen Lane/
   New York: St Martin's Press. For a contrasting interpretation, more
   congenial to the psychiatric powers that be, see Kathleen Jones (1955)
   Lunacy, Law, and Conscience, London: Routledge & Kegan Paul.
2. [John Conolly] (1838) 'Review of *What Asylums Were, Are, and
   Ought to Be*,' *British and Foreign Medical Review*, 5, no. 9: 65–74.
   The lectures' force, Conolly complained, 'is somewhat weakened by a

kind of challenging and declamatory style ... a verbose declamation which should surely have been retrenched before publication. His style is remarkably round-a-bout ... ; becomes ineffective by aiming at the forcible; and his lectures acquire a kind of colouring, as if intended to astonish more than teach ... he overloads with eloquence.' (Ibid., pp. 70–1.) Curiously enough, these were precisely the defects of Conolly's own writing and speech, a preference for verbosity and 'oleaginous periphrasis' that were to be savagely mocked by Charles Reade in his fictional portrait of Conolly as a bumbling, secretly mad hypocrite. (See Reade (1864) *Hard Cash: A Matter of Fact Romance*, London: Ward, Lock, pp. 203–12, 335–9.) The *Edinburgh Medical and Surgical Journal*, in the course of a generally favourable review (1837, 48: 513–18), made similar complaints about 'the faults of Mr Browne's style', which it found 'far too florid for a didactic work like the present'.

3. W. A. F. Browne (1837) *What Asylums Were, Are, and Ought to Be*, Edinburgh: Black, p. viii.
4. Conolly's pre-eminence among English alienists extended over almost precisely the same time period, from his assumption of his duties at Hanwell in 1839 till his death at Lawn House in 1866.
5. See Andrew Scull (1989) 'John Conolly: A Victorian Psychiatric Career', ch. 7, pp. 162–212 in *Social Order/Mental Disorder: Anglo American Psychiatry in Historical Perspective* London: Routledge/ Berkeley: University of California Press.
6. William Parry-Jones (1972) *The Trade in Lunacy*, London: Routledge & Kegan Paul.
7. For the English speaking world, see the discussion in Andrew Scull (1974) 'From Madness to Mental Illness: Medical Men as Moral Entrepreneurs', *European Journal of Sociology*, 15: 219–61, and in William F. Bynum (1981) 'Rationales for Therapy in British Psychiatry, 1780–1835', pp. 35–57 in Andrew Scull (ed.) *Madhouses, Mad-doctors, and Madmen: The Social History of Psychiatry in the Victorian Era*, London: Athlone/Philadelphia: University of Pennsylvania Press; and for France, see Jan Goldstein (1987) *Console and Classify: The French Psychiatric Profession in the Nineteenth Century*, Cambridge: Cambridge University Press.
8. Ironically enough, to a Scots *émigré* named Stirling.
9. Magali Larson (1977) *The Rise of Professionalism: A Sociological Analysis*, Berkeley: University of California Press.
10. Irvine Loudon (1986) *Medical Care and the General Practitioner, 1750–1850*, Oxford: Clarendon Press.
11. Loudon, *Medical Care*, pp. 183–5, 270–1, *et passim*.

12. W. A. F. Browne, 'Application and Testimonials for the Super-intendency of the Montrose Royal Lunatic Asylum', quoted in C. C. Easterbrook (1940) *The Chronicle of Crichton Royal (1833–1936)*, Courier Press: Dumfries, p. iv.

13. cf. G. Cantor (1975) 'The Edinburgh Phrenology Debate: 1803–1828', *Annals of Science*, 32: 195–218; S. Shapin (1975) 'Phrenological Knowledge and the Social Structure of Nineteenth Century Edinburgh', *Annals of Science*, 32: 219–43; *idem* (1978) 'The Politics of Observation: Cerebral Anatomy and Social Interests in the Edinburgh Phrenology Disputes', pp. 139–78 in R. Wallis (ed.) *On the Margins of Science*, Keele, Staffordshire: Sociological Review Monograph No. 27.

14. Browne was to serve as a Vice-President of the Edinburgh Phrenological Society in 1830–31 and again in 1831–32, and as one of the founding members and President of the Edinburgh Ethical Society for the Study and Practical Application of Phrenology. His close friendship with the dominant figures in Edinburgh phrenological circles, George and Andrew Combe (to the latter of whom he dedicated *What Asylums Were, Are, and Ought to Be*), was subsequently rewarded with their powerful sponsorship at a critical moment in his career. In the early 1830s, Browne was one of the most popular lecturers on phrenology, an activity from which one could derive a substantial income. Conolly was a founding member of the Warwickshire and Leamington Phrenological Society in the 1830s, and in 1843 served as chairman of the Phrenological Association.

15. cf. Roger Cooter, 'Phrenology and British Alienists, ca. 1825–1845', pp. 58–104 in Scull (ed.) *Madhouses, Mad-Doctors, and Madmen*.

16. Andrew Combe (1797–1847) was the fifteenth child and seventh son of an Edinburgh brewer, George Combe, and grew up in a rigid and emotionally stultifying Calvinist household. He qualified as a surgeon in 1817, became a convert to phrenology shortly thereafter, and spent the spring of 1819 at the Salpêtrière in Paris, where he attended Esquirol's lectures on mental derangement. One of the four founding members of the Edinburgh Phrenological Society in 1820, he received his MD from Edinburgh University in 1825. President of the Phrenological Society in 1827, he was much in demand as a public lecturer, and wrote two hugely successful popular treatises on hygiene and domestic medicine, as well as *Observations on Mental Derangement: Being An Application of Phrenology to the Elucidation of the Causes, Symptoms, Nature and Treatment of Insanity*, Edinburgh: Anderson, 1831. For most of his adult life, he suffered from tuberculosis, the disease which eventually killed him.

17. George Combe (1788–1858), older brother of Andrew, was an

Edinburgh lawyer converted to phrenology on the occasion of J. G. Spurzheim's visit to Edinburgh in 1816–17. Made a wealthy man by the stupendous commercial success of *The Constitution of Man* (Edinburgh: John Anderson, 1828), which once sold 2,000 copies in the space of ten days in Britain and went through twenty American editions by 1851, he enjoyed a world-wide reputation as a social reformer and advocate of phrenological doctrines, and possessed an ego to match.

18. Shapin, 'The Politics of Observation', p. 147.
19. See, in addition to the studies referred to in note 13 above, David A. De Giustino (1975) *The Conquest of Mind: Phrenology and Victorian Social Thought*, London: Croom Helm; Robert Young (1970) *Mind, Brain, and Adaptation in the Nineteenth Century*, Oxford: Clarendon Press; Roger Cooter (1976) 'Phrenology: The Provocation of Progress', *History of Science*, 15: 211–34; *idem* (1984) *The Cultural Meaning of Popular Science: Phrenology and the Organization of Consent in Nineteenth Century Britain*, Cambridge: Cambridge University Press; and Terry Parssinen (1974) 'Popular Science and Society: The Phrenology Movement in Early Victorian Britain', *Journal of Social History*, Fall, pp. 1–20.
20. E. H. Ackerknecht (1967) *Medicine at the Paris Hospital 1794–1848*, Baltimore: Johns Hopkins University Press, p. 172.
21. Shapin, 'Phrenological Knowledge', p. 232.
22. For George Combe's own commentary on this phenomenon, see his *The Life and Correspondence of Andrew Combe, M.D.*, Edinburgh: Maclachlan and Stewart (1850), especially pp. 44–8, 183–4, 191–4.
23. Shapin, 'The Politics of Observation', p. 145.
24. Shapin's essays provide the most subtle, sophisticated, and convincing discussion of these connections between phrenological ideas and the social structure of early nineteenth century Edinburgh.
25. Shapin, 'The Politics of Observation', p. 143.
26. Roger Cooter, 'Phrenology and British Alienists', p. 67.
27. George Combe subsequently appointed him as one of the trustees of his estate.
28. W. A. F. Browne, 'Application and Testimonials Presented to the Managers of the Montrose Lunatic Asylum', quoted in Easterbrook, *Crichton Royal*, p. iv.
29. See John Conolly (1830) *An Inquiry Concerning the Indications of Insanity*, London: Taylor. Conolly's critique of the asylum, and advocacy of domiciliary care, are discussed in Scull, *Social Order/ Mental Disorder*, ch. 7.

30. Andrew Combe to George Combe, 22 March, 1834, reprinted in George Combe, *Life of Andrew Combe*, pp. 228–9.
31. Ibid., p. 229.
32. Eliot Freidson (1970) *The Profession of Medicine: A Study in the Sociology of Applied Knowledge*, New York: Dodd, Mead, p. 10. For an insightful analysis of the processes of claiming, competing for, and controlling jurisdictions as constitutive of 'the real, determining history of the professions', see Andrew Abbott (1988) *The System of Professions: An Essay on the Division of Expert Labor*, Chicago: University of Chicago Press. And for a useful comparative perspective on how American 'doctors acquired sole jurisdiction over this large and costly new medical establishment', see Nancy Tomes (1984) *A Generous Confidence: Thomas Story Kirkbride and the Art of Asylum-Keeping, 1840–1883*, Cambridge: Cambridge University Press.
33. Easterbrook, *Chronicle*, p. 616.
34. W. A. F. Browne (1864) 'The Moral Treatment of the Insane: A Lecture', *Journal of Mental Science*, 10: 312. Conolly was, if anything, still less prepared for his new tasks at Hanwell. Given his disastrous track record of managing his own life in the years prior to his appointment, and the extraordinary size of Hanwell's patient population (already verging on a thousand), his success was perhaps even more remarkable than Browne's.
35. Browne, 'Moral Treatment', p. 313.
36. Ibid.
37. Browne, *Asylums*, p. 1.
38. See 'Facts Regarding the Statistics of Insanity', *The Lancet* 2, 8 July, 1837, pp. 543–4, pp. 555–6. (Excerpting some portions of Browne's text, Wakley praised the book as 'filled with instruction on a most important subject, and [one that] appeals, irresistibly, to the benevolent sympathies of the public, and is destined, we trust, to be widely circulated and universally read ...'); [John Conolly], 'Review'; Anon. (1837) 'Review of *What Asylums Were, Are, and Ought to Be*', *Edinburgh Medical and Surgical Journal*, 48: 513–18. Not surprisingly, Browne also received a generally laudatory review in the *Phrenological Journal* (1836–37, pp. 687–95), where his discussion was hailed for putting 'the various divisions of the subject into a shape, attractive at once to unprofessional and professional purposes'.
39. See, especially, Roy Porter (1987) *Mind Forg'd Manacles: A History of Madness in England from the Restoration to the Regency*, London: Athlone; and Andrew Scull (1983) 'The Domestication of Madness', *Medical History*, 27: 233–48.

40. cf. Ida MacAlpine and Richard Hunter (1969) *George III and the Mad-Business*, London: Allen Lane.
41. Abbott, *The System of Professions*, p. 40. As Abbott points out, 'the sequence of diagnosis, inference, and treatment embodies the essential cultural logic of professional practice. It is within this logic that tasks receive the subjective qualities that are the cognitive structure of a jurisdictional claim.'
42. In 1823, Morison began his own annual course of lectures on insanity, petitioning Edinburgh University to allow them to 'be attached to the course of study of medical students' and launching the proposal that 'there should be a professorship of Mental Diseases' three years later. His self-promotion, so successful in other directions, on this occasion was without result. The syllabus of his course, together with the substance of his lectures, appeared in published form in 1825 (*Outlines of Lectures on Mental Diseases*, Edinburgh: Lizars), and had appeared in four revised editions by 1848 (though the course itself, by his own admission, had attracted scarcely 'one hundred and fifty ... gentlemen' in the first two decades he offered it). Morison's career and activities in and around London are ably discussed in Nicholas Hervey (1987) 'The Lunacy Commission, 1845–1860, with Special Reference to the Implementation of Policy in Kent and Surrey', unpublished PhD dissertation, University of Bristol.
43. [W. H. Fitton] (1817) 'Lunatic Asylums', *Edinburgh Review*, 28: 431–71.
44. Here again, the *Edinburgh Review* had played a major role, its lengthy notice of Samuel Tuke's *Description of the Retreat* (York: Alexander, 1813) serving to introduce most of its readers to the new approach to madness. See [Sydney Smith] (1814) 'An Account of the York Retreat', *Edinburgh Review*, 23: 189–98.
45. See Andrew Scull, 'Moral Treatment Reconsidered', ch. 4, pp. 80–94 in *Social Order, Mental Disorder*; and Roy Porter, *Mind Forg'd Manacles*, especially p. 277.
46. Samuel Tuke (1813) *Description of the Retreat: An Institution near York for Insane Persons of the Society of Friends*, York: Alexander, pp. vi, 158. In W. A. F. Browne's words, the task of those employing moral treatment was 'to offer temptations to the lunatic to cooperate in his own restoration'. Quoted in the *Phrenological Journal* (1836–37), 10, No. 49: 248.
47. Tuke, *Description of the Retreat*, pp. 110, 111, 115.
48. Among other misfortunes, the hearings revealed the profession's utter inability to agree on even the most basic issues. The spectacle of internecine bickering and the wildly discrepant and contradictory

assertions made by medical witnesses could only have served to undermine public confidence in their claims to possess expertise in the treatment of the mad. As David Uwins ruefully remarked,

> Nothing could be more inconsistent than the reports made by medical men before the commissioners of inquiry, as to the curability of insanity. This one lauded one plan of treatment, that another; emetics were to do everything, according to the opinion of some, purgatives were reported by others, as almost the only medicinals upon which any reliance could be placed. This party talked of reducing, that of exciting; cold bathing was almost the catholicon of some physicians, others were avowedly more partial to warm bathing – but the most remarkable circumstance was, that many respectable men expressed their opinion, that very little could be done in madness by any medicinal measures, while others asserted insanity to be the most curable of all the maladies to which man is subject.

(David Uwins (1833) *A Treatise on those Disorders of the Brain and Nervous System, Which are Usually Considered and Called Mental*, London: Renshaw & Rush, p. 189.)

49. Bynum, 'Rationales for Therapy', p. 43.
50. See Godfrey Higgins (1814) *A Letter to the Right Honourable Earl Fitzwilliam Respecting the Investigation Which Has Lately Taken Place, into the Abuses at the York Lunatic Asylum*, Doncaster: Sheardown; *idem* (1816) *The Evidence Taken Before a Committee of the House of Commons Respecting the Asylum at York; With Observations and Notes, and a Letter to the Committee*, Doncaster: Sheardown.
51. Jonathan Gray (1815) *A History of the York Asylum, Addressed to William Wilberforce, Esq.*, York: Hargrove.
52. Samuel Nicoll (1828) *An Inquiry Into the Present State of Visitation, In Asylums for the Reception of the Insane*, London: Harvey & Darton.
53. Edward Wakefield (1812) 'Plan of an Asylum for Lunatics', *The Philanthropist*, 2: 226–9; *idem* (1813) 'Sir George O. Paul on Lunatic Asylums', *The Philanthropist*, 3: 214–27.
54. T[homas] H[ancock] (1813) 'Tuke's *Description of the Retreat*', *The Philanthropist*, 3: 326–38.
55. *Report of the Select Committee on Madhouses* (1815), p. 24. Wakefield was to modify this judgement the following year, after a visit to William Finch's establishment at Laverstock House, near Salisbury (see *First Report of the Select Committee on Madhouses* (1816), p. 36),

but it was his earlier judgement that was reflected in the bills introduced into Parliament over the next three years.

56. Godfrey Higgins, *The Evidence Respecting the Asylum at York*, p. 48.
57. R. A. Cage (1981) *The Scottish Poor Law, 1745–1845*, Edinburgh: Scottish University Press, pp. 84–9.
58. The impetus for change was the splitting apart of the Church of Scotland in 1843, when the so-called Disruption led two fifths of the clergy to leave to form the Free Church of Scotland, fatally undermining the ability of the established church to administer poor relief, and putting 'to the hazard the pitifully small sums available for poor relief'. Even then, despite an official inquiry which revealed widespread and abject poverty, legislative changes were minimal, and the fundamental opposition to the provision of relief for the able-bodied remained as firm as ever. cf. Cage, *Scottish Poor Law*, pp. 133–42.
59. E. P. Thompson (1963) *The Making of the English Working Class*, New York: Vintage Books, p. 82, *et passim*.
60. Andrew Halliday diagnosed the basis of the rejection: it arose, 'neither from the parsimony nor the poverty of the freeholders, but from a dread of introducing into the Kingdom that system which had been denominated the nightmare of England, the poor's rates'. (1828) *A General View of the Present State of Lunatics and Lunatic Asylums in Great Britain and Ireland*, London: Underwood, p. 28. As J. Steven Watson points out (1960, *The Reign of George III 1760–1815*, Oxford: Clarendon Press, pp. 280–1), 'Scotland had been ruled, in fact, since the Act of Union by her presbyterian established church. ... The kirk retained the power which in England had slipped from the church to the state. ... Real power in Scotland lay in the elective authoritarian councils of the church and not in the hands of the state'. The general role of Scotland's elected officials in Westminster was to prevent any central administrative interference with this state of affairs, to extract whatever largesse could be obtained from the governing clique in return for political support, and to ensure that authority remained firmly in the hands of the church and local aristocracy.
61. See Francis Tiffany (1890) *Life of Dorothea Lynde Dix*, Boston: Houghton, Mifflin; and Helen E. Marshall (1937) *Dorothea Dix: Forgotten Samaritan*, Chapel Hill, North Carolina: University of North Carolina Press.
62. Besides the Montrose Asylum, founded in 1781, these were located at Aberdeen (1800); Edinburgh (1813); Glasgow (1814); Dundee (1820); Perth (1826); and finally, at Dumfries (1839).
63. Some of these exposures took the form of books or pamphlets

published by ex-patients or disgruntled attendants. See, for example, J. W. Rogers (1816) *A Statement of the Cruelties, Abuses, and Frauds, which Are Practised in Mad-Houses*, London: for the author; John Mitford (1825) *A Description of the Crimes and Horrors in the Interior of Warburton's Private Mad-House at Hoxton*, London: Benbow; John Perceval (1840) *A Narrative of the Treatment Experienced by a Gentleman, During a State of Mental Derangement*, London: Effingham Wilson. Two Parliamentary inquiries provided further examples of the conditions exposed in 1815–16: *Report from the Select Committee on Pauper Lunatics in the County of Middlesex* (1827); and *Report from the Select Committee on Hereford Lunatic Asylum* (1839). And, from 1830, the newly established Metropolitan Commissioners in Lunacy provided annual reports on the madhouses in the metropolis, adding a nationwide survey in 1844 (*Report of the Metropolitan Commissioners in Lunacy to the Lord Chancellor, 1844*, London: Bradbury & Evans).

64. The problem is quite openly recognized and discussed in one of Andrew Combe's letters, written on 13 July, 1840, to the author of a pamphlet attacking treatment in lunatic asylums: 'Your work will strengthen the prejudice against asylums as moral lazar-houses ... [by reinforcing] the popular notion of the cruel treatment of lunatics, and the great aversion thence arising either to have the patients removed to an asylum, or even to admit that insanity really exists. Every effort is consequently made by both patient and friends to suppress and conceal the truth. ...' Only when the public could be 'led to regard asylums as infirmaries for the cure and kind treatment of that disease' and might be brought to view insanity as 'neither an anomalous visitation of a mysterious Providence, nor an affliction involving any stigma, or incapable of cure ... [could] full justice ... be done to the unhappy lunatic'. See George Combe, *Life of Andrew Combe*, pp. 376–7.

65. Compare the London physician John Reid's denunciation of madhouses as 'our medical prisons ... our *slaughter houses* for the destruction and mutilation of the human mind'. John Reid (1816) *An Essay on Insanity, Hypochondriacal and other Nervous Affections*, London: Longman, Hurst, Rees, Orme, & Brown, p. 206, emphasis in the original.

66. Those advocating institutional treatment of the mad frequently commented on the resistance of patients' families to the notion that they should pack their nearest and dearest off to an asylum as soon as the symptoms of mental alienation manifested themselves. George Man Burrows, for instance, urging 'the great utility of separation', portrayed asylum care as the foundation of successful treatment:

There is no general maxim in the treatment of insanity wherein medical practitioners, ancient or modern, foreign or domestic are so unanimous, as that of separating the patient from all customary association, his family, and his home; and there is none wherein the advice of the faculty is so commonly and successfully opposed. Thus cases which in the early stages are comparatively manageable, obedient to medical discipline, and commonly curable, are rendered obstinate, tedious, unnecessarily expensive, and too often incurable.

(Burrows, *Commentaries on the Causes, Forms, Symptoms, and Treatment, Moral and Medical, of Insanity*, London: Underwood, 1828, pp. 696–7.)

67. The term is Ellen Dwyer's: see her *Homes for the Mad: Life Inside Two Nineteenth Century Asylums*, New Brunswick, New Jersey: Rutgers University Press, 1987.

68. In the words of the *Phrenological Journal* (1836–37, p. 688), 'The chief obstacle seems to have been the difficulty of convincing [the political powers that be] of the necessity of the various improvements. Another impediment of no less magnitude has been the want of a cordial cooperation on the part of the relations of the insane[, and] the difficulty of inducing them to consent to the removal to asylums and the early employment of effectual treatment. ...'

69. Thomas Mayo (1817) *Remarks on Insanity*, London: Underwood, p. v.

70. Francis Willis (1823) *A Treatise on Mental Derangement*, London: Longman, p. 2.

71. William Lawrence (1819) *Lectures on the Physiology, Zoology, and Natural History of Man*, London: Callow, p. 114.

72. 'Insanity and Madhouses', *Quarterly Review* (1816) 15: 402.

73. John Haslam (1817) *Considerations on the Moral Management of Insane Persons*, London: Hunter, pp. 2–3.

74. See George Man Burrows (1817) *Cursory Remarks on a Bill Now in the House of Peers for Regulating Madhouses*, London: Harding.

75. See the *Minutes of Evidence Taken Before the Select Committee of the House of Lords on the Bills Relating to Lunatics and Lunatic Asylums*, London: 1828, especially the testimony of William Finch, E. T. Monro, and Edward Long Fox.

76. Mayo, *Remarks on Insanity*, p. v.

77. For a review of these efforts, see Andrew Scull, *Social Order/Mental Disorder*, ch. 6.

78. Browne, *Asylums*, p. viii.

79. Ibid., p. 99.

80. Ibid., pp. 1–2.
81. [George Combe] (1819) *Essays on Phrenology*, Edinburgh: Bell & Bradfute, pp. 304–6.
82. Shapin, 'Phrenological Knowledge', p. 228; de Giustino, *Conquest of Mind;* Cooter, *The Cultural Meaning of Popular Science.*
83. Andrew Combe, *Observations on Mental Derangement.*
84. Andrew Combe to an unknown correspondent, 1830, quoted in George Combe, *Life and Correspondence of Andrew Combe,* p. 189.
85. Combe, *Observations on Mental Derangement,* p. 353.
86. Conolly was, of course, the most prominent English alienist of his generation; Ellis was superintendent successively of the West Riding Asylum at Wakefield, and of the Hanwell Asylum in Middlesex and was the first alienist to be knighted; Alexander succeeded him at Wakefield; Poole was Browne's successor at Montrose (as well as being the first editor of the *Phrenological Journal*); Uwins was the physician to the Peckham Asylum in London and wrote regularly for the *Quarterly Review* on matters psychiatric; and Forbes Winslow, who owned two private madhouses in Hammersmith, later published the first English psychiatric periodical, the *Journal of Psychological Medicine.*
87. cf. Cooter, 'Phrenology and British Alienists'.
88. Cooter, 'Phrenology and British Alienists', p. 62.
89. See W. A. F. Browne 'On the Morbid Manifestations of the Organ of Language, as Connected with Insanity', *Phrenological Journal* (1832–34), 8: 250–60, 308–16, 414–23; *idem*, 'Observations on Religious Fanaticism', *Phrenological Journal* (1834–36), 9: 289–302, 532–45, 577–603; *idem*, 'Pathological Contribution to Phrenology: Case of a Patient in the Montrose Lunatic Asylum', *Phrenological Journal* (1836–38), 10: 45–52.
90. Andrew Combe to W. A. F. Browne, 28 January, 1837, reprinted in George Combe, *Life and Correspondence of Andrew Combe,* pp. 280–1.
91. Browne, *Asylums,* [p. v].
92. Ibid., p. viii.
93. Andrew Combe to Browne, 28 January, 1837, in George Combe, *Life and Correspondence of Andrew Combe,* p. 281.
94. W. A. F. Browne to Andrew Combe, 3 January, 1845, reprinted as an appendix to Andrew Combe (1846) *Phrenology – Its Nature and Uses*, Edinburgh: Maclachan, Stewart, p. 30.
95. Shapin, 'The Politics of Observation', p. 142.
96. De Giustino, *Conquest of Mind,* p. 100.

97. L. S. Jacyna (1982) 'Somatic Theories of Mind and the Interests of Medicine in Britain, 1850–1879', *Medical History*, 26: 248.

98. Browne, *Asylums*, p. viii.

99. [John Conolly], 'Review', p. 70.

100. Browne, *Asylums*, p. 3.

101. Ibid., p. 4.

102. Ibid., p. 7.

103. Compare David Skae's revealing commentary on the significance of a somatic etiology: 'Unless insanity is *a disease,* a disease of the brain affecting the mind, I do not see what we have to do with it more than other people: but if it is a disease, I maintain that we are bound to know more about it than other people.' David Skae (1867) 'On the Legal Relations of Insanity: The Civil Incapacity and Criminal Responsibility of the Insane', *Edinburgh Medical Journal*, 12: 813.

104. Browne, *Asylums*, p. 91.

105. Ibid., p. 69.

106. Ibid., p. 69. As Roger Smith notes, routinely in the discourse of nineteenth century alienists, 'Spiritualist theories of insanity were denigrated by association with therapeutic pessimism', Smith (1981) *Trial by Medicine: Insanity and Responsibility in Victorian Trials*, Edinburgh: Edinburgh University Press, p. 41.

107. See my extended discussion of these issues in *Social Order/Mental Disorder*, pp. 118–61.

108. Browne, *Asylums*, p. 178.

109. Ibid., p. 5.

110. Smith, *Trial by Medicine*. Compare Browne's own earlier modesty about what was known about the physical changes in cases of insanity: 'I have not attempted to penetrate into the means by which disease is produced. Without more extensive experience, and the aid of pathology, such an undertaking must prove vague and visionary.' W. A. F. Browne, 'On the Morbid Manifestations of the Organ of Language, as Connected with Insanity', *Phrenological Journal* (1832–34), 8: No. 38, 422.

111. William Nisbet (1815) *Two Letters to the Right Honourable George Rose, M.P., on the Reports at Present Before the House of Commons on the State of the Madhouses*, London: Cox, pp. 21–2. The primacy of the theoretical preconceptions over the empirical evidence to hand is evident in the insistence of those unable to demonstrate the necessary physical changes that such pathological alterations were nonetheless quite certainly present: 'the indications of physiology point to our imperfect powers of observation, and assure us that cerebral lesion, although in some cases inappreciable to our senses,

must exist in every instance of disordered mind'. John Charles Bucknill (1857) *Unsoundness of Mind in Relation to Criminal Acts*, 2nd edition, London: Longman, Brown, Green, Longmans, & Roberts, p. iv.

112. William Neville (1836) *On Insanity: Its Nature, Causes, and Cure*, London: Longman, Rees, Orme, Brown, Green, & Longmans, p. 18.

113. George Man Burrows (1821) *An Inquiry Into Certain Errors Relative to Insanity, and their Consequences, Physical, Moral, and Civil*, London: Underwood, p. 7.

114. Browne, *Asylums*, p. 4.

115. Smith, *Trial by Medicine*, p. 43.

116. As William Bynum has noted, such conflation of mind and soul has an ancient lineage, and can be traced even in the physical model of mind offered in David Hartley (1749) *Observations on Man, His Frame, His Duties, and His Expectations*, London: Leake & Frederick, 1749. See Bynum, 'Rationales', p. 38.

117. A few broke ranks and adopted a more thorough-going materialism. William Lawrence, for instance, spoke dismissively of the 'hypothesis or fiction of a subtle invisible matter, animating the visible textures of animal bodies'. This was, he continued, 'only an example of that propensity in the human mind, which has led men at all times to account for those phenomena, of which the causes are not obvious, by the mysterious aid of higher and imaginary beings ... and ... the immediate operation of the divinity'. Scientifically speaking, 'the mind, the grand prerogative of man' was nothing other than an aspect of 'the functions of the brain ... symptoms [of insanity] have the same relation to the brain, as vomiting, indigestion, heartburn, to the stomach; cough, asthma, to the lungs; or any other deranged functions to their corresponding organs'. (See William Lawrence (1816) *An Introduction to Comparative Anatomy and Physiology*, London: Callow; *idem* (1819) *Lectures on Physiology, Zoology, and the Natural History of Man*, London: Callow.) Such heterodox and atheistic opinions almost cost Lawrence his appointments at Bethlem and Bridewell and at St Bartholomew's Hospital (see Oswei Temkin (1963) 'Basic Science, Medicine, and the Romantic Era', *Bulletin of the History of Medicine*, 37: 97–129), notwithstanding his attempt to hedge his bets by emphasizing that he was only speaking '*physiologically* ... because the theological doctrine of the soul, and its separate existence, has nothing to do with this physiological question, but rests on a species of proof altogether different'. Even his own mentor, John Abernathy, attacked him for 'propagating

lxiv

opinions detrimental to society, and of ... loosening those [moral and religious] restraints, on which the welfare of mankind depends'. (Quoted in Richard Hunter and Ida MacAlpine (1963) *Three Hundred Years of Psychiatry, 1535–1860*, London: Oxford University Press, p. 748). Either because their own theological convictions barred such materialism, or from motives of prudence, few of Lawrence's medical colleagues publicly adopted his stance.

118. Compare, for instance, Sir Andrew Halliday's discussion of this point. In attempting to ground the medical profession's *a priori* insistence on the somatic roots of madness,

> the anatomist sought in vain for some visible derangement of structure, or a diseased state of the parts in many cases where it was perfectly ascertainable that death had ensued from insanity ... hence the common opinion seemed to be confirmed, that it was an incomprehensible and consequently an incurable malady of mind. Taking this view of the disease, it is not at all wonderful that it was considered as beyond the reach of medical science. ... Besides, we may suppose that many very able men, led away by what appeared to be the general opinion of mankind, would shrink from the investigation of a subject that seemed to lead to a doubt of the immateriality of mind; a truth so evident to their own feelings and so expressly established by divine revelation. If they once admitted that the mind could become diseased, it would follow, as a matter of course, that the mind might die. They therefore refrained from meeting a question which involved such dangerous consequences ...

> (*A General View of the Present State of Lunatics and Lunatic Asylums*, pp. 2–4.)

119. Browne, *Asylums*, p. 4.
120. Ibid.; Morison, *Lectures on Insanity*, pp. 35–7.
121. Browne, *Asylums*, p. 4. For variations on this line of reasoning, which more starkly reveal the ultimately theological basis on which most alienists sought to validate their claim that insanity was a somatic disorder, see Morison, *Lectures on Insanity*, pp. 34–44; and Andrew Halliday (1828) *A General View of the Present State of Lunatics and Lunatic Asylums in Great Britain and Ireland*, London: Underwood, pp. 5–8.
122. For an interesting analysis of parallel developments in French psychiatric theorizing during the Second Empire, see Ian Dowbiggin (1989) 'French Psychiatry and the Search for a Professional Identity:

The Société Medico-Psychologique, 1840–1879', *Bulletin of the History of Medicine*, 63: 331–5.

123. Browne, *Asylums*, pp. 54–5.
124. Ibid., pp. 54–5.
125. Ibid., p. 63.
126. George Man Burrows, *Commentaries on Insanity*, pp. 21–3, was one of the few dissenters from the ruling orthodoxy. Of course, the connections between artificiality, over-stimulation, luxury and madness had been a staple of speculation on the causes of nervous distempers at least since the publication of George Cheyne (1733) *The English Malady*, London: Wisk, Ewing, & Smith. For a general discussion of the persistence of this belief as a staple of nineteenth century psychiatric theorizing, see D. J. Mellett (1982) *The Prerogative of Asylumdom*, New York: Garland, pp. 64–9. David Rothman's mistaken attempts to claim that such theorizing was a uniquely American phenomenon (in his (1971) *The Discovery of the Asylum*, Boston: Little, Brown) at least serve to demonstrate how widely this myth was disseminated.
127. Browne, *Asylums*, p. 52. The point is echoed by his anonymous reviewer in the *Phrenological Journal* (1836–37, 10, No. 53: 691): 'In that state of society which is now termed civilized, the sources of mental excitation and disease are almost beyond computation.'
128. Ibid., pp. 52–3. For a parallel discussion, see J. C. Bucknill and D. H. Tuke (1858) *A Manual of Psychological Medicine*, Philadelphia: Blanchard & Lee, pp. 48, 58.
129. Browne, *Asylums*, p. 55.
130. Compare Johann Gaspar Spurzheim's earlier, and less extreme, formulation: 'no one is secure from [insanity]; ... rich and poor, the laborious and sober labourer and his master who indulges in scenes of luxury are all equally liable to this affliction'. (*Observations on the Deranged Manifestations of the Mind, or Insanity* (1817), London: Baldwin, Craddock, & Joy.)
131. Browne, *Asylums*, p. 59.
132. Ibid., p. 61.
133. Ibid., pp. 56–7. Browne insists on this point: 'the situation, education, and habits of the [wealthy classes] are all more favourable to the development of the moral causes of insanity, than can be affirmed of the condition of the poor'. Ibid., p. 59. In David Uwins' more alliterative formulation, which placed particular emphasis on the vulnerability of the bourgeois and professional classes: 'Pianos, parasols, *Edinburgh Reviews*, and Paris-going desires, are now found among a class of persons who formerly thought these things

belonged to a different race; these are the true sources of nervousness and mental ailments.' (*Treatise*, p. 51.)

134. At a similar stage in the legitimation of the asylum in the United States, such figures as Thomas Story Kirkbride offered virtually identical accounts of insanity as a disease to which anyone was prone, even as the special province of the educated, the wealthy, the most cultured segments of the community. 'Insanity', he informed his readers, 'is truly the great leveller of all the artificial distinctions of society ... an accident ... to which we are all liable, ... no reproach to anyone ... it is found among the purest and best of all dwellers upon earth, as well as those who are far from being models of excellence ... [among] persons of cultivated and refined minds ... high social position, exalted intellectual endowment, the most abundant wealth.' Quoted in Nancy Tomes, 'A Generous Confidence: Thomas Story Kirkbride's Philosophy of Asylum Construction and Management', in Scull (ed.) *Madhouses, Mad-Doctors, and Madmen*, p. 126. In the first half of the nineteenth century, alienists throughout Western Europe and North America faced the same structural task of simultaneously legitimating the asylum and their own position as its governing authority. Kirkbride's *On the Construction, Organization, and General Arrangements of Hospitals for the Insane* (1854, Philadephia: Lindsay & Blakiston) is thus the American, as Conolly's (1847) *On the Construction and Government of Lunatic Asylums* (London: Churchill) is the English, and Maximilian Jacobi's (1834) *Ueber die Anlegung und Einrichtung von Irren-Heilanstalt* (Berlin: G. Reimer) the German counterpart of Browne's book.

135. cf. Scull, *Museums of Madness*, Chs 6 and 7.

136. Henry Maudsley (1879) *The Pathology of Mind*, London: Macmillan, p. 105.

137. Ibid., p. 115.

138. Daniel Hack Tuke (1878) *Insanity in Ancient and Modern Life*, London: Macmillan, p. 152. In Tuke's words, 'On admission, "No good" is plainly inscribed on their foreheads.' By the mid-1860s, Browne, too, had revised his earlier judgement: 'although the blight of alienation falls upon the purest and highest spirit, the blight falls heaviest and most poisonously upon those of imperfect character, or ungoverned passions, and degraded propensities'. Consequently, 'In many senses an asylum should be a grand moral school and reformatory, as well as an hospital.' Browne, 'Moral Treatment', pp. 314–15.

139. Browne, *Asylums*, p. 177.

140. Ibid., p. 172.

141. Ibid., pp. 99, 101. More complex portraits of the *ancien regime* madhouse may be found in Parry-Jones, *The Trade in Lunacy*; and in Porter *Mind Forg'd Manacles*.

142. Browne, *Asylums*, p. 128.

143. Ibid., p. 101.

144. Ibid., pp. 133, 107.

145. Ibid., p. 138. The description Browne gives here of Pinel liberating the insane at the Bicêtre had rapidly become one of the most hackneyed images in the alienists' own version of their history. That modern scholarship has demonstrated its almost wholly mythical character (see Goldstein, *Console and Classify*, pp. 72–119) does not detract in the least from its rhetorical and practical importance in the constitution of Victorian asylumdom. One should note here the political significance of Browne's choice of Pinel as the founding father of moral treatment, and thus of alienism. William Tuke has at least equal claim to the title, and his work at the Retreat was far better known to a British audience. Perhaps the choice in part reflects Browne's Parisian experiences, and his extended contact with Pinel's most famous pupil, Esquirol. But Browne, as his later career and writings were to re-emphasize, was centrally concerned to make the treatment of madness an exclusively medical prerogative. (He was subsequently to accuse medical men who were insufficiently active in this cause of 'treason' to the profession.) The shadowy presence, throughout the book, of the Retreat, and of the tea and coffee merchant who founded it, is thus wholly unsurprising; as is the choice to emphasize a rival who, however sceptical he may have been of the value of a medical therapeutics for madness, at least had the merit of being one of the two or three best-known physicians in Revolutionary France.

146. Browne, *Asylums*, p. 139.

147. Ibid., p. 139.

148. Ibid., p. 176.

149. Ibid., p. 203.

150. Ibid., p. 213.

151. Ibid., p. 183.

152. Ibid., p. 191.

153. Ibid., p. 203.

154. See John Conolly, *The Indications of Insanity*, p. 31: 'the fault of the association of lunatics with each other, and the infrequency of any communication between the patient and persons of sound mind mars the whole design [of employing the asylum to treat the mad]'. See also George Nesse Hill (1814) *An Essay on the Prevention and Cure*

of Insanity, London: Longman, Hurst, Rees, Orme, & Brown, pp. 222, 220: 'congregating insane people together in the promiscuous way which has too long obtained is an evil of the most pernicious tendency ... public charities and private asylums stand opposed to all rational plans of speedy and permanent cure of insanity, and from their very nature are the most unfavourable situations in which ... lunatics ... can be placed'.

155. He emphasizes the expertise necessary to accomplish this task: 'the mind of every individual should be carefully studied, its healthy as well as insane bearings analyzed, and the relations which these may have with, or the influence they may acquire upon the minds of others calculated, and groups formed in reference to the result'. Browne, *Asylums*, p. 200.
156. Ibid., p. 207.
157. Ibid., p. 201.
158. Ibid., p. 199.
159. Ibid., p. 169.
160. Ibid., p. 181.
161. W. A. F. Browne, quoted in 'Miscellaneous Notices – Dundee and Montrose Lunatic Asylums', *Phrenological Journal* (1836–37), 10, No. 49: 248.
162. Browne, *Asylums*, p. 156.
163. Ibid., p. 155.
164. Ibid., p. 50.
165. Ibid., p. 178.
166. Ibid., p. 180.
167. 'Review of *What Asylums Were, Are, and Ought to Be*', *Phrenological Journal* (1836–37), 10, No. 53: 697.
168. The centrality and the necessarily untrammelled power of the asylum superintendent are consistently insisted upon by Browne throughout his career as a vital 'element in curative discipline. He is not merely a dispenser of advice and medicine, he is a moral governor, who identifies himself with the happiness as well as the health of those around; a referee in all disputes and difficulties; a depository of all secrets and sorrows; a source of pleasure, as well as of power and direction, and who gives a tone to every proceedings.' *(Crichton Royal Asylum, 11th Annual Report* (1850), p. 39.) In his 1864 lecture on 'The Moral Treatment of the Insane' (*Journal of Mental Science* (1864) 10: 334), the royal analogy is made overt.

> The power of government by which such communities are ruled should be monarchical. The details, as well as the principles,

should emanate from one central will; while much must be left to the spontaneous good sense and good feeling of subordinates, these subordinates should be chosen, their views and acts should be influenced, their whole bearing determined by the supreme official.

169. Browne, *Asylums*, pp. 229–31. Compare Conolly's equally optimistic portrait of the modern asylum as the place where,

> calmness will come; hope will revive; satisfaction will prevail; ... almost all disposition to meditate mischievous or fatal revenge, or self-destruction, will disappear; ... cleanliness and decency will be maintained or restored; and despair itself will sometimes be found to give place to cheerfulness or secure tranquility. [This is the place] where humanity, if anywhere on earth, shall reign supreme.

(John Conolly (1847) *On the Construction and Government of Lunatic Asylums*, London: Churchill, p. 143.)

170. Karl Polanyi (1957) *The Great Transformation*, Boston: Beacon Press.

171. It was these very features of the reformed asylum regime that were most commonly remarked on when its achievements were advertised to the public at large. Compare, for instance, the *Medical Times'* (20 January, 1844) report on an evening at Hanwell: '[one] could not but have been gratified with the affectionate regard shewn to authority, and perfect attention paid to good order and harmony, by a multitude of human beings, whom society has been accustomed to treat as so little under the empire of mankind's better feelings. Such instances as this give us bright hopes for the present age's achievements in the great field of practical benevolence.' Or the report in the *Glasgow Citizen* (2 February, 1844) on a performance of *Guy Mannering* by a mixed cast of patients and staff at the Glasgow Lunatic Asylum: 'Nothing could be more gratifying than the harmony and good order observable in the establishment, and the friendly, and even affectionate, regard in which Dr Hutcheson seemed to be held by the inmates.' See also *The Times*, 5 January, 1842, p. 5, column f; 'Lunatic Asylums', *Quarterly Review* (1857), 101: 375–6. Compare, too, Browne's own variation on this theme: describing the Halloween celebration that brought the asylum year to a close, he remarks that,

> In watching this scene; in analysing the groups which moved through the brightly lighted and garlanded hall; in scanning the glee and gladness of every countenance, the regularity and joyousness of the dance, and the decorum and propriety, and yet the

unrestrained pleasure of every proceeding, we were accompanied
by a professional friend who could recall the former condition of
the insane ... it may be boldly, yet humbly affirmed, that
the system which inculcates, and permits, and produces such
exhibitions, which can conduct one-half of its pupils through such
an ordeal [sic], cannot be altogether evil, or vain, or visionary.

(*Crichton Royal Asylum, 3rd Annual Report* (1842), p. 31.)

172. [Conolly], 'Review', p. 74.
173. The Crichton Royal owed its existence to a very substantial bequest
from Elizabeth Crichton's husband, Dr James Crichton, the bulk of
whose fortune derived from his service in the East India Company.
On his death in 1823, he left the residue of his estate, amounting to
well over £100,000, for charitable purposes, its precise use or uses to
be determined by his widow. Her initial plans to found a university
at Dumfries were blocked by the existing Scottish universities, and it
was not until 1833 that she decided to build a lunatic asylum instead.
Her plan was not popular locally: 'The Building was commenced
amidst much ridicule, and in so far as public opinion went, even
some opposition.' *Dumfries and Galloway Courier*, 29 August, 1838.
174. Sir James Crichton-Browne, 'Some Early Crichton Memories',
foreword to Easterbrook, *The Chronicle of Crichton Royal*, p. 3.
175. His long tenure at the head of a sizeable asylum forms a marked
contrast with John Conolly's career. Conolly assumed the superintendency of the Hanwell County Asylum in Middlesex, with its
thousand pauper patients, the same year that the Crichton Royal
Asylum received its first patient. By 1844, however, threatened with
the prospect of having to divide his authority with a lay superintendent, he had resigned, staying on as 'visiting and consulting
physician' for a few years more, before severing his connection with
Hanwell entirely in 1852. From the mid-1840s, Conolly was forced
to earn his living from the private madhouse trade. Notwithstanding
his eminence, this permanently debarred him from an appointment
as a commissioner in lunacy. Legally such appointments were
frowned upon, reflecting the still-disreputable overtones of the
profit-making asylum business, with the consequence that not a
single proprietor of a private asylum was recruited to the ranks of the
Lunacy Commission during the nineteenth century.
176. On asylum reports and their audiences, cf. Nancy Tomes, 'A
Generous Confidence', pp. 125–39. In Browne's own words: 'We
conceive that the chief use of such annual summaries as the present, is
to introduce the public to the interior of an Asylum; to expose
transactions which cannot be witnessed, or even conjectured, by any

other means, and to explain principles which otherwise can only be gathered from their results. They are not addressed to professional men, and are not, therefore, intended to be scientific treatises. . .'. *Crichton Royal Asylum 3rd Annual Report* (1842), p. 5.

177. There is, nonetheless, something distinctly odd about his incessantly reiterated insistence on his own selflessness and un(self)conscious references to his 'God-like' qualities. The self-congratulatory tone is evident, for instance, in the following passage from his *12th Annual Report* of 1851 (p. 36):

> if it be recollected that there is no suspension of these offices and ministrations; that there is no holiday from the vagaries and caprices, and sufferings of the insane, nor from the supervision and anxiety which these exact; that every new case creates new cares; that the seclusion of the guardians is nearly as complete as that of their charges; it must be a matter of satisfaction that individuals have been found capable of such self-denial, and of discharging such complicated and arduous duties, who interpret aright the God-like act of giving a hand to the lunatic and raising him up, and whose chief reward consists in seeing him seated, clothed, and in his right mind.

A half a dozen years later, retiring from the superintendency, he lauds himself for possessing 'the single and unselfish purpose of carrying healing and happiness to the sorrowing and suffering, of restoring useful members to society, and or protecting from themselves, and from evils which they can neither foresee nor avoid, the waifs and strays, the weak and wayward of our race.' *Crichton Royal Asylum 18th Annual Report* (1857), p. 5.

178. *Crichton Royal Asylum, 13th Annual Report* (1852), p. 36.
179. *Crichton Royal Asylum, 3rd Annual Report* (1842), pp. 15–16.
180. Crichton-Browne, 'Early Crichton Memories', p. 4.
181. *Crichton Royal Asylum, 5th Annual Report* (1844), p. 23.
182. The journal was published continuously for over a century, and attracted much contemporary attention, including strongly favourable notices in *The Lancet, Phrenological Journal, Chambers' Journal,* and the *Scotsman* during 1845. See Easterbrook, *Chronicle of Crichton Royal*, p. 40.
183. Ibid., p. 24.
184. Easterbrook, *Chronicle of Crichton Royal*, p. 24; *Crichton Royal Asylum, 12th Annual Report* (1851), pp. 22–8.
185. 'Promenades . . . are recommended to the higher classes as substitutes for employment, to those whom the feelings or prejudices or rank or

profession exclude from the operations in field and garden ...'.
Crichton Royal Asylum, 6th Annual Report (1845), p. 24.

186. In 1842, for example, he reported that 'Sixteen men have been almost constantly employed in the gardens and grounds; and this is a very large proportion of the male pauper inmates of the Establishment.' If inclement weather kept them indoors, mat-making, basket-weaving, mattress-making, shoe-mending, and watch- and clock-repairing all provided occupation. 'The female patients of all classes are more easily provided with employment, and are, perhaps, from previous custom and the nature of their avocations, more capable of continuous exertion.' *Crichton Royal Asylum, 3rd Annual Report* (1842), p. 24. Between 1842 and 1844, patient labour was used to construct large sand filter beds to purify the water drawn from the River Nith, a precaution which preserved the asylum from cholera when an epidemic broke out in Dumfries in 1848.

187. *Crichton Royal Asylum, 3rd Annual Report* (1842), p. 22.

188. *Crichton Royal Asylum, 11th Annual Report* (1850), p. 7; see also *14th Annual Report* (1853), p. 11 ('it is a well-established fact, that in whatever mode moral causes may act upon the mind, it is through physical changes'); *16th Annual Report* (1855), p. 9 ('It may be held to be an axiom, that there is physical disorder wherever mental alienation is manifested').

189. *Crichton Royal Asylum, 3rd Annual Report* (1842), p. 26.

190. Ibid., pp. 25–6.

191. Ibid., p. 26.

192. *Crichton Royal Asylum, 8th Annual Report* (1847), p. 20; *9th Annual Report* (1848), p. 23. The disease remained defiant.

193. Browne, 'Moral Treatment', p. 335.

194. *Crichton Royal Asylum, 8th Annual Report* (1847), pp. 19–20.

195. *Crichton Royal Asylum, 18th Annual Report* (1857), p. 18.

196. For a discussion of the significance of these dimensions of moral treatment, see Scull, *Social Order/Mental Disorder*, Chapter 4.

197. *Crichton Royal Asylum, 11th Annual Report* (1850), p. 39.

198. *Crichton Royal Asylum, 3rd Annual Report* (1842), p. 17.

199. *Crichton Royal Asylum, 7th Annual Report* (1846), p. 35.

200. *Crichton Royal Asylum, 11th Annual Report* (1850), p. 31.

201. *Crichton Royal Asylum, 7th Annual Report* (1846), p. 35.

202. cf. Browne, 'Moral Treatment', pp. 311–12, *et passim*. At an early stage, he insisted on 'the necessity for rigid, stringent, even stern discipline among the insane ...' (*Crichton Royal Asylum, 3rd Annual Report* (1842), p. 21). Elsewhere, Browne boasted that the use of dormitory accommodation for pauper patients 'continues the

discipline and inspection exercised during active pursuits into the night, and during silence and sleep. Control may thus penetrate into the very dreams of the insane.' *Crichton Royal Asylum, 10th Annual Report* (1849), p. 38. In general, he found pauper patients more malleable (p. 42):

> The plebian insane are more easily guided and governed than those of more cultivated mind, artificial habits, and elevated rank. For the same reasons they are more curable. . . . Perhaps derangement is a less complicated and intractable affection when attacking the limited elements, the plain and unsophisticated tendencies of the uneducated understanding. . . . Accustomed to obey, called upon for constant sacrifices of inclination, and convenience, and comfort, and prone to rely on others for advice and assistance, and to adopt their thoughts and opinions, the members of the working classes lose their individuality in a community like this, are readily influenced and moved in masses, frequently yield up a delusion as they yield up an opinion; and where this does not follow, they are taught and trained by the discipline established all around.

203. *Crichton Royal Asylum, 5th Annual Report* (1844), p. 5.
204. A.B.C. [W. A. F. Browne], 'Letter to the Members of the Royal Commission of Inquiry into the Operation of the Poor Laws in Scotland, on the Condition of the Insane Poor', *Dumfries and Galloway Herald*, 21 December, 1843, reprinted in *Phrenological Journal and Magazine of Moral Science* (1844), 17: 258.
205. Ibid., p. 255.
206. Ibid., p. 256.
207. *Crichton Royal Asylum, 14th Annual Report* (1853), p. 7.
208. *Crichton Royal Asylum, 9th Annual Report* (1848), p. 5. A year later, he concedes that 'it is suspected that modern improvements, or attempts to improve, do not produce commensurate results'; and attempts to console himself with the thought that 'nothing is certain but that love has taken the place of barbarity, that the insane are treated as fellow-men, and not as outcasts, and that, if the various forms of insanity have increased in virulence and frequency [an interesting rationalization of therapeutic impotence], the efforts to meet and overcome the evil have been proportionately multiplied'. *Crichton Royal Asylum, 10th Annual Report* (1849), p. 43.
209. *Crichton Royal Asylum, 8th Annual Report* (1847), p. 23.
210. *Crichton Royal Asylum, 10th Annual Report* (1849), p. 5.
211. *Crichton Royal Asylum, 12th Annual Report* (1851), p. 5.
212. Ibid. Compare David Cassedy, superintendent of the Lancaster

Moor County Asylum: 'the care and alleviation of the condition of the great body of the insane is at least as important a function of Asylums as the so-called "cure" of a small percentage of cases, few of whom remain permanently cured'. *Lancashire Asylum Board Report* (1880), p. 18.

213. *Crichton Royal Asylum, 12th Annual Report* (1851), p. 28.
214. Browne, 'Moral Treatment', p. 322.
215. *Crichton Royal Asylum, 9th Annual Report* (1848), p. 35.
216. *Crichton Royal Asylum, 13th Annual Report* (1852), p. 40.
217. *Crichton Royal Asylum, 15th Annual Report* (1854), p. 5.
218. *Crichton Royal Asylum, 13th Annual Report* (1852), p. 40. In the light of comments of this sort, there is an increasingly hollow ring to his attempts to reassure himself that,

> It is less the amount of good effects, than the amount attempted [that matters] ... the great object of all such sustained exertion and ceaseless treatment is to ameliorate; and even if the results be incommensurate with the effort, as they assuredly ever will be, the public is so fully satisfied of the sincerity of the struggle, that the only obstacle to future progress ... is the lack of accommodation.

(14th Annual Report (1853), p. 33.)
219. *Crichton Royal Asylum, 17th Annual Report* (1856), p. 37. Elsewhere in the same report, he urged legal changes to allow 'retreats', separate from existing asylums, to be set up for those in 'the premonitory stages, or under the milder forms of the malady'. Otherwise, as he revealingly put it, such a patient would find him or herself reduced to the same status as the unambiguously mad already under confinement, 'treated as a culprit and a captive'. Ibid., p. 6.
220. *Crichton Royal Asylum, 18th Annual Report* (1857), p. 5.
221. Ibid., p. 5.
222. Ibid., p. 7.
223. Ibid., p. 8.
224. Ibid., pp. 12–13. One must recognize a bitter truth:

> The subversion of reason involves not only present incompetency, but a prospective susceptibility of disease, a proclivity to relapse. ... The mind does not pass out of the ordeal unchanged. ... Recovery ... may be little more than the exercise of great cunning, or self control, in concealing the signs of error and extravagance. The intellect that recovers its balance may not always recover its strength.

225. Ibid., pp. 24–6.

226. Ibid., p. 40.
227. See W. A. F. Browne (1861) 'Cottage Asylums', *Medical Critic and Psychological Journal*, 1: 213–37.
228. Easterbrook, *Chronicle of Crichton Royal*, p. 64. Browne's adherence to this position was the subject of acerbic criticism in the *Journal of Mental Science* (1856, 2: 413–16). Bucknill, its editor, particularly objected to Browne's claim that room could be found for pauper lunatics in charity asylums, which ought to maintain their monopoly by arranging 'to undersell private speculators' (i.e., proprietors of private madhouses). He pointed out that 'when it comes to a matter of underselling, the screw of parsimony can be pressed tighter in the obscurity of a private asylum, than it will be possible to do in a public one'. And he found equal fault with Browne's references to 'the hard and severe simplicity which necessarily and properly, and the ignorance and vulgarity, if not the wild turmoil and debasement which naturally characterize a pauper asylum ...', seeing such passages as confirmation of a long held opinion among English alienists 'that too large a share of the attention of the officers and governors [of Scottish asylums] has been devoted to patients [of the wealthier classes], and that the state of the pauper patients has been such as to form a striking and painful contrast, not only to the wealthier patients in the same institutions, but to that of insane paupers in this country'.
229. The *Journal of Mental Science* (1858, 5: 205), in welcoming the appointment, commented that,

> The professional men in Scotland engaged in the treatment of the insane are fortunate that the Government has placed the administration of the lunacy law in the hands of a man whose profound knowledge of mental disease will enable him to recognise the nature of the false accusations so constantly preferred against their guardians. We have known the greatest injustice committed in this country from the want of similar knowledge.

230. See, for example, W. A. F. Browne (1865) 'Epileptics: Their Mental Condition', *Journal of Mental Science*, 11: 336–63, delivered at the Inverness District Asylum; and his lecture on 'Moral Treatment', delivered the previous year at the Crichton Royal. Laycock had been professor of the practice of physic at Edinburgh University since 1855, and was to serve as President of the Medico-Psychological Association in 1869. Earlier in his career, while a lecturer at the York Medical School, he had exercised a formative influence over Hughlings Jackson, and his advocacy of psycho-physical parallelism

and of the notion of cerebral reflex action appealed to Browne as a scientific replacement for a now-discredited phrenology. See, for example, Browne to George Combe, 30 April, 1857, Combe Papers, National Library of Scotland.

231. Browne's address (1866) 'On Medico-Psychology', *Journal of Mental Science*, 12: 309–27, marked the change in the official title of the alienists' organization from the Association of Medical Officers of Asylums and Hospitals for the Insane to the Medico-Psychological Association, a transformation of obvious symbolic importance for the emerging profession, 'pointing', as Browne put it, 'to a wider and more legitimate destiny [as something more than] a mere friendly club or a mutual defence society'.

232. Browne, 'Moral Treatment', p. 311.

233. Compare, for instance, J. C. Bucknill and D. H. Tuke (1858), in their *Manual of Psychological Medicine* (London: Churchill, p. 88) – the standard mid-Victorian textbook on the subject:

> Whatever definition of insanity is adopted by the student, it is all important that he should regard disease as an essential condition; in other words, that insanity is a condition in which the intellectual faculties, or the moral sentiments, or the animal propensities, any one or all of them have their free action destroyed by disease, whether congenital or acquired. He will not go far wrong if he regards insanity as a disease of the brain.

See, more generally, the discussion in Jacyna, 'Somatic Theories of Mind'.

234. Browne, 'On Medico-Psychology', p. 311.

235. Browne, 'Moral Treatment', p. 311. The reiterated emphasis is precisely proportional to the flimsiness of the evidentiary basis on which these assertions rested.

236. Browne, 'On Medico-Psychology', p. 312.

237. Browne, 'Moral Treatment', p. 311.

WHAT ASYLUMS WERE, ARE, AND OUGHT TO BE:

BEING THE SUBSTANCE OF

FIVE LECTURES

DELIVERED BEFORE

THE MANAGERS

OF THE

MONTROSE ROYAL LUNATIC ASYLUM.

BY

W. A. F. BROWNE, Surgeon,

MEDICAL SUPERINTENDENT OF THE MONTROSE ASYLUM, FORMERLY
PRESIDENT OF THE ROYAL MEDICAL SOCIETY, EDINBURGH, &c.

———————

EDINBURGH:

ADAM AND CHARLES BLACK,

AND LONGMAN, REES, ORME, BROWN, GREEN, AND LONGMAN,
LONDON.

———————
MDCCCXXXVII.

THIS WORK

IS DEDICATED,

WITH SINCERE RESPECT AND GRATITUDE,

TO

ANDREW COMBE, M.D.,

PHYSICIAN TO THEIR MAJESTIES THE KING AND QUEEN OF THE BELGIANS ;
AUTHOR OF " OBSERVATIONS ON MENTAL DERANGEMENT ;"
" PRINCIPLES OF PHYSIOLOGY, AS APPLIED TO HEALTH
AND EDUCATION," &c.

AS AN ACKNOWLEDGMENT

OF THE BENEFITS CONFERRED ON SOCIETY,

BY

HIS EXPOSITION OF THE APPLICATION OF PHRENOLOGY IN THE

TREATMENT OF INSANITY AND NERVOUS DISEASES ;

AND

OF PRIVATE BENEFITS CONFERRED,

AS

THE MOST ENLIGHTENED PRECEPTOR, THE MOST DISINTERESTED

ADVISER, AND THE KINDEST FRIEND,

OF THE

AUTHOR.

TO THE MANAGERS OF THE MONTROSE ROYAL LUNATIC ASYLUM.

MY LORD AND GENTLEMEN,

To the many obligations which you have already conferred upon me, is now to be added the permission to publish the following pages under your sanction and patronage. In offering them for your acceptance, as a very imperfect proof of the importance which I attach to the office to which you appointed me, and as an equally imperfect acknowledgment of my gratitude for the uniform kindness and support which I have received from you, I have to express the deep respect and admiration which I entertain for the anxiety which you have ever manifested, and the exertions which you have made, and are now making, to promote the happiness and cure of those lunatics whose interests are more immediately confided to your care.

I have the honour to be,

MY LORD AND GENTLEMEN,

Very much your obedient servant,

W. A. F. BROWNE.

Montrose, May 1837.

PREFACE.

My object in publishing the following Lectures, was to draw the attention of the public, and especially of those who are by profession engaged in, or who by philanthropy are prompted to, works of mercy, to the consideration of what has been done, and what remains to be done, for the relief of the most unfortunate of our fellow-men : of those who may be almost literally said to " sit in darkness, and in the shadow of death: being fast bound in misery and iron." My inducements to publish were, first, the countenance and encouragement which I received from the Directors of the establishment under my charge, to whom my observations were in the first instance addressed ; and, secondly, the hope that a plain and clear statement of facts by a practical man might reach and influence those who administer either by their opinion or by their power to the necessities of the " poor in spirit." If my appeal should, even to a limited extent, excite the sympathy of those who are blessed with a sane, a benevolent, and a cultivated mind, and engage them as cordially in the attempt to ameliorate the condition of the lunatic, as similar, and even less clamant appeals have done in behalf of the slave, the oppressed, the destitute ; little difficulty will be found in removing the evils, and in carrying into effect the improvements which I have suggested, and an amount of happiness will be secured to the objects of my solicitude which has hitherto been denied to them, but to which they are as clearly entitled as the slave to freedom, or the poor to pity and relief.

I have no claim to originality, either in the design or the execution of the present production. A large portion of the volume refers to the past, and is necessarily occupied with historical details: that portion which refers to the future I have as scrupulously as was practicable collected and collated from the writings and opinions of others: and when presenting a synoptical view of the different forms under which mental disease may appear, I was indebted rather to the science upon the principles of which that arrangement was founded, than to any peculiar views or philosophical analysis of my own. To those who are acquainted with the doctrines of Phrenology, the extent of my obligations in this particular case, and throughout the work, will be readily recognized; and to those who are still ignorant of these doctrines, I have to offer the assurance that Insanity can neither be understood, nor described, nor treated by the aid of any other philosophy. I have long entertained this opinion: I have for many years put it to the test of experiment, and I now wish to record it as my deliberate conviction. While, however, I have constantly availed myself of the principles, I have avoided the phraseology of the science, first, because my original auditors were not, and my readers may not be phrenologists; and, secondly, and chiefly, because my object was not to advocate or promote particular truths, but to employ and apply these in the elucidation of the object in view, and thereby to place in as clear, and conclusive, and acceptable a manner as possible, the noble cause which I have undertaken.

CONTENTS.

LECTURE I.

WHAT IS INSANITY?

LECTURE II.

WHAT ARE THE STATISTICS OF INSANITY?

LECTURE III.

WHAT ASYLUMS WERE.

LECTURE IV.

WHAT ASYLUMS ARE.

LECTURE V.

WHAT ASYLUMS OUGHT TO BE.

LECTURE I.

WHAT IS INSANITY?

Erroneous views on the Subject.—Propensities, Sentiments, Reflective and Perceptive powers.—The dependence of these on Organization.—Derangement a disease of the Brain.—The changes which occur in the Structure of the Brain—Evidence that such changes take place—Extent of diseased action which constitutes Insanity—Description preferable to definition of the disease where the regulation of the internal economy of Asylums is concerned—Nosological classification of the varieties of the Disease—Arrangements of Arnold, Heinroth, and Author—Idiocy—Its four gradations—Fatuity, partial, complete—Monomania, erotic, homicidal and destructive, proud, vain, timid, suspicious, religious and superstitious, desponding and suicidal, imaginative, avaricious, benevolent, and affectionate—Incapability of perceiving the relations of ideas—Incapability of perceiving the relations of external objects—Incapability of perceiving the qualities of external objects—Mania, with and without increased activity—Conclusion.

GENTLEMEN,—The pages which I am about to submit to you, and subsequently to the public, possess one quality which many regard as a merit, but which I am inclined to think is a misfortune. It is that of originality. No attempt, so far as I know, has yet been made to condense, in a plain, practical, and still popular form, the results of observation in the treatment of insanity, for the specific and avowed purpose of demanding from the public an amelioration of the condition of the insane. The motives which have actuated me in bestowing a very careful, and, I humbly trust, a candid examination on the subject, have been a profound sympathy for the misfortunes of the insane, and a keen feel-

B

ing of indignation that these misfortunes should often be
multiplied through the apathy, or ignorance, or cruelty of
those who have it in their power to become benefactors, in
the noblest sense of the term, and in the noblest cause which
can arouse virtuous ambition. Should this attempt to enlist in that cause the feelings of justice and mercy in every
bosom, in any degree succeed, as by the blessing of a just
and merciful God I trust it may, and should the cry for improvement in public Asylums be raised where hitherto the
silence of indifference has reigned, the only reward which I
covet will have been obtained.

What is insanity? The question may be put and answered in two senses; either philosophically or practically; either as directed to ascertain the actual condition of the
mind which constitutes disease, or to determine that amount
of diseased action which compromises the safety of the sufferer, and justifies legal interference. Our chief concern is
with the aspect which the disease presents, after the law has
interfered. In order to arrive at just conclusions on such a
subject, it is incumbent to understand something of the nature, the powers, and the laws of the mind while in possession of health and vigour. This is generally overlooked in
the investigation, and the verdict of the public and of a jury
is as recklessly and ignorantly pronounced respecting mental strength, as if the points at issue were the discovery of
the perpetual motion or the utility of a comet. It is not to
be expected that either of these tribunals should be composed of metaphysicians; but it is highly desirable that
every man, qualified by his station in society to judge or
legislate in such matters, should be competent by education
to found and form his judgments on a knowledge of what
consciousness and observation shew to be the laws of our
spiritual nature. So vague are the ideas generally entertained, or, rather, so destitute is the great majority of even
educated men of any ideas or definite opinions as to mental

philosophy, that very recently the capability of repeating the Multiplication Table was gravely propounded in an English court of law as a test of sanity. This looks like satire on the reputed money-making propensities of this nation, but the proposal had no such origin. And to prove how momentous the interests are which hinge upon a clear comprehension of what insanity is, it may be mentioned that in the very case where this arithmetical crux was suggested, immense property and the reputation and affections of many individuals were at stake.

So far as our present purpose is concerned it may be sufficient to know, that the mind consists of four classes of powers. The first of these are mere instincts or impulses, manifested by us in common with the lower animals, capable of being directed by reason, or the moral feeling, to great and noble ends, but in themselves prompting merely to love, to combat, to acquire, and so forth. The second class comprehends the sentiments where there is a vivid emotion superadded to a propensity to act ; among these are feelings of pride, vanity, veneration, hope, &c. The purely intellectual powers constitute the third class. By them we recognise the relations of ideas, of the impressions of the mind itself; we are enabled to trace effects to their causes, to ascertain the difference or agreement of propositions, and to conduct what is commonly called a process of reasoning. In the fourth class are the observing powers, those by which we perceive the qualities and relations of external objects.

Now it appears that all these feelings and faculties are gradually developed and that they gradually decline ; that they are weak in infancy, strong at maturity, and again weak in old age ; that their evolution and decay correspond with the changes in organization. Farther, it has been ascertained, that the condition and intensity of these powers is influenced by the state of the body, by external and internal stimuli ; that in certain affections of the nervous system, as intoxication, their energy is impaired; and that in certain other affections, as phrenitis and ramollissement, their operation is altogether destroyed. Lastly it is proved, that the integrity and health of these powers depend upon the structure of the brain and its coverings; that if this organ be prevented from attaining a certain size, no mental manifestations appear; that if by accident or disease, the nervous mass should be directly or indirectly injured, these manifestations are diminished in number, impaired in strength, or annihilated. In what manner this connexion between mind and matter is effected, is not here inquired into. The link will, perhaps, ever escape human research. Enough has been disclosed to teach us the importance of recognising the connexion, and of making it the foundation of all inquiries into the nature of mental alienation, and of all attempts to improve the condition of the insane. From the admission of this principle, derangement is no longer considered a disease of the understanding, but of the centre of the nervous system, upon the unimpaired condition of which the exercise of the understanding depends. The brain is at fault and not the mind. The brain is oppressed by blood; it is irritated; it is softened; and the ideas are confused, the feelings exalted, because that part of the system with which their healthy manifestation has been associated in this world, has undergone an alteration. But let this oppression be relieved, this irritation be removed, and the mind rises in its native strength, clear and calm, uninjured, immutable, immortal. In all cases where disorder of the mind is detectable, from the faintest peculiarity to the widest deviation from health, it must and can only be traced directly or indirectly to the brain. The change may exist in its own structure, or in distant organs which influence its condition, but that which renders it impossible that the mental operation should be continued with regularity, or equanimity, is to be referred to the brain. For

example, if a blow is received on the forehead, the skull is depressed, the brain is lacerated or contused, and the individual
passes at once from the possession of a sound and powerful reason, from a clear and correct perception of the position which
he occupies, the plans he has formed, and of the knowledge
and energies he can put forth, into a dark fatuity, a bewil-
derment of thought, an ignorance of all he has done, can do,
or is required to do. Here the two facts of cerebral mutilation, and of deprivation of intellect stand so distinctly in the
relation of cause and effect, that all men are accustomed to
regard them, and are warranted in regarding them in this
light. Again, if the dissolute and reckless debauchee per-
severe for long years in the practice of gratifying his palate,
and destroying his digestive powers, and keeping his nervous and circulating systems in a state of excitement, alike
inimical to virtue and to health, the first indication of the interruption to his enjoyments, and of the incursion of disease
may be in the stomach. Uneasy sensations, pain, disorganization will attract his attention ; his reason will in vain
attempt steadily to contemplate his situation, his fears are
up in arms, the whole mind totters and ultimately falls.
After a few years of raving madness, or helpless idiocy, he
dies. On dissection, the stomach may exhibit traces of
deep-seated, long-continued morbid action, the obvious consequences of frequent exposure to stimulants. But will this
be the only lesion discoverable ? Can such changes, which
are found to follow other causes without disturbing the
functions of the brain, in this particular case produce insanity ?—Experience proves the reverse of this. In, or
around the brain will be detected some obvious alteration
of structure, with the existence of which health was incompatible. The incessant determination of an accelerated or
vitiated current of blood to the head, or the condition of
the nervous system consequent on repeated intoxication,
accounts for the production of this alteration. Occasion-

ally, cases occur where the lesions are very slight, have
been overlooked, or, according to some authors, have not
existed. The disease, in the latter case, is called functional,
or is supposed to depend upon some change in the proportion or qualities of the elements of which the brain is composed, not appreciable by our senses, nor detectable by che-
mical agents. Neither of these explanations is satisfactory.
The prevailing opinion at present is, that no cases do occur
where no pathological condition can be observed : that those
recorded owe this feature to the negligence or ignorance of
the narrator, and that, should such cases really exist, the
brain must be affected similarly to the rest of the body in
fever, where the alterations are evanescent, disappearing on
the extinction of life. But what does history contribute to
the settlement of the question. Greding noticed thickening
of the skull in one hundred and sixty-seven out of two hundred and sixteen cases, besides other organic disease. It
ought to be observed, that Greding was in search of a particular morbid appearance. Davidson, of Lancaster Asylum, in the examination of two hundred cases, scarcely ever
met a single instance in which evident traces of diseased
action were not found. Dr. Wright, Bethlem, dissected one
hundred cases, and saw disorganization of the brain, &c. in
all. Dr. Haslam, St. Lukes, says, insanity is always connected with organic changes. Georget, Falret, Voisin, Cox,
Crighton, Crowther, Burrows, &c. entertain the same opinion.

Insanity, then, is inordinate or irregular, or impaired action of the mind, of the instincts, sentiments, intellectual, or
perceptive powers, depending upon and produced by an organic change in the brain ; the extent of the disease corresponding to the extent of the destruction or injury of the
nervous structure.* It is here particularly worthy of notice,

* " A great error has arisen," says Newnham, " and has been perpetuated even to the present day, in considering cerebral disorder as

that being strictly a bodily disease, the nature, intensity and aggravations of insanity must be regulated, in a great measure, by the relation of the brain to the other organs of the body, and the relation of both of these to external agents: and that if such a dependence exists, an equally intimate connexion must be concluded to obtain between the means of cure and the state of these organs and external agents.

But, in determining what treatment ought to be adopted in cases of lunacy, how is the degree of diseased action to be estimated, or rather, what departure from the healthy standard is to be recognised and treated as disease? There appears to be a necessity for some estimate of this kind, however vague, and upon whatever principles founded, in every case where confinement is advised, or resorted to. But, first, is there a healthy standard, or if there be, how is it to be ascertained?

In the well known trial relating to the lunacy of Miss Bagster in 1832, Dr. Haslam gave two rather startling answers when urged by Mr., now Sir F. Pollock. He is reported to have said, " I never saw any human being who was of sound mind ;" and subsequently, on being pressed hard for a more explicit statement, he concluded, " I presume the Deity is of sound mind, and *he* alone." This is

---

mental; requiring, and indeed admitting, ONLY of moral remedies, instead of these forming only ONE class of curative agents ; whereas the brain is the mere ORGAN of the mind, not the mind itself: and its disorder of function arises from its ceasing to be a proper medium for the manifestation of the varied action and passion of the presiding spirit. And strange as it may seem, this error has been consecrated by a desire to escape from the fallacies of *materialism.* Yet it is manifest that they alone are guilty of the charge of attachment to materialism, who consider the disorder of the cerebral functions as *mental,* for then, indeed, the brain must be *mind itself,* and not simply its organ."— *Christian Observer,* vol. xxix. p. 266.

next to asserting that no palpable distinction exists, no
line of demarcation can be traced between the sane and the
insane. It must be confessed, that the line is either ideal
or purely geometrical. If the two most widely separated
conditions of mind, its greatest strength and serenity, and
its most abject imbecility or fury be contrasted, the distance
appears enormous and impassable; but if we gradually recede from these extreme points towards the medium, it will
be found, so imperceptibly do the distinctive marks disappear, and so insensibly do eccentricity on the one hand,
and enthusiasm on the other, blend together, that the task
of declaring this to be reason and that insanity is exceedingly embarrassing, and, to a great degree, arbitrary.
People have puzzled themselves to discover this line, a *terra
incognita*, in fact, which does not exist; the mind being susceptible of as many shades of difference in the strength and
relations of its powers as the body; and the attempt being
as feasible to define the precise health-point in the one as
in the other. Another enigma has been propounded of
somewhat similar import. An enigma which Œdipus could
not have solved. It is to establish a definition of insanity.
That is, to discover one form of words expressive of the nature of a hundred different things. I humbly think, that
however interesting and edifying these investigations may
be to mere philosophers, the philosophical practitioner ought
to make the inquiry invariably bear reference to the question, whether isolation would be for the benefit of the patient. The criteria, however, in forming a judgment are
supposed to be various and adequate. Is a man able to
manage his own affairs, is he violent, virulent, extravagant
or troublesome? are the questions addressed to medical
witnesses. It is rarely demanded, whether confinement will
conduce to the restoration of health. That incompetency
for business, or irritability, do occasionally require the interference of the law, may be true. Property and the

public peace of society must be protected. And where either the one or the other is threatened, or disturbed, no difficulty can be experienced as to the propriety of coercing the violator. Insanity is evidently the cause of such outrages, and insanity of a kind that cannot be efficiently treated without isolation. But even in such cases, the offender sometimes proves to be a delinquent: a criminal rather than a lunatic, and an Asylum becomes more of a penitentiary than an hospital. This is a minor evil. A much greater results from the universal application of such tests leaving lunatics at liberty, and incarcerating sane, or comparatively sane, individuals. This will be better understood from the following illustrations. The cunning vindictive maniac, for example, may be perfectly competent to conduct mercantile, or even more complicated affairs, with ability, he may even prosper in his enterprises ; and yet his treatment of those dependant upon him, of all who may have offended him, of all whom he suspects, may be marked by the maliciousness of the demon, and the indiscriminate ferocity of the maniac. He, if subjected to such tests, may never be suspected, until some out-burst of fury, when he is deserted by his habitual caution, consigns those around to death or misery. This man ought to be confined, but escapes, until the evil is done. Again, the man who from natural inaptitude to details of business is incapable of conducting his affairs advantageously, may be in all other matters rational and praiseworthy : he may be a good mechanician, an artist, a man of strong affections and irreproachable manners. This man ought to be free, but being subjected to the same tests, is confined, until his whole mind is as much enfeebled as his business powers. All chances ought certainly to be in favour of the lunatic ; for a greater injury is done by the sacrifice of one sane individual, than by the freedom of many lunatics. The test ought to be as general as possible, and to have reference not to the abstract question of what insanity is, but to the probable consequences which may accrue from the declaration that it exists in every given case.

Entertaining these opinions then, in place of endeavouring to define, I have described the different forms which insanity assumes, believing that by such a course the interests of science and of humanity will be better served, than by straining after what the failure of all previous writers nearly proves to be a nonentity.

As an enlightened system of classifying lunatics must depend on the accuracy of the classification of the varieties of the disease with which they are affected, I have here presented three: the most ancient, at least the most ancient which has any pretensions to be complete, the most recent, and the best. We shall adhere to the latter.

I. ARNOLD'S TABLE OF THE SPECIES OF INSANITY.

I. *Ideal.*   I.   Phrenitic.
            II.   Incoherent.
            III.   Maniacal.
            IV.   Sensitive.
I. *Notional.* V.   Delusive.
            VI.   Fanciful.
            VII.   Whimsical.
            VIII, Impulsive.
            IX.   Scheming.
            X.   Vain or Self-important.
            XI.   Hypochondriacal.
            XII. Pathetic.
                     1. Amorous.
                     2. Jealous.
                     3. Avaricious.
                     4. Misanthropic.
                     5. Arrogant.
                     6. Irascible.
                     7. Abhorrent.
                     8. Suspicious.

II. *Notional* continued.

> 9. Bashful.
> 10. Timid.
> 11. Sorrowful.
> 12. Distressful.
> 13. Nostalgic.
> 14. Superstitious.
> 15. Fanatical.
> 16. Desponding.

xiii. Appetitive.

II. Heinroth's Division of Insanity.

I. Disorders of the Moral Dispositions.

   1. *Exaltation, or excessive intensity.*
     Undue vehemence of feelings, morbid violence of passions and emotions.

   2. *Depression.*
     Simple melancholy, dejection without illusion of the understanding.

II. Disorders of the Understanding, or intellectual faculties.

   1. *Exaltation.*
     Undue intensity of the imagination, producing mental illusions and all the varieties of monomania.

   2. *Depression.*
     Feebleness of conception ; of ideas.
     Imbecility of the understanding.

III. Disorders of voluntary powers, or of propensities, or of will.

   1. *Exaltation.*
     Violence of will and of propensities; madness without lesion of the understanding.

   2. *Depression.*
     Weakness, or incapacity of willing.
     Moral imbecility.

Note.—To these unmixed forms others are added under each division, displaying combinations of several simple varieties.

III. The Author's Arrangement.

I. Idiocy.   Non-development of faculties.

    1. Gradation.   Non-development of all the powers.
    2.   ~~~~   External senses developed.
    3.   -----   A propensity or affection developed.
    4.   -----   An intellectual power developed.

II. Fatuity.   Obliteration of Faculties.
    1. Partial.
    2. Complete.

III. Monomania.   Derangement of one or more faculties.

SECTION I.

    1. Satyriasis.
    2. Homicidal and destructive.
    3. Proud.
    4. Vain.
    5. Timid.
    6. Cunning and suspicious.
    7. Religious and superstitious.
    8. Desponding and suicidal.
    9. Imaginative.
    10. Avaricious.
    11. Benevolent or affectionate.

SECTION II.

    12. Incapability of perceiving relations of ideas.
    13. Incapability of perceiving relations of external things.
    14. Incapability of perceiving qualities of external objects.

IV. Mania.   Derangement of all the faculties.
    1. Mania with increased activity.
    2. Mania with diminished activity.

I. Idiocy.   The first of these classes comprehends the manifestations of all those unfortunate beings, who, dead to sensation, or, with the external senses perfectly faithful and active, appear to possess no mind to which the impressions thus received can be communicated, or one so closely assimilated to that of the lowest gradations of animal existence, that the impressions pass away without becoming objects of thought, or causality, and without calling forth a single propensity or sentiment. The mind may not be, nay rarely is, so utterly undeveloped as this description would convey, but, while there may remain an attachment to some favourite place or person, or a delight in harmonious sounds, or constructive powers, or the irritability of anger, every other faculty is blotted out: no appeal can be made to reason, no progress can be made in education, there is, in fact, nothing to educate. So great, occasionally, are these privations, that the individuals cannot articulate, nor acquire language, and literally do not differ, we repeat, from the lower animals, with which they delight to associate.* Hitherto these helpless creatures have been permitted to remain at liberty, the sport of fortune or of their own imperfect instincts and ill-regulated passions, the prey of the designing, the butt of the idle, or the cruel. According to a public print,† two individuals of this neglected class who had long roamed through Rosshire, quarrelled, fought, one died of the wounds received in the struggle, and the other was, of course, consigned to prison. This took place in January 1835.

Rational and true humanity would have suggested their protection from these sources of pain and annoyance by seclusion, where their humble and limited wants might be supplied, their wishes, so far as might be compatible with their safety gratified, and all the vegetative happiness of which they are susceptible, secured.

There are, however, gradations in the scale of idiocy. Certain individuals advance farther towards the maturi-

---

*Art. " Idiotisme," by Esquirol, Dict. des Sciences Med., vol. xxiii. —Pinel on Insanity, Eng. Trans., p. 126—169.—Voisin, Journal de la Société Phrenologique de Paris, April 1835.

† Scotsman, January 1835.

ty of mind than others, and yet fall infinitely short of what
our intellectual nature is intended to be, and even what the
most neglected and degraded sane individual actually is.
The lowest state in which humanity appears, is when neither
reason nor sensation has been bestowed. Where the imperfect being does not appear to be conscious of light, or
sound, or hunger, and where sleep and a swaying motion of
the body alternate, during the long protracted lifetime which
many of these unfortunates are required to endure. The
next gradation is where the external senses exist, but without the co-existence of any faculty by which the sensations
thus obtained can become objects of reflection. The individuals of this class prefer light to darkness, experience great
pleasure from odours, and occupy a great part of their time
in moving their hands along smooth surfaces, an act which
in the child is supposed to contribute to the idea of extension. The third gradation consists of patients, who, besides
exercising their senses, contract affections, display desires,
and feel the first throbs of ambition. The last gradation is,
where in addition to these feelings, there is a certain, but very
contracted power of ratiocination, a facility in acquiring a
mechanical art, or an aptitude for arithmetical or mathema-
cal studies, without any corresponding evolution of the
other powers of mind.

II. FATUITY is generally the effect of apoplexy, chronic
inflammation of the membranes of the brain, or of some signal alteration in the texture of the nervous substance. The
extent to which such deviations from the healthy condition
of structure may be borne with impunity, has not been ascertained. But whenever both hemispheres are implicated,
and the parts affected are actually disorganized, the annihi-
lation, or, to avoid any mistake as to our meaning, the suspension of mind inevitably follows. It should be understood
that these alterations are general and not local, or are at

least of such a nature as to affect the whole of the contents of the encephalon.

The progress of the malady is often slow, always insidious. Half a lifetime may elapse, marked by gradually increasing inconsistencies and imbecility, which are kindly attributed to humour or eccentricity, before the understanding is suspected to be undermined, or the glaring approach of a second childishness be more than surmised. When the keen and easily awakened sensibility of affection is struck by some unusual petulance, loss of attention, or inability to exercise judgment, the source may be conjectured, but some momentary gleam of returning reason, or the occurrence of circumstances where, from there being no demand for intelligence the mental weakness may not be betrayed, will lull the fears to sleep, and not until after repeated follies and irregularities, does the truth, that an utter obliteration of the faculties is on the eve of taking place, become manifest. Even when succeeding another form of derangement, which very frequently happens, the decay steals on as insensibly as the approach of old age. The amount of deprivation can only be measured by comparing distant periods. Furious mania is probably more exposed than other varieties to this termination. The change in this case is indeed astounding: when the outrageous, ungovernable desperado loses his attributes one by one—suffers first the extinction of the memory of his grievances, then of the inclination to hate or injure, and ultimately sinks into complete tranquillity and reverieism. Men of genius often share a similar fate, and from a similar, though, in their case, a voluntarily incurred affliction. They overtax, exhaust, and destroy their powers. And the contrast here is still more distressing. The brilliant wit, the impassioned orator, even the calm philosopher become dotards, imbeciles, puling children, and by their own act, by their own ignorance of the mind, which they pretended to improve and ennoble.

Fatuity may be partial or complete. It may comprehend one or all of the intellectual energies, and enfeeble all or destroy all. The powers may remain, but their strength, and especially the strength acquired by cultivation, is gone. They no longer act in concert; and the indistinct description of a discovery in mechanics, or a transaction in business, is associated with a prayer, or a passionate ejaculation. Some solitary power, or accomplishment, or favourite train of thought occasionally lingers behind the rest, or survives their destruction. Imbecile weavers are sometimes met with, who occupy themselves with the trade in which they have been originally trained. Musical imbeciles, and affectionate but one-ideaed imbeciles might be mentioned, who diffused a happiness around them which they did not feel, and from their peculiarities created a bustling and merry activity among their companions in which they could not participate. But as great infirmity of frame, in the majority of instances, accompanies fatuity, a more insurmountable obstacle is opposed to such manifestations than even the intrinsic decrepitude of the mind itself. Dementia and general paralysis go hand in hand, and patients borne down by such complicated misfortunes, are seldom able to leave their beds or chairs.* From this circumstance, and from being at once harmless and independent of society from the extinction of their social powers, a separate ward is appropriated to their use in many hospitals, where their existence glides on towards its peaceful but humiliating close, undisturbed by cold, or hunger, or darkness, or pain, or any of the few strictly animal irritations of which they are susceptible. Notwithstanding the apparently hopeless condition of patients labouring under fatuity, cures occasionally take place. Their rarity may be gathered from the fact, that of 518 cures effected at Charenton, only four of those restored had been fatuous.

* De la Paralysie considerée chez les Aliénés par L. F. Calmeil.

III. MONOMANIA. The attempt to reduce the tints, and shadings, and combinations of tints which meet the eye, to the rudimentary colours, must appear to the unscientific impossible. In the same way to a stranger who examines a populous asylum, and perceives the thousand modifications of disease of the moral sentiments and feelings which are there presented, a classification of these under some ten or twelve primitive powers or states of mind, must appear sufficiently daring. Yet by the aid of a careful analysis this may be readily done. You will not find the delusions of two madmen alike, is a common remark. True, the particular succession of ideas will not and cannot be the same, for that is determined in each case by education, pursuit, and extraneous circumstances; but the source, the emotion, by which these ideas are suggested, and in consequence of the derangement of which they are morbid, will frequently be found to be identical. One man conceives himself to be our Saviour, another that he is Louis XIV.; the first rails against his imaginary persecutors, his fellow-patients, whom he designates unbelieving Jews; the second pays court to the chambermaid as Madam de Maintenon, or mourns over his defeat at Blenheim; the one walks about without shoes or stockings; the other has turned his coat inside out as a fitting vestment for royalty. Two cases can scarcely be imagined more remote in their characteristics; but if the deportment of each be traced back—if the assumption of elevated rank, the mock dignity, the hauteur, be analyzed, excessive activity of the feeling of self-esteem, accompanied by an inability to perceive the relations subsisting between the impressions in the mind and real circumstances, will be discovered to be the ultimate cause, and adequate to account for all the phenomena. Pride acting in the one case, on dispositions originally religious, and strengthened by cultivation; and pride, acting in the other, on the ambitious longings of an enthusiastic spirit. If all cases of insanity be

dealt with in a similar manner, the specific distinctions
shrink within a very small compass.

Before proceeding to sketch a few of the distinctive marks
of the varieties of monomania, it is expedient to warn you that
this term is generally understood in a sense altogether unphilosophical. It is applied to cases where there exists only *one*
delusion. And it is intended to imply the disease of only one
power. Should a man declare himself to be Julius Cæsar,
and be clear, and consistent, and cogent on all other points,
he is called a monomaniac, and is concluded to possess all
his powers sane and sound, except the feeling of pride. The
conclusion is erroneous. Pride communicates nothing more
than a vivacious, an intense feeling of haughtiness and disdain, a desire for exaltation ; but the delusion whereby this
desire is gratified, on a supposed metempsychosis into the
body of the Roman emperor, must result from the diseased
action of the intellectual powers,—from an incapability, in
fact, of perceiving the relations of ideas. A feeling cannot
give an *idea* that a man is a different person from what he
actually is. The word, then, is not here restricted to one
delusion, but means the disease of certain classes of mental powers, in contradistinction to mania or disease of the
whole.

SECT. I.—1. *Satyriasis.* The first form of Monomania, to which
it is necessary to advert, is Satyriasis, or inordinate sexual desire
uncontroled and incontrolable by any governing power within,
or by admonitions, threats, punishment or coercion.   This
loathsome and most humiliating spectacle is fortunately rare,
and occurs in consequence either of organic alteration in the
brain, or of a long course of debauchery. We forge the bolt
that is to destroy us. The history of mental disease reveals
awful truths. And one of these is, that the mind may be trained to insanity, to destroy itself. And by the wise and ever just
arrangements of Providence the punishment is proportioned

to the offence, the effect corresponds in nature and in degree to the source from which it originated, the awards of
justice are inflicted on the criminal by means of the very
weapon with which his offence was committed : he cultivated his passions and propensities, and these, on arriving at
the maximum of their energy, destroy him. Nay more, it
would appear that the lower the propensity to the gratification of which his other powers have been but ministers, that
the more gross and injurious the violations committed against
the powers which regulate his own being, or connect him
with his fellow-men, the more signal and striking is the termination to such a career, the more grovelling and disgusting the condition to which the offender is reduced. Has
sexual appetite polluted and paralyzed his mind ? He becomes the victim of a loathsome species of mania, to characterize which we have been obliged to borrow the name of a
fabulous monster from the Roman mythology.

The erotomaniac is generally furious and inaccessible to
any moral influence ; the mind is concentrated upon one
point, and, as is always the case when profoundly affected,
is blind and deaf, and closed against every less powerful
motive. Sometimes there is mere sallacity attended by
shame at the degradation of such an enslavement,—a conviction of the diseased condition of the feelings,—a struggle
to resist the incursion of the attack, and long intervals of
health. All objects which address, excite the propensity ;
all alterations in the functions of the system which tend to
produce plethora or irritation, and all associations which
divert the mind *from* occupations purely intellectual, are
calculated to give force to the disease. Conceive, then, the
situation of a maniac of this description in an institution
where there was no separation of the sexes, little attention
to the connection of the nervous system with the other
functions, and no employment. Instances of pure monomania of this kind are certainly rare ; but the inordinate

desire is often exhibited where other morbid feelings have
the predominance and give a name to the disease. Here
the regulating faculties are extinct, or suspended, and the
passions assume the sway as the only, or most energetic
mental impulses remaining, in the same way as a craving
for food, or pleasurable sensations, rise above the general
wreck in imbecility. Certain powers only, however, may
suffer obscuration. The suggestions of these, although undiseased, become vitiated by the over-ruling propensity ;
they become instruments at the disposal of a mightier energy ; they are bent from their natural course and directed to
objects, and visions, and hopes, and fears, which sympathize
with the impulse. Recollections, in themselves pure and
connected with periods or events long antecedent to the
commencement of the disease, are. inextricably mingled
with the existing gross conceptions. Trains of associations
which originate in subjects the most remote from lascivious-
ness, and appear to tend towards an elevation of sentiment,
are found actually to terminate in and to inflame the feeling. The dreams are voluptuous. Even the automatic
movements of the body are indelicate or indecent. The
terminations of this form are three. The victims are either
cured, sink into fatuity, or exhibit symptoms of another and
more benign species of insanity.*

2. *Homicidal,* or *destructive mania,* is asserted to be more
prevalent in this country than elsewhere. Were we inclined to form our opinion on the revolting descriptions contained in a book, once too popular, we might conclude
every second or third madman to be ferocious, sanguinary,
a maimer, a murderer, or a parricide.† But this is not a
correct exposition of the case. The Asylum from which

* Dictionnaire de Médecine, Art. " Satyriasis," " Folie," vols. xix.
and viii. Buffon, vol. i. p. 222. Smellie's translation. Heckar,
Epidemics of the Middle Ages, p. 105.

† Sketches of Bedlam.

these sketches were drawn was a receptacle for criminal lunatics, and, to a certain extent, adhered to the old regime of manacles and punishment which render men furious and dangerous. Our national character may render us more prone to this than to other forms of alienation; and the present demoralised habits of certain sections of the population, their dog-fights, bull-baitings, pugilistic contests, and so forth, may assuredly predispose to the excitement of the very lowest passions; but my own experience would lead me to believe that homicidal mania is as frequent in France at least as in Britain. The lowest and least formidable degree of this malady is an irresistible inclination to destroy clothes, furniture, every article that will tear or break. This instinct attends the acute stage of many species of mania, but I here speak of it as idiopathic and permanent. A man who was otherwise tolerably well, once told me that the only words he liked to use, and the only things he liked to do, were " crush, smash." The second variety is where the patient is incorrigibly quarrelsome; where he seeks grounds of dispute and antagonists; throws all around into turmoil and confusion, and will fight with his shadow rather than allow his aggressive powers to continue dormant. The third variety combines with these qualities an indomitable hatred to human life; the thirst for blood is insatiable, and every other feeling seems subdued by the desire for victims.

In many countries and codes of law the majority of those horrible atrocities which place man below the level of the tiger are attributed to madness, and their perpetrators are committed to the charge of the physician instead of the executioner. For a long period the Romans had no law against parricide. They thought the crime impossible. That the insane have been immolated as criminals there exists too melancholy proof; and whenever an adequate motive is wanting to explain the commission of such an act, or where the act is opposed to the generally prevailing motives of the actor, it is certainly humane and just to consider him as irresponsible.* Without entering into the legal question, it is necessary to observe that there exist very marked differences in the mental condition of individuals instigated by this blind impulse. There is the intense desire to kill ; but at the same moment a sympathy for, a wish to save, and an effort to warn the intended victim. There is this desire without any such sympathy, but attended with a violent internal struggle to resist the temptation. And again, there is the desire unmitigated either by sympathy or struggle, burning for gratification, pausing, it may be from fear, but ever watching for opportunities. Examples of these distinctions occur every day. Dr. Otho of Copenhagen relates that Peter Nielson, the father of seven children, *was seized with a desire* which he felt he could not resist to destroy four of his children, whom, nevertheless, he tenderly loved. He took them to a turf pit, and after passionately embracing them, pushed them into the water and remained until he saw them drowned. Esquirol had a patient who acknowledged that he experienced a desire to shed blood, and especially that of his own friends, to whom he was, notwithstanding, much attached. He deplored the tendency ; but could only frustrate his own designs by crying, when the fit returned, " Mother, save yourself, or I will cut your throat." The third degree may be illustrated by the history of a man given by Dr. Caldwell. He had been guilty of *nine* murders, the whole of which he acknowledged he had committed from an inherent love of slaughter. The flowing of blood he declared to be " delightful to him." To such desolators, or rather to the absence of any attempt to distinguish and separate them from their less blood-thirsty or vindic-

* Simpson on Homicidal Insanity : Appendix to Necessity of Popular Education. Archives de Médecine, vol. viii. p. 177. Georget's various Medico-legal works. Annales d'Hygiène Publique et de Médecine Legale, vol. xv, p. 128, and vol. xvi. p. 122.

tive associates, is the loss of life in asylums to be referred. Within the last twenty years, two medical men and many keepers and patients have been sacrificed from this cause.

The secondary incentives to, or reasons for such desires, are very numerous. One deadly blow is inflicted to save the soul of the sufferer, another is given to rid the world of a monster, and a third that a sacrifice may be offered up for the sins of all concerned. The effect which companions entertaining, and known to entertain such designs, must produce upon those labouring under the mania of fear or despondency, must be most distressing. To have the keen, cruel, blood-thirsty gaze of the glaring eye : the grinding teeth, the clenched hand, and the threats of vengeance of such a being constantly obtruded on the attention, might excite madness. It may be supposed that patients of this disposition are beyond the pale of humanity—beyond the reach of art, or of alleviation. It is not so. They may be, and often have been, humanized. By aiding the sympathy, the virtuous resolves and sane convictions during the struggle—by binding the mind to a certain routine of purely intellectual or mechanical tasks, and thus excluding the operation of the propensities, these unfortunates have been reclaimed, have been intrusted with instruments which might have served to wreak their fury, and finally have been replaced in that position in society from which they had fallen.*

3. *Monomania of Pride*, &c. There may be in this variety either the exaltation of the emotion of self-conceit—the deep and impregnable notion of superiority, and indifference or contempt of all that is beneath, or that does not minister to egotism, or to the affairs of the egotist,—or there may be these feelings, coupled with delusions as to the character,

* Médecine Legale relative aux Aliénés et aux Sourds-Muets par J. C. Hoffbauer, p. 135.—Note sur la Monomanie Homicide par M. le Docteur Esquirol.

circumstances, rank and claims, upon which this pride is based. The self-satisfaction may be felt, the inattention to business, the squandering of property, and other irrational acts, may be resolved upon by the lunatic in his own proper person, or as a king or a conqueror. The latter is the most frequent form. There is, however, in the most pertinacious contenders for imaginary rank, no loss of the consciousness of personal identity. The individual may conceive himself to be Socrates or Sappho, a prince or a philosopher. He may conduct himself with all the dignity, and speak and think, as far as his abilities admit, in keeping with the assumed character, and spurn the slightest insinuation that Socrates is dead, that he himself is A. B., or that there is no real ground for his pretensions. But should his friends be presented to him, they are recognized and received as such : or should old scenes and former associations be recalled, he will uniformly place himself in the same relation to these as when they were previously before his mind. He will, for example, readily describe how Socrates sold a sheep to C.D., or took a dose of medicine at a certain time, and in a certain place, but will never dream of referring the sale of the sheep to the pastures of Mount Hymettus, or the swallowing of the drug to the prison of the Acropolis. I have under my care a female, who declares herself to be the wife of George III. ; but then it is as Queen Elspeth, born in the parish of Benholm, that she ascended the throne. The proud maniac, where his peculiar reveries or hallucinations are not combined with other feelings, is generally silent, and is regarded as sullen. He is wrapped up in the magnificence of his own importance and authority, or in the contemplation of his own attributes. He is independent of the world's humility or kindness : he feels himself immeasurably removed from its approaches, and despises the trifles which engage its inhabitants. But he is not unapproachable. Regulate your advances by the prevailing feeling of his mind, which must be the foundation of all intercourse ; put into your addresses that respect and deference which he demands ; appear by the tone and style of your remarks to admit the point at issue between him and the sane part of the community, and you will perhaps find him a condescending patron, an adviser, or a protector. His happiness resides in thoughts of personal magnificence : he is, therefore, concluded to be selfish. But it is not the selfishness of aggrandizement or monopoly. His most marked symptom indeed is, that within himself centre so many excellencies, that he can dispense with all the ordinary objects of man's desire and ambition. He neglects his dress, he is solitary, he seeks no kindness ; for what avails the foreign aid of ornament, or companionship, or attention, to one who possesses unbounded wealth, a descent of twenty quarterings, the wisdom or the eloquence of all antiquity, everything. in short, which nature or fortune could bestow. Such are his delusions : they may, nay, must be varied, by the constitution and cultivation of his mind ; but they will be found to revolve without deviation round one point, the feeling of pride. The ease with which such patients are bent from their own purposes towards those of others, by persons who understand the human mind, and can use their knowledge practically, is beautifully shewn in a statement of Pinel's. He had no less than three Louis Sixteenth's in Bicêtre at one time. Their majesties unfortunately met in the courtyard : a dispute ensued as to the right that each respectively had to the title which they all assumed : and as a scuffle appeared likely to take place, the matron interposed, took one of the disputants aside, and said with great gravity, " How happens it that you should think of arguing with such fellows as these, who are evidently out of their minds ? we all know well enough that your majesty alone is Louis Sixteenth." The appeal produced the desired effect on each

c

real sovereign in succession, each retiring triumphant and supreme.*

As a cause of insanity, wounded self-love, under the different aspects of disappointed ambition, jealousy, and insult, is prolific. Of 492 cases given by Esquirol, sixty-one, or about one-eighth, were attributable to these states of feeling.†

4. *Monomania of Vanity.* Consists in an irrepressible craving for praise, homage, and admiration. This is the original germ ; but from this there spring a thousand grotesque manifestations of the appetite and the modes by which it shall be gratified. The actions of the great are imitated, their manners travestied, and there is an affectation of all accomplishments and virtues, with the view of extorting approbation. The courteous bow, the rakish swagger, the ostentatious display of a scrap of old ribbon, are all intended to excite astonishment and admiration. The mind's errors all tend towards what is called eclât : they bear reference to the judgment of the world. The vain lunatic often suffers a moral metamorphosis as well as the proud ; but when imagination has suggested the delusion of being some very important personage, it is not enough : the qualities upon which this importance depends must be exhibited in order to attract notice. If the idea of a celebrated singer has predominated, the harshest notes will be screamed out in the hope of an encore : if the maniac be converted into a Demosthenes, you are assailed with the most incoherent, but probably the most impassioned harangue that ever fell from the lips of the most enthusiastic and successful orator : if a person of fashion be imitated, rags are arranged in their

---

* Pinel on Insanity, p. 96.—Davies' Trans.

† Observations on the Nature, Kinds, Causes, and Prevention of Insanity, &c. By Thomas Arnold, M.D., vol. i. p. 251.

most elegant folds—ribbons, and stars, and orders, load the breast—there is the mincing step, the stoop, the lisp—all the frivolity of the character: if kingship be personated, it will be popular kingship; for although legitimacy may suffice the proud, popularity, or living in the hearts of the people, will alone satisfy the vain maniac. He is a cringing beggar for the smallest mite of respect.

Females are more subject to this description of derangement than males: and the French hospitals are crowded with examples. These facts are accounted for by the strength of the feeling of vanity in the female sex, and by the injudicious encouragement which it receives from the present state of society. The misery of this class of lunatics is often extreme. They demand a tribute which is never paid, and which it might prove injurious to pay. Their disappointment is acute. They are discomfited to find that their loathsome rags are not regarded as cloth of gold, their croaking voice as melody. This discomfiture may be turned as a weapon against the disease.*

5. *Monomania of Fear.* The agitation of fear and anxiety frequently produces the monomania of fear; but the designation here used refers to the nature, and not to the origin of the complaint. Its essence is vague, exquisite terror. It may be definite, and have an object, real or imaginary, frightful or not; or it may be an irrepressible apprehension of present or prospective evil, without any conception of what is feared, or why it is feared. The object dreaded, when there *is* one, is external and connected with certain persons, events, or influences; or it is internal, a part, a condition of the diseased mind itself. Hence, there is the fear of some persecutor, plot, or awful calamity; or the mind quails at its own resolves, at what it is, at what it may

* Pinel. Quoted by Dr. A. Combe.—Observations on Mental Derangement, p. 174.

become. Haunted by self-created torments, the lunatic spends his days in seeking protection, in attempts to escape from the incubus of ever-present danger—his nights in the anguish of abandonment and despair. The wailings which are heard in asylums, are oftener the petitions of the terror-stricken for succour, or inarticulate cries of consternation at what is seen, heard, or felt—than shouts of defiance, or expressions of sorrow. The timid are likewise the most sleepless inmates; the night comes to them with its awe-inspiring darkness and silence, but not with its repose. The furious exhaust their muscular powers by their struggles during the day, and obtain the deep sleep of fatigue; but the timid know no remission of misery, even during their disturbed slumbers—for their terrors rise up before them as vividly in dream as in their waking thoughts. The things dreaded are proteiform. Occasionally, the same delusion, be it a spectre, or the deep laid plan of a conspiracy, will remain for months or years. More generally, every circumstance is successively construed into a source of alarm, until no impression reaches the mind, save through this distorted medium.

Fear is well known to render the system defenceless in the case of contagious diseases; and while it actually causes many attacks of insanity, it predisposes to a still greater number. What I mean is, that the suspense, the apprehension, the actual terror incidental to many situations of life, sap the foundations of mental strength, and leave the nervous system a prey to the exciting causes of mania. It appears that of nearly five hundred cases of insanity depending on a moral cause, forty-six or one-eleventh proceeded from terror. A fact not less illustrative of the influence of fear, is drawn from the history of the French revolution. Females, although they did not share so prominently in the dangers of that period, could not escape from the panic and misery which it created. They heard the howling of the tempest, though they felt not its fury. They had husbands, children to be guillotined, property to be confiscated, ties, and hopes, and happiness to be sacrificed. The consequence was, that an infinitely greater number of those who were pregnant at the time, gave birth to idiots, or children who afterwards became lunatic, than during times of order and tranquillity. The year 1793, in which the most frightful events of this convulsion took place, was likewise remarkable for the number of suicides. Fear is known, by those who have studied the feelings under which self-destruction is attempted, to be one of its most frequent causes. Strange to say, the apprehension of death itself leads to this act. "It would seem," says Reid, "as if they rushed into the arms of death in order to shield themselves from the terror of his countenance."* Now, in Versailles, a town, the population of which even now does not exceed 30,000, and where the Revolution may be said to have commenced, and upon which it repeatedly recoiled from the capital, not less than 1300 suicides occurred during the year mentioned.† Public events, or private misfortunes often determine the character of the object feared. Dr. Voisin affirms, that in France, those who formerly would have trembled at ghosts, the guillotine or Robespierre, now fear the police. The timid maniac is little susceptible of cure; but his sorrows may be soothed; his desire for society and protection may be opposed to his imaginary horrors; and the distraction of having something to do may be made to counteract the delusion of having something to fear.‡

6. *Monomania of Cunning and Suspicion.* Wonder is often expressed that madmen should say such shrewd, and

---

* Reid's Essays on Hypochondriasis.

† Art. Suicide, Dict. des Sciences Med. Burrow's Commentaries, p. 438.

‡ Perfect—Annals of Insanity, p. 243. Guislain, Traité sur les Phrenopathies, &c. p. 122.

do such cunning things. Those who have felt any surprise
at a circumstance so common, are ignorant, first, that the
powers which give shrewdness may remain uninjured while
all the others are extinct ; and, secondly, that cunning, the
wish to mystify, deceive, or conceal, and likewise the suspicion that deceit is practised or designed, is itself a modification of madness. We believe the terms cunning and suspicious to be convertible ; for in mania, as in the healthy
discharge of the mental functions, he who is disposed to
over-reach is jealous of the intentions of others, and while
shrouding his own feelings and projects, makes every effort
to penetrate those which he suspects. The cunning maniac
places no confidence in any one friend. He sees a sinister
meaning in every act ; he gathers insinuations from every
word ; he is the victim of some plot, the meshes of which
surround him, but which he will break through and baffle.
He will outwit all machinations. If a smile appears on the
face of a companion, it is held to be a secret sign. If a letter is delivered in his presence, he is certain that it implicates him in some mysterious transaction. He glories in
circumventing, in assuming an aspect different from the true
expression of his feelings—in concealment and insincerity.
His friends are his dupes ; and while he writhes under the
idea of their falsehood and connivance, his delusions revert
to schemes by which they may be deceived in retaliation.
If in confinement, he may disturb the concord of a whole
asylum, by disclosing conspiracies and schemes, and snares
which have no existence but in his own suspicion. He will
bend every energy to escape, and will display a great deal
of ingenuity in devising the means. An old spoon will
assume the office of a key to open the door ; a few stray
threads will be converted into a rope to scale the walls, and
some propitious moment will be chosen for the enterprise. The
apartment, bed and wearing apparel of such a Mephistopheles
will afford ample proofs of his dominant propensity. Every

thing will be hidden. Whatever he does will be attempted in secrecy, and the success of a stratagem will prove the maximum of enjoyment. Although men so actuated cannot well understand open dealing, candour and disinterested kindness—all marks of which they will believe to be the mask of a selfish purpose—yet they are accessible in many ways. Flattery, humanity, honour, command, may all, in different cases, find a responsive feeling in their breast. They may even be cajoled, deceived into an exercise of reason, although this should be the last resource. When cunning is associated with malicious or suicidal intentions, the case is distressing. A lunatic affected in this manner, known to cherish a design to destroy himself, and deprived of all ordinary means of executing his purpose, triumphed over all these obstacles in the following manner. He complained of a total want of sleep, restlessness, and headache. An opiate was prescribed. He every evening received about a grain of opium, and after a show of reluctance, put it into his mouth. He did not, however, swallow it. By retaining it in the mouth until his attendants left the room, he at last accumulated nearly a scruple, swallowed the whole, and died.*

7. *Monomania of Religion and Superstition.* The engrossing sentiment in this variety is a blind devotion and awe; the delusions rest upon the relation which the patient holds to Deity, his laws and providence, and to other supernatural beings. Acts of worship, really solemn, extravagant or horrible, according to the extent of the disease or the character of the other predominating feelings, are often attendant on the paroxysm. Vision seeing, miracle working, claims to the possession of the divine afflatus, are among the symptoms. The belief that as a missionary, a preacher, or a prophet, he is to achieve the conversion and regeneration of mankind,

---

* Esquirol, Des Illusions chez les Aliénés, p. 16. Guislain, p. 194.

is ever before the philanthropic, while his personal interests
and salvation are the cherished hope of the selfish maniac.
The vagaries of the vacillating powers often lead the individual back to some far distant period in the progress of religion ; and standing on a heap of rubbish, he imagines himself a heroic Hebrew fighting for his faith on the crumbling
battlements of Jerusalem ; or, transported to the palmy days
of Rome, he declares himself to be the head of the church.
In the majority of instances the delusion bears a resemblance
to any recent demonstration of enthusiasm, or to any description of fanaticism which may be current. When I studied at Salpetrière, the Jesuits were in deep disgrace ; the
St. Simonians were popular and fashionable ; and almost all
the religious maniacs admitted, laboured under the impression that they were Jesuits or St. Simonians.* The minor
features of this kind of derangement differ in different countries, and as it occurs in different sects : the insane Catholic
enfeebles his body with stripes and penance ; the insane
Protestant is more contemplative, but in essential points the
disease is the same in both. When complicated with the
belief in the visitation, or interference of spiritual existences,
fear may or may not be experienced. This is determined
by the courage of the party, or the attributes of the being
conjured up. The demon may be met by execrations, or
shouts of joy, this matters not ; the deviation from health consists in the firm conviction that the eye sees what is the shadowy creation of a distempered fancy, and that the heart
feels the inspiration and strength of divinity when it is agitated by its own erring suggestions. Lunatics affected in
this manner appear to be supremely happy. The very intensity of their feelings protects them against anxiety or depression. They believe that their constant humility and
adoration will be rewarded ; that they are favoured more than

* 1832.

other men, and that their communication with higher intelligences is proof and foretaste of this. This fine spun tissue of error cannot but yield joy and security. There are, accordingly, few suicides from religious Monomania. Occasionally they do occur, and under circumstances which correspond to the peculiarity of the individual or of his situation. A Venetian shoemaker conceived that he was destined to be a sacrifice for the human race. He prepared and planted a cross, procured a sponge, nails, spear, and in fact imitated the representations of the death of our Saviour so often seen in Catholic countries. He wounded his side, transfixed his feet and hands, and then raised himself up to the cross by some mechanical contrivance, and hung impaled for upwards of twenty-four hours before he was discovered.

Wherever lunatics are collected together, a great many cases are always designated religious, and supposed to be attributable to enthusiasm. This partly proceeds from the difficulty of obtaining correct information as to the history of each case, and partly from the philosophical blunder of concluding that in insanity the cause is invariably of the same nature as the effect. We are the more anxious to expose this error as it seems to set limits to religious instruction, to the cultivation of pious dispositions, and to cast a doubt on the propriety of the promulgation of certain high and holy principles of our faith. Now all men must, and practically do, admit that the kind and degree of religious training should be adapted to the capacity and the education of the proselyte. By forgetting this principle, this " tempering the wind to the shorn lamb ;" and by treating the desponding and presumptuous, the weak and the strong understanding alike, madness may have been produced. Yet even after allowing this system all the evil influence it can possibly possess, and adding to it the injurious effect of the theological speculation in which the ignorant engage, the cases of insanity produced by these means are comparatively

few. Burrows states that no case of mania resulting from a
religious source ever fell under his notice which could not
be referred to the conflict accompanying a *change* of opinion
in religion.* To every one who can analyze this proposition, it must be clear that the tendency to insanity is given
by the change, by the overthrow of long established principles, and not by the nature of the thing *from* or *to* which the
change is effected. A change in politics or fortune would
be equally prejudicial. Scepticism produces a greater number of maniacs than enthusiasm. The authority just quoted
appears to coincide in this view, as he affirms that the cases
of which he speaks were developed during the interval of
doubt occurring between the relinquishment of old, and the
adoption of new principles. But to appeal to facts. Esquirol states, that of 492 patients insane from moral causes,
in nine only could the alienation be traced to religious fanaticism. This calculation was made in France at a period, it
is true, when a moral pestilence had swept the feelings and
symbols of Christianity from the land. Previous to this
period, that is, during the desecrations of the revolutionists,
the proportion was greater, Pinel attributes 25 in 113 cases
to fanaticism. But now, when the ordinary tone and character of society and its institutions have been, to a certain
extent re-established, that proportion has scarcely at all increased. Of 528 cases admitted to Charenton, from 1826
to 1832, produced by moral causes, only 24 arose from
"exalted devotion." In Holst's tables, only 28 of 384 cases
are traced to this cause. In this country, statistics are very
deficient. Of 40 cases in a neighbouring institution, not
one is referred to this origin. But I am convinced from
observation, that although this *cause* does not operate more
powerfully, the number of religious maniacs is greater in
Britain than elsewhere. The explanation is obvious. Re-

* Burrow's Commentaries, p. 38.

ligion has here its due exercise and awful importance; the
mind is trained, thinks and feels under its influence; and
when from misfortune or ambition, or physical injury, the
place of reason is usurped, it may always be predicated,
first that the delusions which succeed will correspond to the
natural disposition, and secondly to those impressions which
have been most powerful and permanent; and hence there
are not a greater number of maniacs; but there are a greater
number of maniacs exhibiting a certain class of delusions,
because our countrymen are, whatever may be their errors,
naturally and habitually devout.*

8. *Monomania of Despondency and Suicide.* This form is
often classed with religious mania upon the very inadequate
ground that the patient may accuse himself of inexpiable
guilt, of having offended God, and therefore despond. But
the derangement consists in the depression and prostration
of energy; the delusion of criminality, &c. follow, and are
adduced but cannot be received as reasons for the disquietude. The simplest form in which morbid despondency is
manifested, is as a want of confidence in the talents and prospects which previously had been regarded with satisfaction;
an utter abandonment of hope, a miserable lethargic despair.
There is no delusion or incoherence present; there is a settled and horrible conviction of the approach of ruin and desolation, to which the mind gives itself up, against which it
can make no effort, but for which no cause, not even an imaginary one, can be assigned. This, when an individual has
the fortitude to control, or the cunning to conceal the expression of the full extent of his sufferings, or when they do
not interfere with the common affairs of life, is called lowness
of spirits. It ought to be regarded and treated as insanity,
and not dreaded as its forerunner. For it is at this stage
that suicide is resorted to. Should this not be the case,

Perfect, Annals of Insanity, p. 87. Arnold's Observations, p. 228.

specific hallucinations may speedily appear, and the agony
of mind will be indured as a consequence of bankruptcy, the
unfaithfulness of a friend, the persecutions of enemies, or the
ravages of an incurable disease. No demonstration of the
untenableness of such grounds, no picture of brighter and
happier circumstances will avail to refute or encourage. The
sufferer clings to his hoarded misery. There is generally
great loss of physical strength in cases of this kind; and the
pale, emaciated countenance, dull and sunken eye, and list-
less dejected form, tell as plainly as the querulous complaint,
or the long intricate description of sorrows and anticipated
evils, to what class the patient belongs. These unfortunate
beings are often persecuted by their fellow-maniacs, and have
real added to imaginary sources of uneasiness. I have conjoined the cognomen of "suicidal" with this species of madness, because the propensity to self-destruction appears more
frequently in the desponding than in the religious, the suspicious, or even the homicidal maniac. In a table given by
Professor Casper of Berlin, 103 cases of suicide are attributed to mental affections; 30 of these may be classed under
this head, and 32 under that of fear and despondency combined. In the same table, containing in all 412 cases, the
causes of which were known, a corroboration of the opinion
that suicide is rare among religious maniacs is found, one
case only having followed religious excitement.* In Paris
where there have been 3185 suicides in ten years, and the
annual mortality from this cause now amounts to 477, M.
Guerry, the eminent and accurate writer on the statistics of

* A somewhat different result appears to have been recently arrived
at by Dr. Sc. Pinel. He has published a table in which 11 of 125
cases of suicide depended upon religious excitement. His conclusions
are, however, much less valuable and satisfactory from his having taken
a particular class of suicides, that in which the attempt was unsuccessful,
as the ground of his observations. But even waiving such an objection,
the proportion is still small.

crime, says that gambling, and of necessity the defeated hopes and dejection which it entails, produces a greater number of self-inflicted deaths than any other cause. He hazards the opinion that it is almost the sole cause.* Next to despondency, offended honour and domestic disappointments appear as the most fertile source of suicide. But such reasonable causes do not always exist; a mere disgust at life, an uneasy sensation, a disturbed digestion may be conceived by the unhinged mind sufficient to justify the act. Such reasons have been acknowledged by those who retained intelligence to know and describe their intentions; and it should be recollected that in proportion to the impairment of intelligence, the danger increases, for to him who cannot distinguish the real position in which he stands, who cannot estimate either the present or future consequences of the act, and who is wholly delivered up to one series of ideas, or to two, pleasure and pain, the most insignificant event, the most ridiculous and incongruous motive, may precipitate the attempt. The desponding maniac consequently requires unremitting attention. No ordinary precaution will frustrate the success of his designs, for every object may by ingenuity be turned into a means of destruction; and the moment, apparently the most inauspicious, and from that reason the least suspected, will be chosen for the purpose. For years will such a design be cherished in silence, until the fears and care of those around are lulled to sleep, and then executed.

I have noticed a very interesting fact connected with the utility of isolation and superintendence in this variety. We learn from Guerry that suicides are annually effected in Paris in the proportion of one to every 3000 inhabitants. This takes place among individuals accredited sane, and in possession of many of the things which endear the continuance of life.

* Essai sur la Statistique Morale de la France. The statements of M. Brouc, Annales d'Hygiène Publique, vol. xvi. p. 243, do not countenance this view.

Esquirol states, on the other hand, that among 12,000 lunatics confined at Salpetrière, during a series of years, and exposed by their malady to constant temptations to escape from
suffering by death, only four suicides took place; that is, one
in 3000. The proportion is apparently the same; but the advantages of restraint, and the actually low rate in asylums
must become manifest, when the circumstances of the cases
and the conditions of the persons compared are considered.*

9. *Monomania of Imagination.* This may be defined the
mania of accomplishments. It is displayed in attempts to do
every thing, and a pleased conviction that every thing is
done perfectly. The maniac is a poet, a painter, a mathe-
matician, as the case may happen, he pants after excellence,
and struggles indefatigably to attain it; he writes verses
which would disgrace a valentine; he scratches hideous
figures on the wall, his calculations cover every slip of paper;
these efforts of his genius do not satisfy his longing after im-
mortality, but he is resolved to improve. He lives in an atmosphere where the distorted objects appear to him of gigan-
tic size, sublime magnificence, and surpassing beauty. Every
thing with him is superlative. This is the madness of Don
Quixote. He does all odd and eccentric things to satisfy his
humour, and if reprimanded for his extravagances, he will,
in all probability, reply in some impassioned strain to the
lady of his love, or to the keeper, as Shakspeare or the Emperor of Morocco. He literally

> " Finds tongues in trees, sermons in stones."

He is, to use a word in a new sense, a transcendentalist. His
reasonings are so subtile as to escape the ordinary power of
the mind's eye; and his refinements upon excellence would
astonish an optimist. His plans for human improvement are
original, and on the grandest scale. Whatever is new he

* Burrow's Commentaries, p. 412.—Perfect's Annals, p. 26—297.
Falret du Suicide et de l'Hypochondrie.

prizes, and, in fact, his grand desire and delusion is to act differently from the common herd, in order to do it well and with eclàt. This, in less marked outline constitutes the oddities and eccentricities of society. A Frenchman passed twenty years in cogitating a plan whereby the whole human race could be accommodated under one roof in one sumptuous building. The rulers were to reside in the centre, and the nations over which they presided were to radiate in their various interminable abodes from this point. His calculations and arrangements for this vast pantisocracy were repeated again and again, but on his pulling down his house in order to apply these practically, his splendid visions were dissipated by confinement. The disease evidently consists in the inordinate activity of those feelings called romantic which aim at an unreal, a perfect state of existence, without any counterpoise on the part of reason. Poets and novel writers have certainly done, or attempted to do much towards the elevation of the human race ; but over the unprepared, ill-balanced and sanguine mind, their works exercise a pernicious dominion, and sometimes cause the madness now delineated. In the Charenton table, thirteen cases are traced to novel reading.[*]

10. *Monomania of Avarice.* This is not simply the vice of the miser in excess. There is the propensity to acquire, by any means, legitimate or otherwise, as well as the propensity to hoard. The day-dreams of avaricious lunatics are all directed towards wealth, property, or aggrandizement in some shape. Their air castles are built of gold. But although panting after riches, they may be styled omnivorous : they will derive pleasure from receiving or taking any article without reference to its nature or value. The only condition necessary to secure this gratification being, that the

* Tuke, Description of the Retreat at York, p. 182.—Perfect, Annals, p. 47.—Guislain sur les Phrenopathies, p. 204.

coveted possession is not theirs, but is about to become theirs.
They only, of all men, have discovered the philosopher's
stone; every straw and rag and pebble becomes precious, is
transmuted into gold, or silver, or gem, when it passes into
their hands. Did they actually possess this flux, their belief would be justifiable, that they are owners of half the
land in the kingdom: that the occupants are appointed by
them as agents; that their food is served on plate and china;
and their straw pillow filled with rubies. The rooms they
inhabit are littered, their clothes are loaded with collections
of indescribable trumpery, which they hold to be of incalculable importance. If possible these treasures are concealed, and the hiding places would puzzle a French police
agent. The point of the shoe, the lining of the coat, the
sleeve, the mouth, even the stomach, are made depositaries
of these ill-gotten gains. They, of course, make no use
whatever of such acquisitions; it is the act of accumulating
which constitutes their happiness. The pocket-handker-
chiefs of every one who visited a large Asylum disappeared,
no one could imagine how or where. At last they were
discovered bound round the waist of an avaricious maniac,
who had abstracted them so dexterously as to have eluded
suspicion, and who, though from his notorious character he
was searched every night, had outwitted the inquisitors by
placing the stolen goods next his skin. Stealing is delightful to these men; they rob their fellow-patients, seize upon
everything within their reach, and boldly justify their conduct on the ground that all they have taken is theirs *de
jure.* In the supposed plenitude of an ample fortune, such
men are sometimes generous. They offer to pay the board
of all the patients, and the wages of all the servants in an
asylum; or present you with bills for an enormous amount,
sometimes for your own behoof, more frequently for their
own. For the last five or six years a patient has regularly,
every week, presented the physician at Charenton with

scraps of paper, designed to meet all the disbursements of that vast institution. It is almost needless to say, that this class of patients may be bribed to do any thing.*

11. *Monomania of Benevolence and Affection.*—Even the un-restrained exercise of the powers giving a name to this variety must be classed with madness. It may be described as an over anxiety for the welfare of the whole human race, or for that of the narrower circle of friends and acquaintances. A visionary who neglects his own duties and concerns in order to eradicate poverty, and sickness, and sorrow from the world, or gives up his soul to anguish, because the attempt has failed, and the mother who, distracted for the safety of her children and acquaintances, can neither act, nor think, nor sleep, because she cannot relieve them from some evil or misery of which they do not complain, and by which they are sub-jected to no annoyance, are both instigated by similar morbid feelings. The affectionate maniac is a melancholy spectacle. There is a nobleness and magnanimity in his phrenzy; he strips himself of his clothes; he starves for days in order to relieve the supposed wants of his associates; his mind teems with projects to alleviate their condition, to render them happy; or he wanders about declaring that his whole kin-dred is destroyed, or in misfortune, and searches for their mangled bodies in every hole and crevice. They often look upon themselves as physicians, nurses, or overseers of the poor, and the asylum, or their place of abode whatever it may be, as an hospital, or house of refuge, where they are commissioned to diffuse comfort and contentment. Such ministrations are often highly beneficial; but so far as the kind ministrants are concerned, the labour never ends, for they never fail to detect new wants and require to devise new methods to relieve them. Men of this stamp often

* Guislain, Traité sur les Phrenopathies, p. 209. Esquirol, Des Illusions chez les Aliénés, p. 18.

squander a noble fortune before confinement is resorted to.
As it is they who see the want and not the objects who feel
it, the charities which they bestow must be indiscriminate.
" To endow a college or a cat," affords to them nearly the
same satisfaction. This, however, is the most pleasing
view of the case. They are generally rendered unhappy by
the delusions of wretchedness which are ever before them,
but which they have no means to alleviate, and bemoan the
hard fate of being unable to execute the munificent and merciful behest for which they were sent upon earth. Or, torn
by apprehensions for the misfortunes of friends, by disappointment from their want of affection, and by grief from
their ingratitude, they commit suicide.*

Sect. II.—12. *Incapability of perceiving the Relations of
Ideas.*—The second section relates to disturbance of the reflecting and perceptive powers, and the first division of it to
the incapability of perceiving the relations of ideas. This
disorder of the thinking, may be consentaneous with the
perfect health of the emotive or feeling part of our nature.
The man who cannot recognise the relevancy of the most
obvious argument, or the agreement or disagreement of
two of the simplest propositions, may experience no exaltation or depression of his sentiments; may act with the same
integrity, love with the same fervor, and hope and fear as
intensely as if no change had taken place. Popularly it is
named confusion of ideas. The diseased process seems to
consist of the following steps. The mind receives perceptions accurately. The senses convey their reports with the
customary clearness and fidelity, and the representations of
the external world are accordingly exact, and known and
acted upon as exact. The suggestions of the propensities
are neither exaggerated nor irregular, and they impel to cer-

* Perfect's Annals, p. 54.

tain actions, become objects of thought and memory, without any interruption to the laws by which such conditions are regulated. But at the point where the mind seeks to arrange, contrast, compare, or analyze the ideas thus acquired, the error which constitutes derangement occurs. The qualities which associate or separate ideas are no longer appreciable, and reasoning is at an end. For example, vision has at some period made an individual acquainted with the effects of galvanism upon others, the image conveyed to the mind was at the time distinct and correct, and the recollection preserved of it is equally so. At the same, or some subsequent period, misfortunes have assailed this person and produced all the pain of disappointed hopes and aggrieved self-love. Now the calamities were real; the melancholy and wounded pride were no more than proportioned to the circumstances which called them forth, and the impressions of these states received and retained were true indices of the existing feelings. But when the maniac thinks of galvanism, there is probably suggested some portion of his own distressing history; he does not and cannot see that these events have no possible connexion; they immediately become objects of reflection, finding them associated, he believes them to be connected, and the issue may be, I shall assume that it is, a conviction that the galvanism was the *cause* of his ruin; that the contortions which he witnessed in the subjects of this experiment, upon which his attempt at ratiocination is founded, were proofs that the process of destruction was going on in them; that the uneasiness which he experienced on recalling the past is the thrilling and tingling sensations communicated by this agent; that every man in pain and poverty is galvanized; that the nation is on the eve of bankruptcy, and that galvanism is at the bottom of it. The total absence of concord, connexion, or sequence in these thoughts, the inability to assort, if such a vague expression be admissable, the classes of ideas before

the mind according to their qualities and natural order, is
the principal feature of this form of insanity. The incoherence of maniacs often depends on this cause; it is that
plausible incoherence, however, which seems to have a meaning could it but be discovered. Men so affected may continue to mingle with society and to be useful citizens; when
confined, so much of the mind remains vigorous and sound
that they may, with perfect prudence, be intrusted with even
responsible situations in the management.

But the disease is occasionally more limited in its scope
than what I have described it. The incapability to perceive
relations being apparent only when certain classes of ideas
are presented to the mind. Such is the case of Matthews,
who imagined that he was the victim of what he learnedly
called " pneumatic chemistry." By means of this tremendous agent, mercenary blood-hounds employed to torment
him, though residing at a distance, introduced notions into
his brain, intercepted the communication between his brain
and heart, distended his nerves with gas, and so forth.* Of
the same kind is the case of the clergyman who believed
that he had lost his rational soul, refused to join in worship
as an act of impiety for a being destitute of a spirit, and who,
in dedicating a book of great merit to the sovereign of the
time, subscribes himself as one " who was once a man, and
of some little name, but whose thinking substance wasted for
seventeen years, and is now utterly come to nothing."†
Both of these men retained sufficient intelligence to perceive the relations of other ideas, or were, to vary the expression, rational upon all other subjects.‡

13. *Incapability of perceiving the relations of external objects.* A man cannot divest himself of the belief that the
house which he has inhabited for years has changed its po-

* Haslam's Illustrations of Madness.
† Conolly's Inquiry concerning the Indications of Insanity.
‡ Burrow's Commentaries, p. 299. Guislain, 310.

sition, that the windows are diminished or increased in number to a frightfu' xtent, that the trees planted by his own hands, and firmly rooted and flourishing for years in the same spot, move off suddenly in various directions, crowd together, or circle round him in the mazes of a dance. He hears the most ravishing melody, or the harshest discord emanating from every object around; voices address him, and counsel, or threaten him, where there is no tongue to speak. But during all this the mind may be very sceptical of the reality of the appearances presented to it, and is only startled into an unwilling and conditional belief by the difficulty of answering the question, can I doubt the evidence of my own senses. But there is more than the senses at fault. The powers which take cognizance of their reports must be diseased. For we are well assured that, from the nature of vision, the retina must receive the picture of the errant house as it is, that the actual number of windows must be depicted, and that the impressions corresponding to sounds which reach the mind do not reach the ear. It is in the combining these, the faithful communications of sense, that the infidelity is committed. The idea of a house may be well defined; but the idea of the relation which the house bears to the surrounding trees, &c. is vague, indistinct, or erroneous; the idea of windows may be clear, but the interminable multiplication of these is the result of the diseased conception of that idea. There is no fear, or superstition, consequent on such extraordinary visions as that described, the patient supposes them to be the real, everyday working of nature, and neither looks for, nor detects in them magic, nor divine interposition. The delusions of the superstitious maniac conjure up objects which do not exist, the present class see real objects through a false medium. The individual mentioned may be found to reason sensibly on all subjects abstracted from external objects, and to act as if his house were a fixture, and the trees budded and blossomed in their

original soil. The man who saw in his own house the Inquisition, and in his chairs the instruments of torture, but
acted as if he never had heard of St. Dominic or the rack,
was a complete exemplification of this malady.*

14. *Incapability of perceiving the qualities of external objects.* The mind, otherwise unimpaired, sees a hunting field,
for instance, the horses, the dogs, and the sportsmen, of gi-
gantic or microscopical size ; they resemble mammoths or
ants at full speed ; the colouring of the scene is uniform, a
brilliant scarlet, perhaps, or it is infinitely varied. The individual thus affected either cannot perceive the quality of
an object at all, there is a suspension of the power to do so,
as where no impression is communicated to the mind by
several colours ; or the quality is perceived in an imperfect
and erroneous manner, as when objects appear larger or
smaller than their actual size ; and grotesque shapes occupy
the place of familiar pieces of furniture.† A great inaptitude is likewise felt to arrange all the visual impressions into one whole, they start up contrary to the will, in irregular
succession, and as isolated sensations, so that the hallucination, besides being a hallucination, is a thing of shreds
and patches. When this species of madness is accompanied
by bodily uneasiness, these morbid perceptions are extended
to the personal condition and feelings of the lunatic, and he
declares his head to be a lantern, his body red-hot, or made
of glass. A royal maniac conceived himself to be a tea-pot.
Saussure believed that he had increased to so enormous a
size, that he could not pass out of the door of his apartment,
and caused the partition to be taken down in consequence.
I have under my care a sturdy soldier, metamorphosed by
his own disordered perceptions into a louse ; and Zimmerman

* Esquirol, Des Illusions chez les Aliénés, *passim.*
† Phrenological Journal, vol. viii., p. 44. Phrenological Transactions, p. 209.

mentions a lunatic who, supposing himself a barley-corn, was terrified to venture into the open air lest he should be picked up by the sparrows.*

IV. MANIA may be defined the irregular action of *all* the mental powers. Its ravages are not confined to certain groups of feelings or perceptions, to associations more or less extensive, but spread to all. They may not be all equally injured; but so deeply rooted is the perversion as to enfeeble that which it does not overthrow. The ideas are chaotic, but amid the confusion there may be observed the struggle of maddened propensities and extravagant feelings, and the jarring of the elements of memory and perception. The recollection of some scene long past is mistaken for a present impression, there is a want of discrimination between what is reflected and what is felt; the passions are involuntary; anger bursts forth without provocation; sorrow arises the next moment, terror succeeds without a single cause for alarm, and the whole terminates with the loud hollow laugh of brutal merriment. There are three things to be considered here. First, the want of power to control or direct the mental operations. Secondly, the absence of all harmony or sequence between these operations. And, thirdly, the incessant activity with which these operations are carried on. To this last consideration have all the other phenomena been referred. In whatever way induced, whether by wine, emotion, or disease, excessive activity is known to affect the propensities and feelings by increasing their excitability and by rendering their suggestions intense, irresistible, and involuntary, and, in some cases, if the cause continues to exist, permanent. Upon the reflective and perceptive faculties the effect of hyperactivity is altogether different. Carried

* Esquirol, Des Illusions chez les Aliénés, *passim.* Perfect, Annals, p. 333, &c.

beyond a certain point, it disturbs, impedes, or arrests the healthy operation of the understanding. The excited judgment may attempt to compare two facts, but the laws under which such a step can be made are abrogated. The whole of the intellectual powers are simultaneously active, and, in place of two, there are twenty propositions to be examined, each of these being distorted by the medium through which it arrived, and withal, neither the power to exclude what is extraneous, nor the power to perceive what is essential to the examination, remain. The violent excitement of the propensities must materially contribute to this disturbance. The process of intoxication amply illustrates the explanation given of the psychological cause of mania, the excessive simultaneous activity of all the mental powers. The drunkard, as he swallows repeated draughts of some exciting liquor, under its influence waxes valiant, or vain, or generous, according to his character. His wrath is fierce, his mirth boisterous, his kindness overpowering. Every sentiment is extreme. This is clearly a description of the irrepressible activity of the propensities. Gradually, and in proportion to the augmenting intensity of the emotions specified, the ability to perceive the merits of an opinion is affected; then the perceptive powers fail, and double vision and erroneous impressions of all kinds follow. The total confusion of mania closes the scene. What tends not a little to give force to the comparison here instituted, and to shew that the states compared are to a certain extent identical, differing only in duration, is the great development of physical strength and insensibility to pain which occur in both. The maniac is in most cases furious as well as incoherent. His strength is tremendous, and cannot be restrained or subdued by ordinary means. It is not, however, necessarily exerted for malicious purposes, otherwise death and desolation must follow his track, and the coercive measures so long recommended might appear to be justified. Passive as well as active strength appears to exist in maniacs. Many bruise and lacerate their bodies, either with a stoical indifference, or with an expression of delight. A sect of insane fanatics at one time occupied much attention in France, who endured all kinds of torture without a murmur, and among other ingenious contrivances for immolation, they received blows on the back, limbs, &c., from sledge-hammers, which, so their historians tell, would have crushed a stone wall to powder. These symptoms all bespeak increased activity; but there is also a species of mania with diminished activity. Under this denomination are included cases where the propensities are in abeyance or extinct, while the powers purely intellectual are diseased with increased activity. The combination of fatuity of the propensities with incapability of perceiving the relations of ideas or things will convey a notion of this form of disease. There is the same incoherence, preposterous grouping of recollections and actual impressions, as in the preceding variety, but there is neither wildness, nor vehemence, nor irritability, nor terror. The incongruous imaginings which the maniac conceives to be opinions, or observations on what is presented to his mind, are poured forth volubly, but he has neither pride, nor vanity, nor irritability to be aroused, either by external or internal impressions.*

The subject is not exhausted. For these varieties of insanity are found in every possible state of combination, exhibiting new and characteristic symptoms. Proud monomania may thus be found conjoined with that of vanity; or both these states of feeling may exist in the same mind which has been deprived of the power to judge of its own operations, or of the impressions which it receives from without. But although it would require a voluminous treatise on the philosophy of insanity to comprehend a description of these combinations,

* Calmeil de la Paralysie considerée chez les Aliénés, p. 56, No. xv. Art. Folie, Dict. de Méd. tom. ix. p. 237.

D

my present object is gained if the sketch here submitted has
served to indicate the most striking distinctions between the
different varieties, and how readily and humanely, and pro-
fitably a separation of the inmates of asylums founded on
such broad distinctions could be carried into effect.

I have mentioned that until this evening, no attempt has
been made to address an unprofessional, but well educated
audience, on the subject of Insanity. Until very recently
the care of the insane was monopolized by medical and other
adventurers: a ridiculous stigma, created by the character
and proceedings of the very persons engaged in this monopoly, deterred regular and well educated practitioners from
attempting to compete, and even from qualifying themselves
to do so. Indeed, it has only been since the voice of the
public has been raised against this monopoly and its consequences, and the philanthropic of every profession interfered
in behalf of those who most required their protection, that
justice and mercy have, in any degree, dictated the treatment which these unfortunate beings received. Until then,
a thick and almost impenetrable veil was cast over the workings of the " mind diseased :" a species of awe and sacred-
ness was attached to the person of the maniac, as one on
whom the hand of his Creator had visibly, and fearfully, and
in a peculiar manner, fallen : the precincts of his prison-
house were regarded as holy and peculiar ground, and the
secrets of that mysterious dwelling remained untold, or only
whispered in accents of horror and reverence. But " the
day-spring from on high" of knowledge which is beginning
to diffuse its cheering light on every the most distant land,
has visited even the benighted sky of a madhouse, and fallen
like healing on the hearts of those, whose doom, in other
days, must have been imprisonment, solitude, and despair.

LECTURE II.

WHAT ARE THE STATISTICS OF INSANITY?

The numbers and distribution of Lunatics in Britain—Is insanity increased by civilization—Does it increase in a greater ratio than the population—Does it attack men of particular professions, or of particular ranks—Does it prevail chiefly under free, or under despotic forms of Government—What period of life does it principally attack —Does Marriage diminish the liability to the Disease—Are Males or Females most exposed—What is the proportion of cures—Rate of Mortality—Does Insanity prolong or shorten life—Influence of season on Mortality—Diseases affecting Lunatics—Proportion of Furious, Paralytic and Epileptic, Fatuous and Idiotic, Dirty, Noisy and Suicidal Madmen—Lucid Intervals—Relapses—Complete isolation—Early confinement—Employment as a means of cure—Proportion of Lunatics that may be employed—Does it promote the cure? —The kind of occupation—Is it safe?

WHAT are the statistics of insanity? What are the numbers, the rank, the occupations, the ages of those who display the varieties of disease enumerated, and are committed to the care of the physician; and in what proportion are they susceptible of cure, alleviation or employment?

In England there are probably not less than 10,000 lunatics; while in Scotland the numbers are certainly not below 4000. Of the latter, 1338 are confined in private asylums, or licensed houses, unworthy the name of asylum, 21 linger out their miserable existence in the jails of some of the remote counties, 500 are in public establishments, and the remainder, about 1500, are at liberty, subsisting upon charity, but in general exposed to the greatest privations.*

By the calculations of Sir A. Halliday, which, although perhaps merely approximations to the truth, have the merit of being the only data we possess, it appears that the proportion of the insane to the sane population of Europe, is 1 to 1000. In Wales the proportion is 1 to 800, in Scotland 1 to 574. The Americans, so closely allied to us by descent, language, national character and customs, it is computed by Dr. Brigham, present 1 lunatic in every 262 inhabitants.† This disparity probably depends upon the rapid acquisition of wealth, and the luxurious social habits to which the good fortune of our transatlantic brethren has exposed them. With luxury, indeed, insanity appears to keep equal pace. Nay, the opinion has been hazarded, that as we recede, step by step, from the simple, that is, the savage manners of our ancestors, and advance in industry and knowledge and happiness, this malignant persecutor strides onward, signalizing every era in the social progress by an increase, a new hecatomb, of victims. Is insanity an inseparable adjunct to civilization? I spurn the supposition. The truth seems to be, that the barbarian escapes this scourge because he is exempt from many of the physical, and almost all the moral sources of mental excitement; and that the members of civilized communities are subjected to it, because the enjoyments and blessings of augmented power are abused; because the mind is roused to exertion without being disciplined, it is stimulated without being strengthened; because our selfish propensities are cultivated while our moral nature is left barren, our pleasures becoming poisonous; and because in

* A general view of the present state of lunatics and lunatic asylums in Great Britain and Ireland, &c., by Sir Andrew Halliday, M.D., pp. 16 and 27.

† Remarks on the Influence of Mental Cultivation and Mental excitement upon health, by A. Brigham, M.D., p. 52.

the midst of a blaze of scientific light, and in the presence of a thousand temptations to multiply our immediate by a sacrifice of our ultimate gratifications, we remain in the darkest ignorance of our own mind, its true relations, its danger and its destiny. With civilization then come sudden and agitating changes and vicissitudes of fortune ; vicious effeminacy of manners ; complicated transactions ; misdirected views of the objects of life ; ambition, and hopes, and fears, which man in his primitive state does not and cannot know. But these neither constitute, nor are they necessarily connected with, civilization. They are defects, obstacles which retard the advancement of that amelioration of condition towards which every discovery in art, or ethics, must ultimately tend. To these defects, and not to the amount of improvement, or refinement of a people is insanity to be traced. Statistics, the best guide in such an inquiry, support this view. Esquirol's Tables of the moral causes of insanity clearly show that a great majority of these are identical with the vices, passions, corruptions, and weaknesses of our nature, or with deviations from what all good or great men understand to be the objects of civilization. Few cases can be traced, except where hereditary predisposition exists, to the well-regulated efforts, the virtuous contentment, or the settled principles of a highly educated mind, or to the affluence, the enterprise, the information, or the polish by which these may be accompanied ; and these, it is conceived, are the legitimate products of civilization. And even when a hereditary taint creates danger where it would not otherwise exist, it must be remembered that it may have been originally contracted through the ignorance or error of some individuals, in cherishing some predominating passion, or by intermarriage with an impure stock. Vicious as the effect unquestionably is of over exertion of the intellectual powers, or of giving an undue preponderance to any faculty, and much as the prevailing systems of education tend to encourage such a practice, I find that out of a total of 472 cases given by Esquirol, 13 only are referred to an excess of study, while about 100 are the fruit of the excess of the propensities, and 90 result from an uneducated and ill-regulated state of the sentiments.* Georget's lists afford similar evidence. He enumerates 25 victims of mental labour, 20 of an ill-conducted education, 106 drunkards, and 470 affected from other moral causes, out of about 1000 cases.†

One of the most interesting questions to be decided by the statistics of insanity is, does the disease increase, is the poisoned stream larger, and wider, and deeper than former-ly ? Does it like other streams deepen the channel as it flows ? As population is doubled in certain periods, so will be the number of cases of disease. But this is not exactly the question at issue. Has insanity, like some other dis-eases, a greater number of victims in proportion to the po-pulation at present existing, than at former periods ? The question has been answered in the affirmative. Dr. Powell entertains this opinion, and shows that while, in the lustrum be-tween 1775 and 1776, the number of registered lunatics was 1783, in that between 1805 and 1809 it amounted to 2271.‡ It must be confessed, however, that his investigations tend rather to point out the fallacies which enter into all such cal-culations, than to support his own views, or to determine the question. Sir A. Halliday asserts, that the number of lunatics has been tripled within the last twenty years : and Esquirol states, that while the patients in the public hospitals in Paris in 1801 were only 1070, in 1821 they amounted to 2145. These startling facts, on the other hand, have been declared to be inconclusive, and those who have adduced them desig-nated alarmists. More careful examination is, without doubt,

---

* Dict. des Sciences Méd., art. " Folie."   † De la Folie.

‡ Observations upon the Comparative Prevalence of Insanity at dif-ferent Periods.   Medical Transactions of the College of Physicians, London, vol. iv. p. 130.

required to establish the proposition : but this, at least, is proved, that a much greater number of cases is known to exist, and to require treatment, than formerly, whatever may be the relative proportion of any given periods. But there are many presumptions in favour of Sir A. Halliday's opinion. We do not speak of the additional asylums building, or recently built, in almost every county in England. The majority of those were required and ought to have been erected fifty years ago. Nor do I allude to the acknowledged increase of other nervous diseases: but to the too palpable multiplication of the causes which produce mania itself. The occupations, amusements, follies, and above all, the vices of the present race, are infinitely more favourable for the development of the disease then at any previous period. We live under the dominion of the propensities and must pay the penalty for so doing : and madness is one of these. There is one feature which has often struck me in examining tables of the causes of insanity in reference to the matter under discussion. One half of these is resolvable into crime, follies, and ignorance. If we consult Esquirol's Table, published in 1835, comprehending 1557 cases, and exclude 337 instances of hereditary taint, as the exciting circumstances under which this burst forth are not noted, it will appear that 579 are attributable to the excess or abuse of the passions, or to the weakness of the uneducated intellect.* The writings of the recent statistical authorities, Guerry and Quetelet, strongly corroborate this opinion. The latter, in quoting from M. Pierquin the observation, " les crimes sont toujours, par rapport aux populations dans une proportion en rapport avec cette de la folie," says, " En général je pense effectivement chez lui, que les causes qui tendent à produire l'aliénation mentale, influent aussi sur le nombre des crimes et sur le nombre des crimes contre les

* Annales d'Hygiène Publique, Janvier, 1835.

personnes surtout, mais sans qu'il y ait un rapport direct et nécessaire entre le nombre des fous et celui des criminels, parce-que tous les crimes ne prennent point nécessairement leur source dans l'aliénation mentale."*

In the table formerly given by this author of the causes of alienation, the abuse of intoxicating liquors is scarcely mentioned ; in the present 134 are attributed to it.† Are these indications of progressive demoralization ? From this calculation are excluded 278 cases proceeding from family affliction, although in these, vicious dispositions, ill-temper or indiscretions must frequently have produced the evils from which afflictions arises. In Holst's tables, the observation is still better illustrated. Of 469 cases, the origin of which had been ascertained, 323 may be shown to depend upon ill-constituted or ill-regulated dispositions.‡

Such then is the general extent of the malady, upon what classes do its ravages fall ? Are there any proscribed or privileged orders recognized in the invasion of madness, or are there any circumstances over which we possess control that appear to promote or prevent that invasion ? There are both. And it conveys an impressive truth that the professions which are most intimately connected with temporal and selfish interests, and the dispositions which are vicious or lead to vice, are precisely those upon which the infliction falls most heavily. It may fall as a punishment ; I must regard it simply as a consequence,—and believe that certain classes of society, and certain courses of life, are exposed to insanity, not because they are worldly or wicked, but because they expose to excitement and tend to the formation of habits of thought and action inimical to the preservation of mental serenity and health. Rank, riches, and education,

* Quetelet, sur l'Homme, p. 126.

† Dict. des Sciences Méd., Art. " Folie."

‡ Official Report of the State of Lunatics in Norway in the year 1825—quoted in the British and Foreign Medical Review, No. I.

afford no protection against this disease as they do against others; nor do they increase the danger otherwise than by giving rise to hopes and fears, and exertions and vicissitudes which the humble and illiterate escape. Statistics must decide this question likewise. And so far as our information extends, the privileged orders, to continue this mode of expression, are merely those who, from the nature of their employments, or their station in life, are farthest removed from the causes of the disease. The proscribed orders live in and by moral agitation, There is no preservative virtue in particular professions, as has been imagined. Mathematical study is not an antidote. The science may become as fatal a poison to certain intellects as the gaming table or ambition. The cultivators of the earth are not so liable to derangement as the cultivators of the mind itself; but it is not because there is anything peculiar or injurious in the latter, but because, from accessary circumstances, it is more calculated to destroy that tranquillity and equilibrium of the powers which is favoured in the former. An eminent writer on this subject has made the startling assertion, that among the educated classes of patients admitted into Bicêtre, no instances of insane geometricians, physicians, naturalists, or chemists are to be found, while priests, poets, painters, and musicians, occur in great numbers.* This can be proved to be an error. Bicêtre is an asylum for the poor; and, from its records, no legitimate conclusions can be drawn as to the liability of the educated classes, or professions. Ignorance of the fact may have led to the error; but from whatever cause proceeding, the reasoning which has been founded upon it, and the obloquy thereby cast on some of the noblest pursuits, is triumphantly exposed by a comparison of the tables published by different authorities, and especially by consulting one given by Esquirol, the most accurate observer and the most cautious philosopher who has written

* Conolly.

upon the subject.* It comprehends 164 cases treated in
his private asylum, which is appropriated to the wealthy
and educated, exclusively. Among these we find neither
priests nor poets. There are, however, two engineers, four
physicians, four chemists, and several others whose investigations had been directed to the observation of the qualities
and relations of external objects. Although, however, the
assertion, here combated be inaccurate it is perfectly true
that priests and poets are more frequently attacked by, or
are more exposed to, insanity, than either physicians or naturalists. And this for three reasons. First, the study and
exercise of religion, and the indulgence of the imagination,
arouse all our most energetic emotions, keep them in constant activity, and in this way, tend towards the condition
most favourable to the appearance of the disease. Secondly, those who from choice adopt and prosecute such subjects, are naturally and constitutionally more liable to excitement. And thirdly, the nature of the subjects themselves affords greater provocations to excitement than the
description of a butterfly, the solution of an arithmetical
problem, or the diagnosis of a loathsome disease. In speaking of men of certain professions being *naturally* more liable
to excitement, I mean that they are so in consequence of
the nature of the powers by which they are led to adopt
these professions, and of the temperament by which these
powers are influenced.

If these observations be kept in view, and applied to the
moral relations and numerical proportions of the remaining
elements of the same table, the characteristics of the privileged and proscribed classes, of which we have spoken, may
be understood. The most numerous classes are, students
25, military men 33, merchants 50. An ascending series
indicating the degree of excitement and the source of mental disturbance to which the members have been subjected.

* Dict. des Sciences Méd , art. " Folie."

Then follow public functionaries 21, advocates 11, artists 8, and so on, illustrating the same proposition. The same author gives the professions of 500 patients admitted into the Asylum at Charenton. Of these 96 belonged to the army, 63 had been engaged in trade, 60 were proprietors, 31 were farmers or gardeners, 15 were students, 6 ecclesiastics, 6 physicians, and 2 chemists.* A table in my possession, containing the admissions to Dr. Duncan's asylum, Ireland, for eighteen years, confirms this view.† The number amounts to 130. Of these, 1 is a schoolmaster, 5 are physicians or surgeons, 7 are farmers, 11 are collegians, 11 are lawyers, 14 are men of property, 14 are clergymen, 29 belong to the army or navy, and 37 are merchants, or connected with mercantile affairs.

We do not possess sufficient data to determine the relative proportions of the insane rich and the insane poor. The information which has been obtained tends to show that the former are most numerous. Esquirol and Georget have adopted this opinion. At the first stage in the inquiry, it must be apparent, that while the poor and the wealthy classes are equally exposed, or rather expose themselves equally, to the physical causes; the situation, education and habits of the latter are all more favourable to the development of the moral causes of insanity, than can be affirmed of the condition of the poor. Poverty enjoins a compulsory temperance; it shuts out the longings of ambition; it acquaints with the realities of life, and excludes the effects of sentimentalism; it often trains the body to vigour, and in all these respects may be styled prophylactic. The agricultural population, which presents poverty in its most attractive forms and enjoys its best privileges, is to a great degree exempt from insanity. The returns published by Halliday show, that in twelve of the agricultural counties of England, the propor-

* Annales d'Hygiène Publique, tom. i. p. 119.
† Statistics of Insanity by Mr. Duncan. Paper read before the Royal Medical Society, Edinburgh, 1835.

tion of lunatics to the whole population is as 1 to 2245, while in twelve non-agricultural counties the proportion was 1 to 1965. Tables given by Esquirol and Duncan establish the same relation. The former states the profession in 164 cases, only three of these were cultivators of the soil. The latter has met with only seven farmers in 130 patients. This exemption has been explained by a reference to the active habits and out-of-door occupations of this class. But this is only one cause. The deportment of a great majority of the individuals belonging to it is virtuous, their amusements are not of an exciting character; they are abstemious, and the amount of their wages seldom fluctuates. All these circumstances are favourable to the continuance of sanity.

Another consideration is equally clear,—the affluent and exclusive classes pant after the preservation of caste; they intermarry for this purpose, and thus transmit through an endless succession of channels the predisposition to insanity wherever it may arise. The state of our own peerage amply confirms this statement. Hereditary taint is the most frequent cause of this disease, and it is here established to a vast extent in that very position of society which abounds with those sources of mental disturbance which are calculated to rouse such a taint into activity. The ancient nobility of all lands are said to inherit this along with, and in as regular succession as, their patents. But it is not to the ordeal of the ordinary moral causes alone that the higher orders are subjected. Besides wounded pride, jealousy, speculation, they have to meet, and indeed court, the excitement of public affairs. And it needs not to be told that the tempest of political strife,' or civil dissension, which passes over the peasant and the artisan unheeded and almost unnoticed, shakes and desolates the breasts of those who have honours or property to lose or gain, with all its fury. For example, the years 1830 and 1831 were marked in Paris for producing a greater number of cases of insanity than had occurred during the five previous years. Of the 367 admissions at Charenton, during these two years, twenty-eight cases were traced to political events.* The very great number of Retreats, &c., in this country, which are mere speculations, and have been intended for the reception of those who can afford to pay for such an investment of capital, has been assumed as a good reason for believing that the rich are most liable to madness; and, in the absence of better grounds for forming a correct judgment, the fact may be interpreted in this manner. From the impossibility of obtaining accurate accounts of the state of private establishments, and from the fact that vast numbers of lunatics are at large, or under the care of their friends, nothing more than an approximation to truth can be expected from such an inquiry. A very imperfect mode of estimating the respective numbers of the two classes, is by comparing the cases admitted into private asylums, where board is paid, with those entering public establishments, supported by government or by subscription, within a given period. This can be done only in respect to Paris. But as it is a metropolis, having in its bosom all the good and evil of other densely inhabited and highly artificial communities, and presenting nearly the same distribution of property as elsewhere, the results of the comparison may be received as evidence of the condition of all other places similarly situated. Thus, during eight years, from 1804 to 1813, there were 2749 admissions to Salpetrière, a pauper female asylum. During the same period, there were about 1883 admissions to Bicêtre, a pauper male asylum, making a total of 4632 lunatics supported by charity, and, of course, belonging to the most indigent classes. M. Esquirol treated about 300, and M. Dubuisson about 240 in three institutions appropriated to the rich. Into Charenton, during the eight years from 1826 to 1834, 1557 cases were received.† These, with very few exceptions, belonged to the better ranks, paying an annual

---

* Charenton is a large and excellent asylum in the vicinity of Paris, under the superintendence of M. Esquirol.

† Burrow's Commentaries, p 512.

board, varying from £35 to £65. These are not all the private asylums in Paris; but they are all to the records of which I have any access. A total of 2090 is thus given. If it be borne in mind that the poor generally constitute nine-tenths of every community, it must be very evident that the pressure of the disease falls upon such classes at least as are removed from absolute poverty.

Another mode of inquiry may be resorted to. Several years ago, and before the erection of Haawell, it was computed that there were residing in confinement in and around London the enormous number of 7000 lunatics. Now, supposing each of the large public asylums capable of containing 500, which they are not; and supposing further that the dependencies at Hoxton, Bethnal Green, &c. contained another thousand, or even fifteen hundred, there will still remain 4500 who cannot be ranked with paupers, and accordingly must be concluded to pay for their maintenance, and in a great majority of instances to belong to the wealthier classes.

Léveille has recorded a very curious observation on this subject. In examining the French hospitals in 1803, he found that, of the lunatics rendered insane by the events of the revolution, the males belonged to the aristocracy, the females to the democracy. Disappointed and successful ambition had thus produced a similar result; and that equality which pulled the one down, and raised the other up, had proved fatal in the same way.*

Esquirol supposes that the rich are less exposed to relapses than the poor, as they have it in their power to distract and give tone to the mind, and to avoid the exciting causes.

The assertion of the greater prevalence of mental disease under free than under despotic forms of government, may be treated in the same spirit as that displayed in examining the alleged connexion of insanity with civilization. I admit the

---

* Rapport fait au Conseil Général des Hospices par un de ses membres, sur l'état des Hopitaux des Hospices, &c., depuis le 1er Janvier, 1804, jusqu'au 1er Janvier, 1814.   Paris, 1816.

fact, but deny the inference. Tyranny has no protective influence—liberty is not the foe of mental health. Consumption has doubled its ravages since the use of tea prevailed,
and cholera has invaded the country since the passing of the
Reform Bill; and these facts have nearly the same connexion that the prevalence of insanity has with the nature of the
constitution under which a people lives. But although the
form of government which, it will be observed, is generally
the result and representation, and not the cause of the existing state of feeling, exercises no influence in the production
of insanity, the mode in which it is administered, the social
relations, the tranquillity or the fluctuations in the habits,
value of property and rank, the degree of prosperity, and the
moral and religious condition which arise out of it, must obviously do so. In that state, then, be it monarchical or repub-
lican, in which the sources of moral agitation and excitement
are most abundant, will the proportion of insanity be the highest.
Panics in the commercial classes, civil commotions, war,
rapid influx and reflux of wealth, and ambitious projects,
which are the most fertile and frequent moral causes of the
disease, may occur, and have occurred, under every form of
government, and affect mankind, not because they are slaves
or citizens, but because their bodies are weak and vitiated,
their minds excitable and ill-balanced. A state in which
wide-spreading changes did not and could not take place,
would afford, to a certain and great extent, a guarantee against
madness. Were despotism another word for tranquillity, and
freedom for turmoil, the line of exemption would be clearly
defined. But public order and disorganization, although
undoubtedly favoured by political relations, flow more from
the character than the actual condition of a people, and accordingly affect indiscriminately the bond and the free. Thus
the free American is comparatively more liable to derangement than the free Swiss;—cretinism is, of course, excluded
from the comparison. The enslaved Turk is exempt; the
conquered Hindoo liable. The act of liberation, however, is

certainly inimical to mental peace. It operates, like all other great political movements, by powerfully affecting the interests of the mass, by calling forth the deepest sympathies, the most ungovernable passions of the human breast. The French Revolution is said to have filled the asylums to overflowing. The immediate effects of the Crusades, the Reformation, and the retreat from Moscow, were similar. These statements, from the remoteness or the peculiar character of the periods to which they refer, are necessarily vague and unsupported by proof. But on turning to the Irish rebellion, the traces and history of which are still fresh and before us, we find from Halloran that of 693 cases, 108, or nearly one-seventh, were produced by the terror, the hostility, and the hopes then prevailing.* From Esquirol we learn that of 492 cases, forty-five resulted from public events; and that of the same number, ninety-one were occasioned by reverse of fortune, an event often dependent on the current of political affairs, and ranking next to them in its detrimental influence on the mind. Georget shews that of 1079 cases, 116 were attributable to political changes, and that these are among the most fertile of the moral causes. This is not the general opinion, nor is it countenanced by experience. Esquirol's observations, we have said, go to shew that while of 492 cases, only forty-five could be traced to popular commotion, not less than 136 were caused by domestic affliction, and the enormous number of 178 originated in the predominance, or non-gratification of such passions as self-love, ambition, anger, jealousy, and sensual desire. This is as good a commentary, and probably contains a more impressive lesson on the necessity for a virtuous and well-regulated mind, than a homily, or a treatise on ethics.

The number of lunatics is said to be much greater in America than in any European country. Can this be the effect, it has been asked, of the acquisition of independence, or of the operation of the constitution under which the people live ?   I am

* Halloran on the Causes and Cure of Insanity.

disposed to believe that a concurrence of causes may have produced this result. First, the abuse of ardent spirits, and especially dram-drinking, is reported to prevail to an awful and destructive extent. Secondly, money is gained easily and rapidly, and the abject and the ignorant become suddenly rich, without becoming better or wiser ; the means of enjoyment thus increase more quickly than the means of moral training, and there are the effects of unexpected prosperity, and the gross and unrestrained gratifications of an ill-regulated mind to contend with. Thirdly, without wishing to repeat the heartless sneer that the Adam and Eve of the United States were born in Newgate, the fact cannot be overlooked that the sources of the tide of population, which has been flowing for so many years uninterruptedly towards America, have been impure and poisoned. The refuse of other nations has been poured forth. I do not wish to speak disparagingly, nor do I allude merely to the criminal outcasts of the old communities, but to the ruined, the unfortunate, the disappointed, the adventurous, all those, in fact, whose minds are predisposed by previous circumstances to excitement and disease. Fourthly, the intenseness of political feeling, and the agitating nature of the civil contests in which the inhabitants generally are from time to time engaged, must decidedly contribute to the development of the disease.

The most useful and active period of life is that most exposed to the incursion of mania. Its activity is the cause. All the mental energies are then excited, the affections find objects, the passions are roused, and if there be a weak or imperfect part of our nature, it is then shaken and may be cast down in the struggle for subsistence, or wealth, or power ; or by the anxieties which will arise in the even tenor of the most humble and unambitious career. Sources of disquietude, altogether unconnected with the constitution of the mind, are then most abundant. Man emerges from the moral nonage of youth into the awful responsibility of indepen-

dence, and new scenes, new situations, new feelings are the
consequence: and changes, and misfortunes, and sorrow, inevitably come.   If the mind has been originally vigorous and
consolidated by a good education it withstands the shock,
but if there exists a hereditary predisposition or debility, a
proneness to excitement, an exalted state of feelings at the
expence of the intellect, that is, the absence of a well adjust-
ed balance between the emotive and reflective powers, it
totters and falls.   The body is, at the same time, more subjected to the physical causes of the malady.   The accidents
of an active profession, the pernicious customs of society, the
diseases of mature age, all come into operation, and contribute to swell the amount of attacks in adults.   Extensive
observation shews that the greatest number of cases of
lunacy occur between thirty and forty.   No age is exempt,
for even infants and octogenarians become insane: but the
frequency of the disease during the decade mentioned is
evinced by the fact that of 2507, 572, or more than one-fifth,
occurred within its limits.   Nearly the same proportion is
observed in Holst's tables, where, of 1909 lunatics, 387 became
deranged between thirty and forty.   If it be recollected that
not only is society liable to be deprived of the services of its
citizens at the precise moment when they are most valuable,
but that at this period a vast proportion of the population of
a country become parents, and transmit to their lineage whatever is good or evil, strong or weak in themselves: a still
more urgent reason is perceived, were the awful character
of the disease itself insufficient for guarding against the attack,
and for providing means the most ample and adequate for the
removal of the disease.   The fact is worth recording, and is
connected with this part of the subject, that marriage, and the
peace and happiness which it secures, afford a protection from
insanity.   This conclusion cannot, at least, be held to be unjustifiable, or the grounds from which it is drawn accidental,
when in tables framed in various countries the unmarried or

widowed lunatics always preponderate. Two tables shew
the following relations.   The first refers to the admissions at
Charenton.*

    Unmarried or widowed.......................859
    Married............ 698
                                                    ────
    Difference.......................................161

The second is extracted from Mr. Duncan's manuscript Essay on the Statistics of Insanity.   He does not mention his
authority.

    Unmarried..1779
    Married... 578
                                                    ────
    Difference....................................1201

Marriage may diminish the tendency to mental alienation
in various ways, either by removing individuals from the influence of many of the exciting causes, or by the formation
of regular habits, and the cultivation of virtuous impulses,
rendering that influence innocuous.   To woman it generally
is or ought to be the point towards which all her wishes have
formerly converged, and from which all her future hopes and
happiness are to emanate.   To man it is the shield against
himself and his passions ; he seeks and finds in it joy, solace,
and support, when his own thoughts, avocations, or the world
fail to furnish either. If founded on harmony of disposition,
not only does it create the capabilities of enjoyment, but of
enduring pain ; and on this account, and because it neutral-
izes selfish feelings and pleasures, because it prevents the
mind from retiring on itself, acts as a barrier against hidden
sorrows, gives employment to our noblest qualities, and while
chequered by the ordinary vicissitudes of life, because it
yields no strong or sudden or permanent excitement, it is an
antidote to insanity.

    Of the parties to this engagement females are perhaps most

    * Annales d'Hygiène Publique.   Janvier, 1835.

subject to insanity, both before and after its consummation.
This has been attributed to the peculiarities of their constitution, the delicacy of frame and susceptibility of mind by
which the sex is distinguished. That these act powerfully
in producing insanity cannot be questioned. But if this set
of causes be confined in their operation to women, so are a
large proportion of the physical causes and the influence of
ambition, speculation, and dissipation, confined in their operation to men ; so that upon these grounds no explanation of
the inequality can be received or attempted. The education,
of females is, however, more imperfect and vicious than that
of men ; it tends to arrest the development of the body ; it
overtasks certain mental powers, it leaves others untouched
and untaught ; so far as it is moral it is directed to sordid and
selfish feelings, and substitutes a vapid sentimentalism for a
knowledge of the realities and duties of life. From such a
perversion of the means of training, what can be expected to
flow but sickly refinement, weak insipidity, or absolute disease. That which is intended to impart, and is incapable of
imparting strength and stability, becomes the source of debility and decay ; that which is created as a bulwark of defence, is converted into the open and easy road by which the
enemy may enter. Before any reasoning on this point can
be considered definitive, it will be necessary to know the proportion of the causes affecting the two sexes. This department of statistics is still uncultivated, almost unknown.

The facts are as follow : in one table of lunatics, Duncan's,
there are 752 males, 1625 females : in another of 2507 insane in the Parisian hospitals, 1095 are men, 1412 women.
This great disparity is not uniformly observed in France or
even in Paris, but from the moral condition of that country
it would not have excited our surprise had it been so. For
example, one-twentieth of the patients at Saltpetrière are supposed to be insane from prostitution.* Esquirol has calcu-

* Esquirol—Parent Duchatelet. De la Prostitution dans la Ville de Paris.

lated that of 25,083 persons ascertained to be insane in France, 11,119 are males, 13,964 females. In Milan the numbers are 2699 men, 3207 women. Some other countries present an equal proportion of lunatics in both sexes. In Norway there appears to be a greater number of male than female lunatics.* Scotland, in 1818, had 2311 men and 3339 women insane. In some other instances the males are most numerous ; but a general census would, it is believed, substantiate the view given above.

Medical men long acted as if nothing could be done with any chance of success in insanity. They believed that were the bowels regulated and the organic functions attended to, their duty was discharged, and the vaunted powers of medicine sufficiently vindicated. The suspicion even arose that the disease could not be removed, that it did not come under the ordinary rules of art. Drs. Munro, Burrows, and Ellis, declare, however, that they cure ninety out of every hundred cases. Such a result proves, so far as the practice of these observers is concerned, that instead of being the most intractable it is the most curable of all diseases. The declaration, however, applies only to recent cases, which have not existed for more than three months, and which have been treated under the most favourable circumstances ; as the patients either belonged to the independent classes or were inmates of one of the most deservedly celebrated institutions in England, Wakefield, under the care of one of the most enlightened physicians in Europe. But even where poverty, popular prejudice, indifference, or other obstacles, have deprived the insane of many of those means which it is in the power of benevolence and art to bestow, the proportion of cures is such as to dispel the disheartening and unworthy conviction that this affliction must continue to baffle human skill,

* Quetelet sur l'Homme, tome ii. p. 127.

and to open up a vista of delightful anticipations of what
might be effected by a coalition between the philanthropists
and the philosophers. That proportion, be it observed, invariably corresponds to the degree in which the treatment is
in unison with the laws of the human mind. It does not depend upon, or vary with, local circumstances; it is the same
in Italy as in England ; it bears little relation to the occupation, sex, or age of the patient, and less to the cause of the
malady, unless that be organic ; it cannot even be attributed
to the talents of the physician, save where these are dedicated solemnly and enthusiastically to the task, and made the
instruments by which it is to be accomplished. If all asylums had advanced to that stage of improvement to which
they will ultimately be forced by the irresistible impetus of
public opinion ; and were patients placed under treatment on
the very first and slightest indication, the oddity or eccentricity which ushers in the disease, I have no hesitation in
affirming, that the proportion given by Ellis would become
universal. Even now, contending, as physicians to the insane have almost everywhere to do, with errors and difficulties which none can appreciate save those who have tried to
put the moral machinery of an asylum into operation ; and
taking all cases as they are presented, of long or short duration, simple or complicated with malformation of the head or organic disease, the average number cured is about one-half. Put
out of view the drawbacks mentioned, and consider only the
numbers cured of other diseases, cast up the recoveries from
consumption which is said to destroy *all* its victims, from
cholera which destroys one *half*, from pneumonia which destroys about *twenty-nine per cent.*, or from less fatal ailments ;
and having found that not two-thirds escape at all, and not
one-twentieth without some injury to the constitution, which
embitters, if it do not shorten life ; and the vast benefit conferred on society by that treatment of the insane will be perceived, which restores to the affections of their friends, and

the duties of active life, and the glorious prerogative of serving God with the eye of reason clear, and the pulse of feeling calm, one half of those who would otherwise be lost to themselves and to the world, and lapse into fury or loathsome futurity. We will here introduce a table of the proportions recovered in different establishments.

Number of years on which the average is taken.		Hospital.	Proportion of cures.
25	......	Senavra, Milan............58 in 100	[a]
2	......	Charenton, Paris.........40 ... —	[b]
12	......	Salpetrière and Bicêtre 34 ... —	[c]
12	......	Ivry, Paris.................51 ... —	[d]
13	......	Retreat, York........... 50 ... —	[e]
16	......	Lancaster..................40 ... —	[f]
8	......	Gloucester........... ......48 ... —	[g]
..	......	York, (county asylum)..49 ... —	[h]
5	......	Bethlem, 1748–1794.....28 ... —	[i]
1	......	Bethlem, 1813.............49 ... —	[j]
15	......	Bethlem, 1819–1833.....50 ... —	[k]
5	......	Wakefield..............42 ... —	[l]
10	......	Stafford....................43 ... —	[m]
2	......	Dundee...................50 ... —	[n]
5	......	Perth......... ....46 ... —	[o]
..	......	Hartford, United States $91\frac{5}{10}$ —	[p]

This table has been constructed and is given to the public merely to convey some idea of what has been effected under

[a] Burrow's Commentaries, p. 522.   [b] Dict. des Sciences Méd. art. "Folie."   [c] Ibid.   [d] Ibid.   [e] Pritchard's Treatise on Insanity.   [f] Ibid.   [g] Ibid.   [h] Ibid. and Esquirol, Mem. de l'Acad. Roy. de Med.   [i] Ibid.   [j] Ibid.   [k] Ibid.   [l] Burrows.   [m] Ibid.   [n] Annual Reports of Dundee.   [o] Annual Reports of Murray's Asylum, Perth.   [p] Combe on Mental Derangement, p 323.

different circumstances, but has no pretensions either to rigid
exactitude or to be considered as affording a complete view
of the subject. The calculations proceeded on the number
of admissions and cures annually, and not upon the actual
number of patients in the asylums at one, or within any given
period.

The success at Hartford, which is probably the most perfect example of an asylum conducted on sound principles, is
highly encouraging. The proportion is exactly that which
Ellis and Burrows have met with in recent cases and in private practice, and affords the most irrefragable proof of how
much may be accomplished by employing all the means
within our reach. The table now given refers chiefly to the
results of the current century. No one conversant with the
details of the subject can doubt that the proportion of cures
corresponds to the improvement of each establishment, and
that the gross amount of cures is much greater within the
last twenty years than during any previous period of the same
length, that is, since the recognition of humanity and employment as means of treatment. In the foregoing synopsis
those only are included whose reason was completely re-established. But there are two other classes not noticed which
swell the amount of good : those who, retaining some visionary project or harmless delusion, are dismissed so materially improved as to be capable of engaging in the pursuits
and tasting the pleasures of life, with great additional happiness to themselves and perfect safety to others : and, secondly, those who, although requiring to be protected from themselves and displaying some untameable appetite which would
render liberty a curse, pass, under proper guidance, long intervals of contentment, who are soothed when unruly, cheered when depressed, advised when capricious, and are at all
times and in every mood surrounded by friends.

Mental disease has been imagined to confer longevity.
To bolster up this imagination, for it is nothing more, in-

stances have been cited of lunatics reaching a great age : the same thing has been said and done with respect to gout, but without weakening the principle that any serious structural change, or impairment of function, renders the system more susceptible of disease, and less able to resist its effects. It would be matter for regret, were it true, that life was prolonged by such means ; but the truth is that life is shortened. To understand this statement, it ought to be premised, that it is not my intention to assert that disorder of reason, which is merely a symptom, shortens life, but that the affections of the nervous system, upon which it depends, tend to do so. In this sense it is no paradox to say that no one ever dies of insanity. The bills of mortality announce the contrary ; but it is well known that these are utterly worthless as scientific documents, and that they are the compilation of churchwardens and old women.* The bill for 1834 has the absurd calculation that 170 persons died from this disease.† The meaning of this, or the interpretation which a medical man acquainted with the subject would give to it, is, that 170 persons died while insane. But if you proceed to examine the reports of the asylums in which these 170 were confined, or even listen to the descriptions of their friends, you will discover that they suffered and succumbed under consumption, dropsy, or more frequently apoplexy, epilepsy, or some other malady of definite character, to which all men are liable. All those who have actually practised among the insane, know, and have cause to grieve, that besides derangement, they are required to treat disease in all its forms. There are then two evils to be combated, and hence arises the greater mortality of the insane. There is the irritation, or organic change, existing in the centre of the nervous system, the cause of the insanity, lessening the general tone of the system, and producing great disturbance as a secondary conse-

* Blizard.   Remarks on Public Hospitals, p. 71.
† Companion to the Almanac, p. 37. 1836.

quence, and there is some other affection rendered more intense and more intractable from that lessened tone and general disturbance. But if the presence of the cause of insanity militates so much against the restorative efforts of nature and the remedial means employed, may it not predispose to disease, and promote the frequency of its incursion as well as its violence. I believe that it may. That it directly induces apoplexy, ramolissement, congestion, and so forth, there is not the slightest doubt; and there is every probability that it influences the condition of organs remote from, although, of course, not independent of the nervous system. But other considerations are mixed up with this question. In general the situation of lunatics is unfavourable for the resistance of disease. The confession of a person intrusted with two private asylums, that from want of suitable protection from the weather, nourishing diet, cleanliness, &c. a hundred of his patients perished in one season from typhus fever, will explain the meaning of this observation.* Even when no such maladministration exists, the patients in asylums often take little exercise,—they are allowed to eat immoderately, —their habits are uncleanly,—they pass their days in close heated rooms, and their nights in rooms equally close, but of a low temperature ; they are, in short, placed under enervating and depressing circumstances. Again, when attacked by disease, unless the symptoms be of such a nature as to come within reach of the senses, or of those modes of exploration which are intended to aid or correct the senses, the powers of medicine are, in a great number of cases, sadly trammelled. All the information derivable from the patient's own sensations is denied ; for he may undervalue or exaggerate the pain which he suffers, or he may refer it to a healthy region: the origin and progress of the disease remain a blank from his inability or unwillingness to disclose them. The duty of a

* First Report of Minutes of Evidence from Committee on Madhouses, 1816, p. 9,

physician is, in such a situation, a very painful one : he sees
a fellow-creature writhing in agony, which may be that of a
troubled spirit or result from bodily suffering: he sees the
ravages of a deep-seated malady, but the exact seat of which
he can at best only conjecture : he hears supplications for aid
which he cannot afford : he is obliged to grope his way in
the darkness of empiricism, altering the direction of his steps
every hour, and at last finds that all his efforts have not only
been vain, but injurious.   Such situations cannot always be
avoided ; but the frequency of their occurrence may be lessened by increasing the chances of recovery among the insane, and by placing them in circumstances more conducive
to health.   The rate of mortality will vary somewhat in different asylums according to the locality, the classes admitted,
and the treatment pursued ; but the following table may be
presented, as exhibiting these differences, and their influence.
There die in

Wakefield Asylum,.........24 in 100 patients, or 1 in 4
Lancaster,...................24½.... ....1...4
French Hospitals,...........22..........................1...4½
Senaora, Italy,..............42½......................1...2½
Cork,......................30.......................1...3½
Retreat, at York,...........20........................1...5
Charenton,.................25.........................1...4
Glasgow,.....................10........................1..10
Burrow's Private Asylum,...6½.......................1..15

Now, if these statements be compared with the results of
the practice in any common hospitals, the proposition which
has been advanced will be readily admitted.   From the reports of eight of the principal hospitals in London, it appears
that the deaths per cent. of all patients received, vary from
seven to ten, while in ten provincial institutions, the mortality ranges from three to seven per cent.*   In the Hotel

* British Medical Almanack, 1836.

Dieu at Paris, the deaths amount to seven per cent.; and in La Charité at Berlin alone, of all the continental hospitals to the statistics of which we have access, do they reach so high as 25 per cent.

By far the most fatal seasons to lunatics are autumn and winter. A fact which shews the necessity, should humanity require the lesson, of protecting them effectually against the influence of the atmosphere and its sudden alternations. Of 798 deaths at Salpetrière, 175 took place during the spring, and 174 during the summer quarter, while in autumn there occurred 234, and in winter 207. At Charenton the disparity is equally marked; 119 deaths took place in summer, 160 in winter.

The diseases which destroy lunatics afford cumulative evidence of the positions that the mortality among them is great, and that it is affected by the nature of the circumstances in which they are placed. We learn from a table, embracing nearly 300 cases, that the diseases most prevalent among lunatics, attack them in the following order,—colliquative diarrhœa, scurvy, affections of the liver, apoplexy, typhoid fevers, nervous fevers, phthisis. With two exceptions, these are the results of debility. In another table, including 995 deaths, which took place in a number of the principal asylums in England, the proportions from the following diseases are, exhaustion and old age, 227; apoplexy and paralysis, 152; diarrhœa and dysentery, 132; consumption, 119; epilepsy and convulsions, 104.* Apart from the affections of the chest, abdomen, and fibrous tissues, directly produced by changes of temperature, the cold of winter has a depressing effect upon the system, which indirectly causes ulcers on the legs, loss of motion, and when the clothing is inadequate, frost-biting.

Besides being distributed into the curable and incurable,

* Parliamentary Returns from County Asylums, 1836.

the inmates of an asylum are subdivided into other groups, the precise numbers of which it is of some importance to ascertain, in order to make arrangements suited to their respective wants and habits. The sections of the curable are very obvious, and are considered elsewhere. The incurable may be arranged into various classes. There is, first, the furious madman, thirsting for blood, glorying in the destruction of every thing around, and requiring, for his self-preservation, and the enjoyment of those transitory throbs of happiness of which his soul is still susceptible, to be coerced, leniently, and as rarely as possible, but to be completely deprived of the power of doing injury. Such cases do certainly occur, although not so frequently, nor of such a frightfully irreclaimable nature as the supporters of the old system would have us to believe.* Were we to be guided by a work which appeared about twenty years ago, our conclusions would be widely different.† From this source we learn, that of 1649 maniacs admitted in Bedlam, 743 were mischievous, and 20 had committed murder. There are only three ways of reconciling the discrepancy thus created with the experience of recent observers. Either the inmates of Bedlam must at that time have been chosen on the ground of their turbulence or treachery; or an epidemic of mischief must have lurked within its walls; or, lastly, our national character must have undergone a change. Whatever alternative we may adopt, the change itself is matter for congratulation. For now the largest establishments boast of having only one or two irreclaimable patients, and of having discarded strait-waistcoats as well as stripes. There is clearly a homicidal and destructive mania, in which no kindness, no moral tie whatever, avails aught in preventing the sacrifice of life and property. You will hear of institutions conducted upon principles of freedom and humanity, where there are neither chains

* Brierre de Boismont, Annales d'Hygiène, Juillet 1836, p. 56.
† Black's Dissertation on Insanity.

nor chastisement ; but even under such mild government as this, the furious maniac will be furious still, strew death and desolation around, immolate his friends and protectors, and exult in his deeds of vengeance. The boast of the reformed treatment is, that these unfortunate beings are at once detected, that no one is restrained on suspicion, that the periods of exacerbation are known and provided for, that the precautions adopted are compatible with many pleasures, and often with the personal liberty of the patient. The proportion of such a dangerous species of derangement is not well known : indeed it must vary with the country, the race, class and occupation of the individuals diseased ; but it is estimated, that of a hundred admissions not more than three will remain, under proper management, permanently and immitigably furious.* The number of furious, or rather unmanageable females, is greater than that of males.

Nor is such an inquiry unimportant for practical purposes. Formerly asylums were constructed upon the principle that ninety-five required to be restrained, that five only could be intrusted with freedom. The considerations submitted above shew, that now arrangements must be made in order to afford freedom to the ninety-five, and adequate restraint to the five.

The second group is that of the paralytic and epileptic incurables. They probably amount to one-tenth of the whole. Holst states that of 1422 cases, 245 were epileptics. From the tables of Léveille we learn, that of 3662 cases admitted at Bicêtre, 1292 were epileptics, that is, nearly one-third of the whole. The proportion is not so large in this country. Of 734 deaths which occurred in nine of the principal county asylums in England, 104, or one-seventh, were from epilepsy. The demands of this class on the affectionate care of those around are constant and imperative. There is the helplessness, without the hopes of childhood, to excite

* First Report from Committee on Madhouses, p. 51.

pity. Instead of expanding, their minds contract under your care; their wants diminish, and are at last reduced to the desire for food, and a claim upon some friendly arm to support their tottering steps.

The third is a very numerous class. The imbecile, fatuous, and idiotic constitute in this and some other countries more than one-fifth of all the cases submitted to treatment. In Norway, however, they are more than one-half, the numbers being 682 to 1229. Although placed beyond the reach of all alleviation from medicine, this form of alienation admits of great alleviation from external circumstances. These individuals have many joys, and the circle may be greatly widened. They may be roused to exertion and industry: some last lingering gleam of intelligence may be brought to bear on the pleasing parts of their condition—some half-extinguished habit may be encouraged; the power of tasting the physical enjoyments of existence may be gratified in such a manner that their life may be passed in a succession of useful employments and agreeable sensations. This is, more than all besides, the boast of modern physicians. If they cannot cure the imbecile and fatuous, they can render them happy.

There is a fourth group. It brings us in contact with the humiliating spectacle of the body living and breathing, but no longer animated by the slightest spark of reason, where even the senses are benumbed or annihilated, and, saving the human form, man becomes as the clod of the valley. In this situation patients are insensible to the calls of nature, and put to a severe test the kindness and forbearance of those to whom they are intrusted. A practical man has estimated that of every hundred lunatics, there are ten who have lost all power over the sphincter muscles. But this is probably erroneous. The same authority calculates that every third lunatic, whether curable or not, contracts dirty habits. I believe that this is likewise an exaggerated estimate. To

those who are accustomed to regard with pride the characteristic cleanliness of a portion, at least, of our countrymen,
but have not traced this quality to a national mental constitution, such a statement will appear ridiculous. But the love
of order and neatness share in the common ruin, and may be
extinguished, as well as the love of wealth or of friends, and
the consequence is, although not to the extent, of the kind
described. The slovenliness, the loathsome and disgusting
peculiarities, and utter disregard to decency or propriety
which follow in the train of madness, are astonishing, almost
incredible. The state of abstraction in which many individuals are plunged, and their corporeal weakness, contribute
as much as the disease of the perceptive powers, to this result. With proper care, however, and training—for the insane must be taught their habits anew—this evil may be
great' y modified, and in one-half of the cases where it appears
altogether eradicated. There are some cases where, from a
wish to offend the delicacy of others, or from absolutely glorying in shame, no persuasion or precaution can prevent the
insane from going about in a state of nudity. Clothe them
twenty times a-day, and twenty times will they appear naked.
This generally takes place where lunacy has been engrafted
on vicious and abandoned habits. Some restraint must be
resorted to, but fortunately incurable cases of this kind do not
occur oftener than 1 in 100. Occasionally idiots and epileptics strip themselves from no worse motive than idleness, or
to enjoy a cold air bath.

In every hundred patients there will be five noisy ones:
riotous, not from the desperation of anger or fear, but from
the truly Irish love of fun and mischief, or from irrepressible
garrulity, which is itself a form of madness. This feature, according to Guislain, presents itself in every ninth lunatic.*
Such inmates may be easily tolerated, and soothed into quiet-

* Sur les Phrenopathies, p. 199.

ness during the day, but during the night their cries and lo-
quacity, for they are sleepless, are altogether inconsistent
with that stillness which to the troubled mind is the best
anodyne I know of. Every patient is thus aroused—the furious maddened, the desponding and timid horrified; and the
hours of rest become hours of turmoil and excitement. To
meet such a state of things, a part of every asylum should
be deafened; and so effectually deafened, that all who are
able to obtain sleep may do so undisturbed. Or what is still
better, the noisy and refractory should inhabit distinct buildings. Then their melancholy orgies may proceed without
interruption.

With the furious may be classed those who are dangerous
to themselves, who have attempted, or are suspected of cherishing a design to attempt, suicide. Dr. Black represents
the proportion of suicidal to other maniacs as enormous. Of
1972 patients admitted to Bedlam from 1772 to 1787, 323,
or about one-sixth, are described as having attempted suicide.
It is both a sound and a safe doctrine to regard all who have
meditated or attempted to perpetrate this crime as insane.
Accordingly, many of those here rated as maniacs unquestionably owed their designation and their confinement to
harbouring such an intention, and to no other overt act of
folly or frenzy. The motives to destroy life vary with the
pains and sorrows to which it is exposed, the capability of
bearing these, and the general constitution with which each
individual mind is endowed. But the resolution is often
taken suddenly, and the hand is raised to accomplish the
deadly purpose, while the mind is blinded by intoxication,
tortured by bodily suffering, cast down by disappointment,
maddened by momentary passion. When the poignancy of
such disordered feelings has ceased, with it in a great number
of cases will cease every inclination and temptation to commit suicide, and the mind will remain calm and undiseased;
so that of the 323 persons consigned to Bedlam because they

had yielded to the suggestions of a selfish and unholy cow-
ardice, probably not one-half would continue under the influence of these feelings after the original impulse had been
checked, a result which was very likely to flow from the act
of isolation. This is a distinction of some importance, as
such patients may be treated with confidence corresponding
to what their dispositions are when relieved from the irrita-
tation by which they were disturbed. To hold an opposite
opinion will lead to the enforcement of all those galling precautions, which offer little or no obstacle to the determined,
provoke the vacillating, and harass the innocent.

The number of suicides may be estimated in one of two
ways: either in proportion to the number of patients actually
sent to and inhabiting asylums, or in proportion to the population of a country. The latter calculation affords some information as to the average that may be expected to be
committed to such institutions. There is only one link
wanting to render the chain complete. We would require
to know, but have no data from which to deduce, the proportion of suicides effected to suicides attempted, and the proportion of both to that of suicides meditated. I do not dispute the accuracy of Dr. Black's statement, nor deny that in
a certain period the suicidal amounted to one-sixth of the
whole of the lunatics confined in Bedlam; but I protest
against the impression which such a statement is calculated
to convey. I deny that such a proportion will be found in
any other asylum. That the crime of suicide increases, that
every year adds to the number of victims cannot be doubted.
But the holocaust has not yet reached the appalling amount
here announced. My own experience leads me to think that
suicidal maniacs bear a proportion of about one-tenth to the
other inmates of asylums. In a table of patients who have
been under my own care, I find exactly this proportion. Of
1032 deaths in the English asylums, only seventeen were
brought about by self-destruction; a fact which proves one

of two things, either the rarity of this species of derangement, or the excellence of the means adopted to prevent the fatal consequences which so frequently flow from it.

One reason has already been given for separating suicides into classes—into those who may be trusted, and those who must be watched; another exists.   It likewise proceeds from a consideration of the cause.   Suicidal mania, like many other forms, is hereditary, whole families, generation after generation, perish by their own act, the different members often selecting the same age and the same weapon for carrying their design into execution.   When such a propensity has been transmitted, and is hence identified with the powers of mind, our watchfulness must be tenfold more strict and search-ing than when the incitement has consisted in an attack of the reflective or perceptive powers, which may be controlled, and which cannot recur without very marked premonitory symptoms.

How easily lunatics may be diverted from their purpose by presence of mind, an intimacy with their character, and the tact to employ the destructive feeling by which they are actuated as the means of protection, is well exemplified in an anecdote related of Dr. Fox.   He had accompanied a suicidal and furious maniac, who was at the time calm, to the upper story of his asylum, to enjoy the prospect beyond the walls.   In returning the spiral staircase struck the eye of the patient, the opportunity roused the half-slumbering propen-sity, and a paroxysm of frenzy ensued.   His eye glared, his teeth ground against each other, he panted like the blood-hound for his prey, and clutching the doctor by the collar, howled into his ear, " Now, I'll cast you down, and leap after you."   Standing on the brink of what seemed inevitable de-struction, the doctor's reply was instantaneous, " Bah, any child could do that; come down and I'll throw you up."   " You cannot," was the rejoinder ; but the artifice prevailed, and they both hurried down to put the boast to the proof;

and the sanguinary threat was forgotten before they reached the lobby.

The proportion of suicides to the rest of the population is strikingly different in countries where the condition of the inhabitants is nearly similar. In Denmark it is higher than in Britain; and in some of the German states it is a hundred times greater than in Copenhagen. In London the proportion is one in 5000; in Paris it is said to be one in 2040.* A very patriotic controversy has been waged by these cities as to which the stigma shall attach of presenting the largest catalogue of suicides. The contest is virtuous though idle; and has brought to light facts which impugn even the accuracy of the statements on which it has proceeded, and render it highly probable that no definite conclusion can be drawn. In Paris, it appears every person found dead, and whose death cannot be otherwise accounted for, is ranked as a self-murderer; whereas, in London, the want of evidence, and the complaisance of juries, often screen the suicide under the verdict of "died by the visitation of God."

It is stated that in the departments of France, the number of deaths from suicide is comparatively small; and, what may appear strange, the more primitive and illiterate the district, the smaller the proportion. We will accordingly find that the darker the ignorance the less the predilection to suicide. Thus, while in Finéstre, which appears to be in the most deplorable state as to education, only twelve in a hundred inhabitants being able to read or write, few suicides occur, at least only in the proportion of one in 25,000. Paris, that focus of all that is brilliant and imposing in science and literature, and where gratuitous elementary instruction is accessible to all, gives a suicide for every 3000. Coréze, where only twelve in the hundred can read or write, presents one suicide in 47,000; and the High Loire one in 163,000. On the

other hand, in Oise and Lower Seine, both places in possession
of the highest degree of general instruction, and of the means
of advancing in improvement, suicides occur in every 5000 or
9000 inhabitants.* This is an appalling picture of demoralization, or of disease, but no hesitation can be felt in determining the causes. It is not because these unfortunates can
read or write, or live in a particular geographical position,
that they commit suicide. But, first, because they are members of communities where the excitements to insanity, and
the temptations to crime abound ; secondly, because the instruction communicated is addressed solely to the reflective
and perceptive faculties ; thirdly, because there exists no
provision for the cultivation of the sentiments, by the aid of
which man, as a citizen, is not only preserved negatively innocent, but is rendered positively virtuous ; there is no domestic tuition in France; there are none of the restraints
which a prevailing morality imposes; there are in the semin-
aries and public institutions the means of corruption; fourthly,
because, as a nation, the doctrines of religion have been abandoned. I speak not of a particular creed or form. That
which the bulk of the people, and especially the well-informed, have rejected, was sufficiently objectionable; but the
evil consists in this, that none other, or better, has been substituted. With the superstitions and ritual of Catholicism,
they appear to have cast aside all reverence for things sacred,
and, in great part, the duties which such a reverence imposes.
Connected with this inquiry is the fact that in the north of
France, Catholicism has been nearly extirpated, and there
suicide and crime predominate ; south of the Loire, on the
contrary, it still retains a strong hold on the affections of the
people, and there suicide, and its sister crimes or maladies,
are comparatively rare. This affords a noble proof that the

* Guerry, Essai sur la Statistique Morale de la France. Bulwer,
France, Social and Literary.

effects of Christianity, in whatever form and under whatever circumstances, are peace and joy.

There is still another consideration connected with this subject, as affording some hints, not how far, but with what a suicidal lunatic may be trusted. M. Guerry attempts to shew that every age has its favourite means of destruction; that in youth and old age suspension is resorted to, in middle age fire-arms. The pistol has its maximum, to use his mode of expression, between thirty and forty, while the rope rises progressively, and does not reach its maximum till from fifty to sixty.* Professor Casper's tables prove that in Germany, hanging is the most common mode adopted. Of 525, 234, nearly one-half, died in this manner, while not more than nineteen effected their purpose by throwing themselves from the window.† These two expedients are in consequence of the present construction of our asylums, and of the furniture they contain, by far too accessible to lunatics, seeing that by building that part of the house destined for the reception of this class of one story, and by making the bed-pole incapable of supporting more than a few pounds weight, all danger might be avoided. Esquirol corroborates the conclusions of the authorities previously quoted. Of 198 female suicides, he states that forty-nine employed hanging or strangulation, forty-five precipitation, and forty-eight abstinence. This table presents still another mode by which lunatics may baffle the wisest and most affectionate precautions. Fortunately, however, in an asylum death from voluntary starvation can rarely happen. The darker pages of medical history exhibit horrible scenes of forcing food into the throat, where teeth were broken, and sometimes dislocation of the jaw took place. Modern sagacity has discovered

* Guerry, Essai sur la Statistique Morale de la France. Quetelet, Sur l'Homme, t. ii. p. 155.

† Burrow's Commentaries, p. 447.

many ways of overcoming such stern obstinacy of purpose, few of which bear even the semblance of compulsion. M. Guislain dissents from the opinion now given, and declares that determined abstinence occurs in one-ninth of the insane, and that in more than a thirtieth part of these it is insurmountable.* It is impossible to explain this fact, contradicted as it is by the experience of every British practitioner, otherwise than by referring it to some local peculiarity, to the prevalence of an epidemic of religious monomania, or, candidly, to some circumstance of which we are completely ignorant. In order to obtain the best and most recent information on a subject so important, I applied to the medical officers of two institutions where the most enlightened treatment prevails, and where regular records of the history of every case are preserved. From Mr. Mackintosh of Dundee Asylum, I learn, that among 650 patients admitted since the commencement of that establishment, there does not appear to have been a single case of obstinate refusal to eat, followed by gangrene ; or, to use the gentleman's own expressions, " any thing at all corroborative of what M. Guislain has advanced." Sir W. Ellis writes me, that in Hanwell Asylum, where the daily average of patients is 611, there have not occurred above twelve cases in the last six years ; but that at Wakefield the proportion was about one in forty.

Common observers passing through the parlours or workshops of a properly conducted asylum, astonished by the decorum and business-like air of the scene, often make such remarks as, these people cannot be deranged, why are they not sent home ? Even those who ought to have been acquainted with the real state of matters, have clamoured in a similar strain, and arraigned the detention of individuals whose deportment might appear to elicit such indiscriminat-

* Gazette Médicale de Paris.   Janvier, 1836.

ing interference, as an act of gross oppression and barbarity.
The perspicacity of that mind must be very questionable
which cannot penetrate the thin veil of correct demeanour
which disguises the wandering thought, or wild passions of
the maniac. The tranquillity which reigns among the insane
is not deceptious, it is not the silence of fear, nor the specious
blandness of affectation ; but yet it must not be received as
revealing the healthy serenity of those hearts from which it
springs. Its sources are three: they are all pure and healing. It may flow from the incapacity of the mind to experience any other than present or animal enjoyment; from the
subsidence of the maniacal paroxysm, in other words, the
presence of a lucid interval; and, lastly, from that calmness
which occupation and other modes of abstraction are intended
to produce, and which, when permanently established, renders all subsequent measures comparatively easy. But to
release patients in any of these states, would be to place them
in the very circumstances calculated above all others to
destroy this superficial peace, and agitate the mind in its
deepest recesses. There may be some difficulty in deciding
what shall be called a lucid interval, and how it shall be distinguished from the stage of convalescence. The experience
of all practical men is, that much more is lost than can possibly be gained by an early restoration to society, and their
advice accordingly is to subject a patient to as long a period
of trial and observation as may be consistent with justice.
The only guide to a correct judgment is the fact of the complete disappearance of every symptom of nervous disease.
During a lucid interval there generally linger some aberra-
tion of thought, some bodily disturbance. During convalescence, no irregularity of function can be detected. Relapses have been separated from recurrences of insanity : the
former being limited to all new attacks which occur within
three months after recovery ; the latter including all at more
distant periods. The distinction may be scientifically just;

but it is not practically useful. For, if whenever a patient
is brought into contact with the world, and the rude shocks
which the current of its affairs inflicts upon delicate and retiring natures, an overthrow of reason ensues, it is of very
little importance what the duration of the interval may have
been ; as, whether of three or twelve months, the re-appear-
ance of the insanity in the same form, and from a similar
cause, cannot be regarded in any other light than as a relapse. I have known patients continue perfectly sane for
ten or twelve months, and then fall into the most ungovernable paroxysm of mania on certain emotions being called
up, and whose sanity thus depended upon the discretion of
those around.   There are indeed many individuals who are
comparatively or entirely sane when under the guardianship
of an asylum, who would become furious or melancholic if
compelled to mingle in a busier and more exciting scene, and
to bear the burden of an active life.

The Parisian registers furnish some very interesting facts
on this subject. From them it appears that the relapses are
to the admissions as four to one hundred, and that the relapses to the cures in both sexes are as twelve to one hundred.   But on examining the proportion in the sexes sepa-
rately it is found to be twenty per cent. in males, and only
ten per cent. in females. What is the cause of such a disparity ? it may be asked. The explanation seems to strength-
en the views I have adopted.   " The medium residence," I
quote Burrows, " of each man discharged cured is four
months and fifteen days: that of each woman discharged
cured nine months and twenty-five days."   Now this proves
most incontestibly either that the removal of the disease is
more difficult in women than in men, which is preposterous,
or that the longer the influence of good treatment is continued the greater will be the security of the individual.   Assuredly it is purchasing an immunity from madness at a cheap
rate to reside for a short time with friends whose reputation

is, to a certain degree, interwoven with the health of their
charge, and under a roof which, while it may remind of the
childishness or frenzy of alienation, cannot fail to be endear-
ed by recollections of the return of intelligence and feeling,
of the rising and renewed glory of the sun of reason from the
darkness of despair. To give any practicability or usefulness
to this suggestion, steps must first be taken to assimilate asylums to the homes to which patients are desirous and are
destined to return. They must have within themselves temptations to induce a protracted residence which it might be
hurtful to extort. They must become boarding houses of the
best description, where medical attendance and moral training shall be as unremitting as during the acute stage of the
disease ; and where there shall exist certain outlets, channels
of communication with the external world, through which
old impressions may be gradually revived ; old friends reun-
ited, and the resumption of former habits and pursuits safely
accomplished.

Complete isolation is as pernicious to the curable insane
as to the sane. The experience derived from the American
prisons and penitentiaries proves that the mind, when totally
deprived of the stimulus afforded by social intercourse and
occupation, gives way, and fury and fatuity succeed. Is this
result at all allied, or more closely than by analogy, to the
breaking up of the constitution, observed in the suddenly
reclaimed drunkard ? I have tried the experiment of complete isolation. The effect was tremendous. A noisy and
ferocious maniac was in the course of a few weeks altogether
subdued, even his diseased energies seemed to be prostrated
by their own unrestrained violence ; but at the same time
the mind was enfeebled by the deprivation of every impression from without, and I for some time trembled lest the cure
of furious mania should prove to be fatuity. To the incurable and dangerous insane, whose alienation admits of no alteration from companionship or external nature, who live

within themselves, solitary confinement is neither injurious nor irksome.

The number of cases is very small which would not be benefited by modified isolation, or rather by separation from the places, and persons, and impressions, causing or connected with the origin of the disease. Were all asylums properly conducted ; were they what they ought to be, and pretend to be, hospitals adapted for all forms of mental alienation ; then *all* forms would be alleviated by this mode of treatment.

From mistaken kindness or an erroneous estimate of the soothing and curative powers of friendship and affection, a trial is frequently recommended to be made at home. Several months after the incursion of the complaint are thus spent in an experiment, in hoping, in grieving over the gradual extinction of the noblest attributes of mind, but in doing nothing. The man who would recommend a patient labouring under inflammation of the lungs to try the effects of the kind attentions of his relations, water-gruel, and the nurse's pharmacopœia, would be reprobated as an ignorant fool. The man who gives similar advice to a patient labouring under inflammation of the brain, or diseased action closely resembling it, scarcely deserves to escape from similar reprobation. From this advice being followed, it is comparatively rare for the superintendents of public asylums to have recent cases submitted to their care. Of one hundred and forty-nine patients admitted to the Retreat, at York, in the course of fifteen years, only sixty-one were recent cases.*

The chances of cure are consequently diminished, unjust conclusions are drawn as to the curability of the disease, and the real advantages of judicious treatment rendered abortive. The reasons why we are more successful in cases of short standing are very obvious. After the agitation consequent on a sudden separation from society has subsided, or the acute stage of mania has been mitigated, there are the for-

* Tuke's Description of Retreat, p. 201.

mer habits of the patient still imprinted vividly on the mind,
and arising more naturally to recollection than new combinations of thought ; there is the languor of idleness, the craving for variety ; there is the instructive desire to escape from
self, and the equally instructive suggestions of making the
hands work instead of the head to effect this escape : there
are all these and many more conditions to be worked upon
which do not exist, or do not exist to the same extent at any
subsequent period.   The mind is then more alive to the stimulus of emulation, rewards, punishments, and threats.   I
have not alluded to the paramount, that is, the physiological
reasons for early treatment.

In the application of labour as a remedy, it is of importance to know what number of patients may be expected to
co-operate, and should it be suited to their condition, to work
out their own cure.   By using the proper incentives ninety
out of every hundred recent cases may be induced to do this,
provided there exist no physical disability, such as palsy, to
prevent the attempt.   Even in old cases where the mind and the
muscles have been allowed to slumber, or to struggle in the
restlessness of pain for twenty years, wonderful transforma-
tions may be accomplished ; and so potent and infectious is
imitation, so exquisite is the pleasure of being roused to activity, and of being tranquillized by having a specific object
to action presented, that two-thirds of those affected may be
employed, and the hoary headed lunatic who has dreamed
away a quarter of a century may be converted into a busy,
bustling, and highly useful personage.   It appears from the
report of Sir W. Ellis, that of 610 patients in the asylum at
Hanwell during 1836, 431 were constantly employed.   In Dundee asylum, during the year 1834–35, ninety-two of ninety-six
paupers were engaged in various branches of industry, from
picking oakum and mending shoes up to flowering muslin and
upholstery work.   The Richmond asylum has one half, or 130
out of 377 constantly contributing to the support of the in-

stitution and to their own restoration. In that establishment another principle, that of tuition, is directed against
insanity. Twelve of the 130 were learning to read. This
noble and most philosophical attempt to build the mind anew
on the ruins of outraged feeling, or enfeebled judgment, or
whatever may be the form of the injury sustained, by conveying new ideas to the perceptive powers, and by calling
up, by means of education, faculties which were previously
unknown or dormant, and which may prove to be healthy
or antagonist to those diseased—has been made elsewhere;
and on a more extended scale, patients have been instructed
in the rudiments of science, in drawing, music, have been
taught weaving, shoe-mending, and other common arts, and
have been even tempted to participate in the representation
of comedies.*   The fact is so evident that the mind must be
relieved from sorrow or any other painful impression by distraction that the humanity of resorting to occupation for this
purpose is universally admitted.   But it may not follow that
because the mind is relieved from pain it is consequently
placed in the best condition to recover; in other words, does
employment promote cure?   The presumption that it is
capable of doing so is founded upon a very familiar precaution.   We do not use a leg or an arm that has been bruised
or wounded or is inflamed; we endeavour to save it from
exertion, and allow it rest by employing the other.   In prescribing occupation then to the insane, it is proposed to engage the healthy, the unwounded powers and thereby to save
those which are pained or diseased, and would be injured by
exertion. If a man, who imagines himself an outcast from
society, the object of contempt and scorn, be placed at a
loom, and induced to produce ten or fifteen yards of cloth per
day, it is quite clear, that during the execution of his task, if

* Wendt's Account of Asylums in North of Europe; quoted in
Pritchard.   Annales d'Hygiène; Juillet, 1836.

it be done well, he is forced to exert his whole attention and
no little ingenuity and manual dexterity upon the manag-
ment of the shuttle, beam, &c., that while his mind is so directed, it cannot be under the dominion of its morbid sorrows ; that just in proportion to the degree and duration of
the occupation will be the freedom from disease and the
nearer approach to health.

But there are other objects than abstraction gained by this
system. It gives a regularity to the mental operations, than
which nothing can be more conducive to tranquillity : it
imposes the necessity of self-command and attention, it
communicates new series of impressions, and if judiciously
managed, it may be made, by giving tone and vigour to the
body, to react on the mind, in the same manner that eva-
cuants, opiates, or tonics do. It cannot then be immaterial
what the nature of the employment is which may be recommended. In the selection, let the object be to combine as
many of the objects here specified as possible. It is not
enough to have the insane playing the part of busy automa-
tons, or to wear out their muscular energies vicariously, in
order to relieve the drooping heart of its load. There must
be an active, and, if possible, an intelligent and willing par-
ticipation on the part of the labourer, and such a portion of
interest, amusement, and mental exertion associated with the
labour, that neither lassitude nor fatigue may follow. The
more elevated, the more useful the description of occupation
provided then, the better. It ought not to be complicated,
for that would discourage : it ought not to be purely mechanical, for that frustrates the end in view : it ought not to
be useless and evidently for the purpose of acting as a
means of abstraction, for the artifice is often detected, and
the patient is disgusted. The utility of every thing ordered
should be palpable ; and this argument holds out another inducement to engage every individual in the pursuits to which
he has been accustomed. Pinel mentions the case of a mad

watchmaker, who spent many months in experiments on the perpetual motion. He, of course, failed to solve the problem, but regained his reason in the attempt. With a view to se-cure the benefit of exercise in the open air, as well as mental concentration, field-labour has been much resorted to, and asylums have been surrounded by farms, and parks, and gardens. The plan is unexceptionable, and wherever it can be carried into effect, will promote the restoration of those engaged. But however excellent in certain circumstances, it is quite clear that its application must be partial, that it can only take place during particular seasons of the year, and can include a very small class of lunatics admitted into urban asylums. Military exercise has been substituted in some countries; and however ridiculous it may at first appear, that a battalion of lunatics should perform the evolutions of a well-disciplined corps, the moral result has justified the expedient. I confess to have seen the drill-sergeant work miracles. But even here fine weather is required for the daily drill; and what we are in search of is some employment which shall be ac-cessible and in constant operation, altogether independently of climate, or any accessory circumstance. The best rule is to have all descriptions of occupation at command; and where a sedentary one is chosen, or preferable, to suggest walking or swinging as a recreation and interruption, or to devise means that the necessary amount of exercise be taken. Wherever people of education are confined, a thousand ex-pedients may be adopted to occupy and amuse. But as ar-tisans and tradesmen furnish, and must always furnish, the greatest proportion of the insane poor, all, or at least the principal arrangements should be adapted to their wants, and for their benefit. Whatever the staple trade of the dis-trict, its implements, or the means by which it is carried on, should be found in the asylum; and not only this, but every reasonable provision for engaging those workmen, who must be members of every community, and be found in every district. Weavers, shoemakers, tailors, gardeners, carpenters, watchmakers, have all been tried for years, and found to work as diligently, and to produce as good articles when confined as when at liberty. I cannot indeed see, nor admit, any limit to the application of the principle.

But conceding its practicability, it may be demanded, is it safe? Can the maniac be intrusted with instruments of the most dangerous, and, if he should so incline, deadly kind: which, wielded by the tremendous force that he is well known occasionally to possess, would enable him to sacrifice all around, and then destroy himself? If there be any superiority in the modern mode of studying the dispositions of the in-sane, it consists in the power of discriminating those who may be allowed to be set free from those who would abuse liberty, and those who may be allowed with impunity to use knives, hatchets, &c. in their ordinary calling, from those who may not. No man, unless mad, would place a knife in the hands of a patient of whose character he was ignorant, or whose character for revenge and cruelty he knew. But nine-tenths of madmen are neither habitually malicious nor furious; and if they satisfactorily pass the ordeal of such ex-amination as it is in the power of every man acquainted with the human mind to institute, it would be egregious folly to debar them from a privilege which may contribute to their happiness, and cannot, in ninety cases out of a hundred, in-terfere with the happiness or safety of others. In the Rich-mond Hospital, where 130 individuals are constantly pos-sessed of cutting instruments and other objects which could be readily converted into weapons of destruction, no acci-dent has ever occurred. Murders are sometimes perpetrated in asylums; but far more rarely than among the sane in-habitants of the world; and in almost all cases where such misfortunes happened, they have been traced to one of two causes, either to the intemperate language and brutal con-duct of a keeper, or to the improper classification of the pa-

patients.   At Sonnenstein no accident is recorded.   Sir W.
Ellis has pursued this plan first at Wakefield, latterly at Hanwell, in the treatment of several thousand patients, and his
courage, confidence, and discernment, have been justified
throughout.   With the limitations mentioned, indeed, there
is no respectable establishment where employment, in its
widest sense, is not considered the grand specific, and every
successive improvement grounded upon its extension.

Possessed then, of such accurate knowledge of all that is
to be dreaded and all that is to be hoped in the treatment of
the insane, it remains to be inquired, have the arrangements
made to effect the great end in view been founded upon this
knowledge ? have they been in accordance with the laws of
the human mind, and the precepts " love mercy, do justly ?"
or have they sprung from the less noble sources, ignorance,
indifference, selfish interests ?   To this inquiry the next lecture is devoted.

LECTURE III.

WHAT ASYLUMS WERE.

Character of System pursued previous to 1815—St. Vincent de Paul—
Insane consigned to Monks—Lunatics set at large to beg—Lunatics
in Gaols, in Cages, in Caves, in Dungeons.—Associating of Lunatics
with Criminals—Modes of quieting Lunatics—"Muffling"—Modes
of feeding Lunatics—"Forcing"—Death from this process—Lunatics
in Hospitals—Four or five sleep in one bed—Confined in Venereal
Wards—Lunatics in Workhouses—Want of Medical attendance,
classification, comfort, and cleanliness in these establishments—Sale
of Idiot children—Madhouses at Venice, Nantes—Confinement of
sane individuals—Carelessness of Medical men in granting certificates—Unusual modes of coercing the Insane—Coercion required for
the poor, but not for the rich—Coercion resorted to as economical—
Lunatics exhibited for a sum of money; excited and induced to gorge
themselves with food, or filth, for the amusement of visitors—Gangrene of extremities from cold—Insufficient supply of food, of clothing—No medical or moral treatment—Superintendence confided to
ignorant and dissolute keepers—Terror as a remedy—Cruelty and immorality of servants—No separation of sexes—Unhealthy cells—Concealment of mortality—Deaths from fury of keepers and patients—
Records burned to frustrate inquiry, &c.—A visit to Asylums as they
were.

THERE exists no wish in my mind, as may be supposed
from the details contained in this lecture, to produce a false
impression in order to excite a strong feeling of sympathy in
the fate and fortunes of those whom I regard as my clients.
Their sufferings are, unfortunately, so numerous and so clamant as scarcely to admit of exaggeration. But it is my
wish to tell the whole truth, and to expedite the cause of

humanity, although the sensitive may be shocked, or the fastidious disgusted by the recital, although even the real philanthropist should be conscience-stricken that his energies have been expended on miseries less poignant and pressing, and on objects of compassion less worthy.

What then were formerly the provisions for the cure of the varieties of lunacy, and for the various classes of lunatics which have been considered ? " Nos pères n'ont pas renversé," says a French writer in 1833, " toutes les Bastilles." The atrocities which have been perpetrated within these bastiles, deridingly called asylums, under the pretence, and, in some cases, it is possible, at the dictation of benevolence, and under the sanction of science, are too little known to the public.   Although belonging to the past, and generally repudiated at the time by those who from ignorance, or some less excusable cause, tolerated their continuance, they require to be exposed in order to accelerate as much as possible the progressive improvement, which shall destroy every lingering remnant of the system from which they sprung, every trace of their existence and influence.

It may appear presumptuous that I should volunteer to preach a crusade in this cause : but he who moved and led the whole Christian world in the first crusade, was nearly as humble an individual as your lecturer, and certainly not more sincere. My only justification, if any be required, is, that my professional studies and pursuits have rendered me familiar with the principles upon which institutions for the cure or reception of the insane have been, in contradistinction to those on which they ought to have been conducted. I am likewise actuated by the desire to show, that practical men have been unjustly regarded as inimical to the changes which the theoretical have proposed. At present reference shall be made only to some of the errors, absurdities, and atrocities of the old system, as they obtained previous to the year 1815. Buried in those valuable though little valued monuments of legislative industry and wisdom, Parliamentary Reports, or scattered through periodicals or other works nearly as ephemeral, the facts upon which this exposition will proceed, rarely if ever meet the eye of the general observer or philosopher. As an indication of the better spirit which now prevails they will appear scarcely credible. But though the characters be written in blood, the accuracy of the tale they tell cannot be questioned.

Until the noble efforts of St. Vincent de Paul were crowned with success, the madman was, on the continent of Europe, either expelled from society as an outcast unworthy of care or compassion, or burnt as a sorcerer unworthy even of those rude forms of justice which then prevailed. This pious man was a divine, and is now a saint of the Catholic church. If canonization ever was justifiable or excusable, it was in this instance. St. Vincent sacrificed every thing for these outcasts : he journeyed from land to land to preach and propagate the cause of charity : his mission was to bring back the sympathies of our nature to their proper channels, to proclaim that the darkened mind was as much the visitation of God as the darkened vision, and that Christianity demanded of the humane and virtuous and powerful to protect, and the skilful to relieve, the one as well as the other. The hearts of nations responded to his call. He became the emancipator of the diseased, the reviled and per-secuted, during all succeeding ages. Of the same type and mould as La Rochefoucauld and Howard, he worthily obtain-ed the glorious epitaph, " The father of the poor, the stew-ard of Providence." May the spirit and enthusiasm which actuated, him be ever present to those who are now intrust-ed with the good work which he commenced ! He was at the time of his labours a monk, and from this circumstance perhaps, or because these recluses were then the principal depositaries of all knowledge, scientific as well as religious, in the countries to which his exertions were confined, to monks was the care of the insane confided. For nearly two centuries they discharged this trust;—how ignorantly and barbarously, may be judged from the treatment stated to have been pursued in a monastic establishment in the south of France. There every lunatic regularly received ten lashes per day. To ascetics, however, who, themselves, shrunk from neither lash nor torture, this regimen might appear both beneficial and reasonable. Convents were, until the Revolution, the only receptacles for the insane in France: in Britain asylums existed at an earlier period. But of what kind ?

The reign of humanity in Bedlam commenced only about twenty years ago. Before that period the lunatic might be truly said to live under a reign of terror. Immured in a wretched and comfortless prison-house, and left to linger out a lifetime of misery, without any rational attempt at treatment, without employment, without a glimpse of happiness, or a hope of liberation, he was terrified or starved into submission, lashed, laughed at, despised, forgotten. The great objects were—confine, conceal. Protect society from his ferocity : protect his sensitive friends from the humiliating spectacle of such a connexion. Regarded as wild beasts, all maniacs indiscriminately were treated as such ; nay, the imprisoned tiger enjoys a milder fate, for his keepers have an interest in his health and preservation. That this is a mitigated rather than an exaggerated summary of horrors, will presently appear. Until very recently, such lunatics as could not with safety be suffered to roam at large, were confined in common prisons. Parliamentary returns prove, that a few years ago, there were in Scotland, at least a thousand lunatics at large, and consequently denied all provision for their recovery. It is not a little illustrative of the utter inadequacy of the establishments formerly appropriated to the insane to the end proposed, and of the crude, or cruel views which were entertained of the nature of their disease, that

it was either necessary or customary to discharge from Bethlem a number of lunatics, who, with a dress and manners as
grotesque as their delusions, wandered from house to house
and town to town, a sort of privileged paupers, long known
as Tom o' Bedlams, living no one cared how, and dying no
one cared where.* This hospital-delivery occurred, of
course, at a remote period, and was resorted to for the purpose of relieving the institution of the burden of maintaining a set of incurable madmen.

If those who were cast into gaols were docile and inoffen-
sive, they were permitted to mingle with their fellow-cap-
tives and become their butt : if noisy or furious, they were,
of course, condemned to the deepest and darkest dungeon
which the house afforded, and never visited by a medical
man except when afflicted with some disease superadded to
their alienation, if even then. In Ghent the intractable
were inclosed in wooden boxes or cages. Strange to say,
at Eberbach, where considerable advancement seems to
have been made in classifying patients, a large iron cage is
still constantly used for confining the refractory and dangerous.† At Strasburg these dens were only four feet wide
and six feet in height. Through the spars was tossed the
litter upon which the half naked maniac reposed : food was
conveyed to him in the same manner ; and from the ribald
jest, or harsh commands of the attendants, he had no protection ; he was indulged in neither darkness nor solitude ;
his tormentors were ever before him. But even here misery
had not reached its maximum. At Maréville the cages
containing the patients were placed in cellars : at Lille they
were confined in what are styled subterranean holes : at
Saumur they inhabited cells without windows, and were

* D'Israeli. Curiosities of Literature. First series. Vol. iii. p. 354.
† Bubbles from the Brunnens of Nassau, p. 290.

provided with wooden troughs filled with oak bark as beds.*
Revolting as these disclosures are, 1 feel myself bound to
make them, in order to show from what a degrading state of
ignorance and brutality we have escaped, and from what
complicated misfortunes the objects of our care have been
rescued by the diffusion of knowledge. These examples
were not peculiar to any country. They have been selected merely because they are the best authenticated. But to
what place and to what period would you conclude the following description to apply. "On visiting the gaol of ——,
a high legal functionary found that the gaoler was absent at
work, and being sent for, declined to attend. There was a
vault in the gaol in which a maniac was kept, who, twenty
years ago, had been sentenced to imprisonment for life for
killing a man. The individual who attended broke the key
in attempting to open the door of this vault; but enough
was seen to show, that the place in which the miserable man
was kept, was of the most wretched description."† This
memorable visit was paid in 1834: the prison is in our own
free and enlightened land, the legal officer was the Solicitor
General, and my authority is Mr. A. E. Menteith, universally known for his probity and piety. Now, who will dare
to assert, that this miserable creature, this homicidal maniac,
who, in some paroxysm of frenzy, perhaps unconsciously,
had imbrued his hands in blood, retained, during the long
period of his confinement, the same sanguinary ferocity
which had prompted to the crime : who dare assert, that if,
in place of being chained in a subterranean dungeon for half
a lifetime, he had been placed in favourable circumstances,
a period of tranquillity and serenity, and even of sanity,

* Esquirol. Dict. des Sciences Méd. art. " Maisons des Aliénés."
Sc. Pinel. Traité Complet du Regime Sanitaire des Aliénés, p. 64.

† Speech delivered by Alex. E. Menteith, Esq. advocate, at the
First Annual Meeting of the Prison Discipline Society of Scotland,
Edin. 1836.

might not have arrived, when a feeling of responsibility and
repentance might have given at once strength and humility to
the mind, and formed the commencement of a life of useful
industry and virtuous contentment.   None of these anticipated results might have followed a more lenient and rational
treatment in this case ; but the gravamen of the charge, the
matter for deep regret is, that any human being, labouring
under mental disease, should be abandoned, without an
attempt at cure or alleviation, to the custody of a coarse and
negligent turnkey, and condemned to endure privations to
which the household dog is never exposed.   " The accommodation for the insane," says Mr. Rice, " in the Limerick
Asylum, appears to be such, as we should not appropriate
for our dog-kennels."*   The civil authorities had formerly
no alternative but to confine the pauper lunatics of the district in the nearest gaol, or lock-up house.   The evils of such
a procedure were even greater than that which has been discussed.   There then existed, as there now, I believe, exists,
no classification among the prisoners ; and the lunatics, if
calm and obedient, were forced to associate with all who
might be placed in the common room.   The unfeeling taunts
of the heartless and debased criminals were the least prominent of these evils : such callous persecution could inflict but
momentary pain, could but aggravate the disease ; but to
minds naturally weak, enfeebled by excitement, or recovering from derangement, the constant and friendly intercourse
of such polluted companions must have proved doubly detrimental, by corrupting every virtuous disposition and over-
throwing every principle of religion.   The man who was
cast into prison a moping fool, ran the risk of being discharged a reckless villain.   But in these moral lazar-houses
the witless noise of the maniac was often found to be inimical to the repose of the other inmates, and how, will it be

* Report from the Select Committee on the Lunatic Poor in Ireland, &c. 1817, p. 14.

supposed, were they soothed to sleep and silence? Intimidation is not, it was discovered, an infallible remedy in mental medicine; it will occasionally defeat its own object and convert irritation and discontent into absolute fury and despair. But cruelty is ingenious, and these practitioners adopted the alternative of bleeding their patients to debility, or drugging them with opiates. A less refined mode of obtaining tranquillity was sometimes resorted to in madhouses, designated, in the revolting slang of its inventors, " muffling"—which consisted in binding a cloth *tightly* over the mouth and nostrils, or, as a person who had witnessed its application graphically describes it, " tying a bit of sheet or something round the nose to stun the noise, to see if it would quiet them."* Connected with this infamous custom was another called " forcing." Patients often refuse to take food. They suspect it to be poisoned : they imagine it to be unwholesome, or to be human flesh : they conceive that they are commanded by an angel to refrain from gratifying their appetite; or, finally, from obstinacy and perversity of character, they resist all solicitations to eat. They were, in times gone by, believed to be inaccessible to reasoning or persuasion, and no such means were adopted to overcome their resolution. Strength of arm was then the remedy for all difficulties. And the struggling victim was bound down on a bed, the teeth forced asunder, and the dreaded substance pushed or poured down the throat. Occasionally teeth were broken or pulled from their sockets, and we hear of the handle of a spoon—this was the instrument generally selected for the operation—being forced through the palate during the contest ; but these consequences were looked upon as trifles.† They were in reality so when compared

* First Report of Minutes of Evidence from Committee on Madhouses, 1816, p. 30.

† First Report of Minutes of Evidence from Committee on Madhouses, 1816, p. 2, and 80.

with what frequently ensued. To facilitate the descent of
the food, the head was unavoidably bent backwards and
placed in so unnatural and dangerous a position, that any
sudden or powerful movement on the part of the patient
rendered dislocation of the vertebræ almost unavoidable.
When the throat was strongly grasped in this attempt, suffo-
cation may have taken place, but the instantaneous death of
some of the victims, whose history is recorded, would lead
to the belief, that pressure on the spinal marrow had been
the cause. What adds to the horror with which we must
regard the practice, adopted although it may have been from
a mistaken compassion, is, that it was not resorted to in
desperate cases only, when long continued fasting, debility,
and the prospect of death from inanition might justify or
palliate such violence, but whenever a single meal was refused. The tyrants would permit neither the stomach nor
the mind to be refractory. A female in a private Asylum
expressed her unwillingness to eat : she was immediately
forced, and is said to have died under the hands of the keeper.
Four or five times a-day would the same practice be had recourse to, and if any disaster occurred, there appears to have
been no troublesome friends or coroner's inquest to tell the
tale. The following event is said to have taken place in the
same establishment, and will exemplify both the cruelty and
indifference displayed by all concerned in such proceedings.
A gentleman refused his food : the keeper forces, from no
revengeful inhumanity perhaps, but still he forces him to
take it, the patient calls for assistance in the piteous words,
" For God's sake, Mr. ———, come and help me, or I shall
be killed by this man." No entreaties either on the part of
the sufferer, or the other servants, could induce Mr. ———,
who was seated in an adjoining room and within hearing of
the scuffle, to interfere. All becomes suddenly still : the
keeper quietly reports to Mr. ———, that the gentleman
went off in a fit during the act of forcing, and no further

notice is taken of the matter.* The truth of these statements was denied at the time by the persons implicated.
Could it be otherwise ? I cannot say, strongly as I desire
to disbelieve such a charge, that the evidence adduced of the
inaccuracy of the details, or of the vindictive bias of the ac-
cusers, is by any means satisfactory or conclusive. But my
accusation is not levelled against these or any other parties,
but against the practice. Exonerating those in whose hands
such distressing accidents happened, from all cool, deliberate cruelty, or even disregard for the lives of those committed to their care: and even admitting that the particular
instances cited may have been exaggerated : yet, is it no
less true, that interference of the nature here described is
generally an uncalled-for exercise of authority, is always
attended with severe suffering and some danger, and cannot
be regarded in any other aspect than as the most cruel alternative which the duty of a curator of the insane can force
him to adopt. Nor is it to be concealed, that such means of
administering food were in many respectable asylums conceived to be indispensable, and that injuries were inflicted
where no blame was attachable except to the abominable
custom itself. "It is the general practice in all houses I have
visited," says a medical witness before the Committee of the
House of Commons.†

Hospitals were sometimes preferred to prisons abroad, and
that at a time when they deserved to be regarded rather as
places for the concentration and aggravation, than for the
relief of disease : when four, five, or more individuals slept in
the same bed, and cleanliness and ventilation were treated
as vain mockeries.‡ In the Hotel Dieu of Paris, previous
to the conversion of a part of Salpetrière into an hospital for
the reception of the curable insane, lunatics in whatever

* First Report of Committee, &c. 1816, p. 86.
† First Report of Committee, &c. 1816, p. 5.
‡ Dict. des Sciènces Méd. art. " Maisons des Alienés."

stage, and presenting whatever features of mental derangement, were confined in a hall adjoining the fever-ward, which
contained beds for four persons, and two small beds; this
accommodation being intended for forty-two patients.   Individuals affected with hydrophobia were classed with the
insane and placed in the same apartment.*   A similar disregard to personal cleanliness and comfort, and to those laws
which regulate both the preservation of health and the progress of disease, appears to have crept into some of the es·
tablishments in this country at a comparatively recent period.
The Inspector of Naval Hospitals found, in one house where
insane officers and seamen are received, " in a ninth bedroom three officers, one of whom was totally insensible to
the calls of nature, and slept in a double cradle with an officer who was cleanly in his habits.   I found three officers in
a tenth apartment, containing pauper patients : a private
seaman slept in a double cradle with one of these officers,"†
I believe that a partition of some kind divided these cradles
into two resting places.   Again, the Commissioners for regulating Madhouses affirm, that in one place they found
"not less than twenty persons ill of fever: a young girl
was in the same bed with a woman who was dying : some
women were lying on the floor, and others at different ends
of the same bed."‡   Even one of the Commissioners of
Madhouses makes this singular admission.   " It is a wrong
thing, but it cannot be expected that a man who pays only
ten shillings a-week should have a separate bed."   So recently as 1788, Iberti conceived it necessary to justify the
propriety of separating lunatics from the other patients in a
public hospital, and of placing them in distinct wards; he did
not venture to propose to place them in distinct buildings.
Asylums existed in England at the time he wrote, and ap-

* Tenon. Mémoires sur les Hopitaux de Paris, p. 214.
+ First Report of Committee, &c. 1816, p. 25.
‡ Fourth Report of Committee, &c. 1815, p. 191.

pear, as may be supposed, to have been much more successful in alleviating insanity than the continental receptacles.
Iberti modestly suggests that this success can easily be explained by attending to the eccentricity which distinguishes
the manners of Englishmen; and, of course, by drawing the
obvious inference, that there exists but little difference between the sanity of those who are confined in asylums and of
those who are left at large.* Until the erection of a separate building, lunatics were placed in the Edinburgh Infirmary, where twelve cells were set apart for their exclusive
use, a measure which placed the sick at the mercy of the
insensate, and exposed the insensate to all the dangers of
contagion ; and which rendered all attempts to cure mental
disease ridiculous and impracticable, or if practicable, altogether nugatory.† In 1818, the same practice was pursued
at Lyons, and on principles still more objectionable. There
the lunatic was not permitted to associate with all the inmates indiscriminately ; he was condemned to the society of
those who were at once loathsome from disease and debased
by crime. The most wretched and infamous refuse of the
community mingled with, and, can we avoid supposing, taint-
ed those who, from their situation, could neither recognize
nor repel their friendship.

Previous to 1828, only twelve of the fifty-two counties of
England possessed public establishments for the insane :
and, until 1808, there was only one asylum in Ireland, all
pauper lunatics requiring restraint being necessarily placed
in the prison or work-house, with the indigent and idle, the
robber and the murderer.‡ And so lax were the laws, that
serious doubts have arisen whether many of those treated in
this manner were not altogether free from mental disease,

* Iberti. Observations Générales sur les Hopitaux, p. 41, 42.
† History of Infirmary, p. 9.
‡ Halliday. General View of the Present State of Lunatics and
Lunatic Asylums, &c. 1828, p. 13.

and sacrificed by malice, revenge, or avarice. The inquiry is somewhat foreign to my present purpose: but even the suspicion that such an injustice could have been perpetrated, illustrates the amount of care and solicitude displayed respecting the subject of insanity. It is, however, necessary to make some observations on the distribution and treatment of lunatics in such places of detention. In 1807 the gaols in England were proved to contain 37, the houses of correction 113, and the poorhouses, and houses of industry or workhouses, 1765 lunatics.* Even at the present moment, 127 of the insane poor belonging to the county of Middlesex are confined in workhouses.† It would be ridiculous to imagine, that in such receptacles any attempt was, or could be made to correct the delusions under which they laboured, or even to the physical causes from which these proceeded. If an ulcer appeared upon the leg, I shall admit that the parish surgeon would exert his experience to heal it, but into the mental ulcer he was not called upon to penetrate; nor, had charity or a perfect knowledge of his art prompted him to do so, would interference, under such circumstances, have been of the slightest avail. No kindness, no ingenuity could have triumphed over the series of irritations inseparable from such a situation. But, although destitute of all the means necessary for the subjugation of their disease, there is reason to believe, or rather to hope, that so far as food and clothing and the comforts which many, even of the most degraded lunatics, desire and value, were concerned, they were as carefully and plentifully provided for as the other inmates. There are, however, some known and appalling exceptions to this charitable supposition. Naked patients were found chained to the ground night and day, and this for a long lapse of years: all water for ablution was denied

* Report from Select Committee, &c. 1807, p. 12.

† Sixth Report of the Physician and Treasurer of the Middlesex Pauper Lunatic Asylum, 1837.

them: others passed the whole night in cells, where so pestilential was the atmosphere, that the inquisitors who detected these facts could not remain in them for a few minutes. " Both of them," avers one of these gentlemen, speaking of two lunatics, "were chained down to the damp stone floor, and one of them had only a little dirty straw, which appeared to have been there for many weeks,—the chain was a long one and fastened to the centre, and admitted of her just coming outside where she sat,—she was perfectly quiet and harmless,— she was not allowed water to wash herself."* Another witness states, " that in a workhouse in his neighbourhood, there is a cell which opens outwardly into the yard, but has no communication internally with the house, and where they have no comfort of a fire,—his father knew a person who was chained naked, lying on straw for fifty years in a workhouse."† Still further doubt has been excited as to the spirit in which certain workhouses were conducted, by the discovery of a traffic of so detestable and revolting character, that the soul sickens at the very name. " In a debate in 1815, Mr. Horner, after stating that a gang of factory children had been exposed to sale as part of a bankrupt's effects, said, " Another case more horrible came to my knowledge while on a committee up stairs : that not many years ago, an agreement had been made between a London parish and a Lancashire manufacturer, by which it was stipulated, that with every twenty sound children *one idiot should be taken*."‡ Here, then, in this free and glorious land was the foundling idiot sold into servitude : here, in this Christian land, and under the pretext of charity, were the purposes of benevolence prostituted by the most unwar-

* First Report of Committee, &c. 1815, p. 55, evidence of Henry Alexander, Esq.

† First Report of Committee, &c. p. 124, evidence of Mr. Thomas Bakewell.

‡ Quarterly Review. Vol. lvii. p. 402.

rantable measures for removing a parish burden, or, I ought rather to say, by the most cruel, callous, and systematized indifference to human suffering and infirmity, ever recorded.

Common sense has so far triumphed, that with the exception of some poor and remote districts, the grotesque classification of the insane with the criminal and the pauper has been altogether abandoned in this country. But in some parts of the continent, as Hesse and Hanover, the insane still are, or very recently were, mixed with criminals, shut up in damp cells, the windows of which are unglazed, furnished with beds of dirty straw, but perfectly naked. One of the most primitive and rude houses of detention exists in the vicinity of Venice. On a flat, slimy, and solitary island in one of the lagoons, there is a ruin, which, although deserted by rational men as uninhabitable, is conceived to be sufficiently good for the degraded maniac. The requisite qualities of strength of wall, bars in the loop-holes which admit light, and solitude, are certainly not wanting. In the lower apartments of this building, which are unfurnished, never cleaned, and exposed, from the want of windows, to the extremes of temperature, are confined a few madmen nearly naked, shockingly filthy; haggard and half-starved in aspect, these men seem to realise the ideas formerly entertained of their condition. They are fed once a-day, the food being thrown to them through the bars, as carrion is tossed to a wolf. The continuance of such barbarity on the very confines of civilization, may be pardoned; but how awful the responsibility of that government which permitted mismanagement nearly as gross to exist at Nantes so late as 1818, in the very centre of civilization.* Or what shall we think of the following narration? Sir G. O. Paul states, in 1807, that he was acquainted with the case of a maniac, who was shut up and chained in an uninhabited ruin. His friends

* Dict. des Sciences Méd. art. " Maisons des Aliénés."

resided at some distance, but brought him a daily allowance
of food.*   The darkest chapter in the history of the human
heart might be compiled from the recorded sufferings of the
insane.

Now, I have spoken of prisons being used as asylums; but
the converse is likewise true, asylums having been used as
prisons, with this important difference, however, that in the
latter case the prisoner was guiltless, not even guilty of being
diseased.   In fact, the popular belief that asylums have been
employed to gratify the cupidity or malice of interested or
indifferent friends, appears not to be without foundation.
Men who were sane, or who scarcely displayed a shade of
eccentricity in their conduct, have been entrapped, imprisoned, and confined, in defiance of the most active interference made in their favour.   The spirit which gives a clemency
to the most rigid legal scrutinies, was suppressed ; and the
presumption, instead of being that the accused should be regarded as sane until he was proved to be deranged, was invariably, that the individual must be treated as mad until he
was proved to be sane.   The provisions of the enactment for
the protection of the rights of those suspected of lunacy, are,
notwithstanding, ample and adequate.   Confinement ought
not, according to the intention of the original framers of the
statute, to be resorted to, nor can it be held to be authorized,
until subsequent to the repeated visits of two medical men
to the person under suspicion, and until they have given an
affidavit that such a course is necessary.   Practitioners have
been found so ignorant, or so regardless of their duties to
their fellow-men, imposed by the exercise of their profession,
as to sign this solemn attestation, which condemns to deprivation of freedom, and of the rights and privileges of citi-
zenship, and to separation from home and friends, without
having seen the individual against whom such designs are

* Report of Committee, 1807, p. 21.

meditated; without knowing, except on hearsay evidence, whether insanity exists, or insanity to such a degree as to justify restraint. The poor are protected from such injustice by their very poverty. No one is interested in secluding them; in fact, should selfish feelings predominate, it is the interest of the parish upon which they are dependent, and by the charities of which they must be supported during confinement, to deprive them, when afflicted with insanity, of the superintendence of medical men as long as possible. And is not this hard-hearted parsimonious policy frequently adopted? Upon the rich falls the violation of this law. The act of stealing a man of property, and immuring him for life in a dungeon, in this country, appears, at first sight impracticable. But there exist strong grounds for believing that such a species of kidnapping has been successfully carried into effect.* Of the facility with which agents in such a scheme may be found, I have personal experience. I was employed to obtain medical evidence of the lunacy of a person who retained reason and cunning sufficient to suspect my designs, and had address and means to have eluded them. He was attended by a physician of great eminence, who, although convinced that his patient was insane, from the dread of being dragged into a court of law, refused to participate in the necessary legal steps. To have introduced another medical attendant would have excited suspicion, and precipitated either the retreat or the suicide of the object of my solicitude. From this dilemma, a friend of the patient's kindly offered to extricate me, by procuring the signature of an individual whom he characterized as of great respectability, and as possessing a reputation for intimate knowledge of mental disease. On stating that it would be impossible to bring about an interview between the parties, my adviser assured me that this form was not necessary, that his friend

* Pigott on Suicide and its Antidotes, p. 107. Report of Committee, &c., 1807, p. 10, 14, 19. Ibid. 1815, p. 124.

would grant the requisite certificate of lunacy without any preliminary investigation, and that he was frequently called upon to act in the same manner. That such cases of abduction and inhumation have taken place, is pretty well established; that they still occur, is more than suspected. The opportunities for confining and concealing sane persons in asylums, whether public or private, are very great; and while there exist relatives so inhuman as to consign those who obstruct their selfish interests or thwart some cherished project to such a fate, instruments sufficiently base and infamous will be found to carry their purpose into execution. The only safeguard—it does not amount to prevention—against such abuses, will be in making all asylums patent, not only to the occasional visits and very imperfect scrutiny of the legal authorities, but to the constant surveillance of humane and trustworthy persons, competent by education and character for the duty.

Some adequate remedy should be provided; for even to the partially unhinged mind there is scarcely within the range of human misery an affliction more cruel than such a fate; to the sane it can scarcely fail to prove the cause of derangement. There is the uprooting of every affection,—the disappointment of every hope; there is the anticipated eternal separation from the world, and all its enjoyments and inhabitants, the degradation of caste, and the conviction that all these varieties of bitterness are inflicted by those in whom confidence was reposed, who were objects of love, and who with the right and power to cherish and protect, have betrayed their trust by deserting and oppressing. Besides this there is to be endured a life of solitude and silence, spent amid furious and raving maniacs, without object or pursuit; there is the deprivation of all sympathy; the being ranked and treated as a proud or perverse lunatic, or as a drivelling imbecile; and ultimately there must be endured a death which may be solaced by the common charities of humanity, but which no friend will know of or weep for. Such ideas must be suggested to the sane, even to the partially sane mind, when the first agitation and terror consequent on con-finement have subsided; and are calculated, as I have said, to accomplish all that the conspirators desire.

The victims of persecution in the middle ages were committed to *oubliettes*. Built into the recess of a dungeon, with sufficient air and food to protract life, but not to allay suffering, they were abandoned to linger on for days and weeks, and, as the name implied, were forgotten. I know not on which of these demoniac destroyers of their kind, those who entombed the body, or those who entombed the soul, the deepest execra-tions should be poured. Human law has no punishment for such barbarities; the Christian heart cannot trust itself in condemning their perpetration, in awarding justice to the perpetrators. I have spoken at length on this abuse, because it is the most awful in its consequences, and because it is the most difficult of detection. I have likewise spoken strongly, but I trust it has been with a voice of virtuous indignation.

Closely as the asylums originally erected were assimilated to prisons; the whole array of bolts, bars, chains, muffs, collars, and strait-jackets, were deemed some years back in-sufficient to afford protection to keepers, and a machine was invented, so perfect in its construction and satisfactory in its application that it deserves description. I shall convey the history of this extraordinary apparatus, and of the oc-casion which was conceived to justify such unusual restraint, nearly in the words of a witness before the parliamentary committee: " William Norris had been confined fourteen years; in consequence of attempting to defend himself from what he conceived to be the improper treatment of his keep-er, who was a habitual drunkard, and at the time intoxicat-ed: he was fastened by a long chain, which, passing through a partition, enabled the keeper, by going into the next cell, to draw him close to the wall at pleasure: to prevent this,

Norris muffled the chain with straw so as to hinder its passing through the wall: he was afterwards confined by a stout ring rivetted round the neck, from which a short chain passed to a ring made to slide upwards or downwards on an upright massive iron bar, more than six feet high, inserted into the wall. Round his body a strong iron bar about two inches wide was rivetted; on each side the bar was a circular projection, which, being fashioned to, and enclosing each of his arms, pinioned them close to his sides. This waist bar was secured by two similar bars, which, passing over his shoulders, were rivetted to the bars on his shoulders by a double link to the waist-bar both before and behind. The iron ring round his neck was connected to the bars on his shoulders by a double link. From each of these bars another short chain passed to the ring on the upright iron bar. He could raise himself so as to stand against the wall, or in the pillow of his bed in the trough in which he lay; but it was impossible for him to advance from the wall on which the iron bar was soldered, on account of the shortness of his chains, which were only twelve inches long. He could not repose in any other position than on his back. His right leg was chained to the trough, on which he had remained thus encaged and chained for twelve years."* The unfortunate being thus empaled was of great muscular power; his wrists were formed in so peculiar a manner as to render all manacles useless, and his disposition is described as blood-thirsty. I presume he was affected with homicidal monomania. Notwithstanding these very formidable qualities, when we learn that at one time he was so docile as to be useful to the servants, that during his incasement in iron he spoke rationally, seemed to understand all that was addressed to him, and to recollect all that he had suffered : that he occupied his time in reading, and that when partially liberated he conducted himself with

* First Report of Committee, &c. 1815, p. 12. Evidence of Mr. E. Wakefield.

propriety; the amount and nature of the precautions adopted appears to have been unnecessary and oppressive.* They afforded, it is true, adequate protection to all around ; but on a mind in such a condition, in a condition so favourable for treatment, moral impressions might have been made to become, as in cases of a precisely similar kind they have become, a source of protection as powerful and as permanent; or, if the patient's nature was really so ferocious and irreclaimable as to render all such efforts fruitless ; why was complete isolation not attempted ? Why, during the periods of intelligence and tranquillity, the periods in fact when he was no longer dangerous, was there no intermission, no diminution of these laboured precautions ? I know nothing at all parallel to this contrivance except a mode of restraint very recently employed at Rome for the turbulent and furious. Two iron rings are fixed in the wall of the cell, one of these serves as a collar and embraces the neck, the other passes round the ankle; thus united action compels the prisoner to stand upright, or, should fatigue and exhaustion render that impossible, to hang suspended.† The race of men who could thus see no safety but in chains, drew a line of distinction as to whom they were to be applied. Patricians, we would be led to believe, were calm and tranquil in their frenzy, for Dr. Monro states, that under his superintendence "gentlemen" were never chained, but that such measures were necessary for the poor in public establishments.‡ This was clearly an error in judgment; a pernicious mistake, it is true, arising out of the opinions prevalent as to the nature of mental disease, and as to the inefficacy of moral treatment :

* First Report of Minutes, &c., 1816, p. 41. Evidence of Mr. James Simmonds.   Second Report from Committee, &c., 1815, p. 151. Evidence of William Smith, Esq.

† Brierre de Boismont.   Mémoire pour l'Etablissement d'un Hospice d'Aliénés, Annales d'Hygiène Publique, vol. xvi. p. 104.

‡ First Report of Committee, &c., 1815, p. 93.

but on advancing one step farther into the inquiry, the same timid measures are discovered to have been taken as part of a system, not of cure but of economy. To avoid the lavish outlay that would be incurred by employing additional keepers, "It was stated," says Dr. Fowler, "when the keepers were asked the reason for putting them in irons, that it would require a larger expense than they could afford to keep servants to take care of them if they were not ironed."*

I have rashly, it may be conceived, compared the former treatment of lunatics to that of the animals in a menagerie. From motives precisely similar to those which actuate Polito or Wombwell, the patients in Bedlam used to be exhibited to any one paying four shillings. And that callous and unenlightened curiosity which draws crowds to the one exhibition drew crowds to the other. So strong was this feeling that, until about sixty years since, a large sum, amounting to about L.400 per annum, was raised by this tax.† Throughout France, one or two large towns excepted, this detestable practice is still persevered in, or, if nominally discontinued, the purse always contains a talisman which removes all difficulties. Esquirol adds that the guardians spare neither menaces nor sarcasms in order to rouse the passions of the patients for the amusement of the visitors. It is difficult to say who shall be admitted and who excluded; but no rule of admission, of whatever latitude, should include visitors for amusement. Open to the intelligent and humane as a means of preventing or removing those abuses which I denounce, asylums ought to be closed to the public, and as sacred from vulgar unsympathizing eyes as the secrets they so often reveal. Conceive the feelings of a family whose sister, or father, or friend, had been made the sport or even the gazing-stock of what is, surely in derision, called a party of pleasure; or,

* First Report of Committee, &c., 1815, p. 46.
† Highmore. An account of the various Public Charities in or near London, p. 19.

conceive again the feelings of that sister, or father, or friend, on returning to the world and encountering those to whom their ravings and folly had afforded matter for wonder or merriment. The evil consequences of such treatment in a medical point of view are glaring, but here it is only necessary to expose its barbarity and brutality. But we have not yet arrived at the climax. It has been insinuated that imbeciles have been deprived for some time of food, in order to astonish the spectators by their voracity when it was given to them. This at least is certain, that a miserable creature who was in the habit of eating his own excrement, earth and filth of every description, was furnished with weeds and grass to devour to gratify the curiosity of visitors.* It would be absurd to suppose that this custom of swallowing noxious and indigestible substances was in general encouraged for the reason here alleged, or for any other. But, in proof of how much lunatics have been neglected, it may be mentioned, that, in the dissection of the bodies of those known as earth-eaters, the colon is sometimes found to be distended with earth and clay, and in such enormous quantities that it must have been the accumulation of months or even years. This I have seen. The gross inattention of governors of asylums to the comfort, and of keepers to the helpless condition, of those committed to their custody, it cannot be called care, is seen in the fact mentioned by Esquirol, that idiots and imbeciles often lose their limbs from grangrene produced by cold, and, shocking to relate, from the attacks of rats. Similar accidents used to occur at Bedlam, and Sir A. Halliday states that he saw, in this country, a rat devouring the extremities of a maniac, who was lying naked on some straw, in the agonies of death.† Although inappropriate food is often given to lunatics, so far as I know, there is no instance on record

* Carter. A Short Account of some of the Principal Hospitals of France, Italy, Switzerland, &c. p. 42.

† Letter in the Courant Newspaper, September 1836.

of the supply of food being inadequate in this country. The case is different in France. During the sway of the revolutionary government, the allowance to the lunatics in the public asylums was reduced to the smallest possible amount which could sustain life. The most marked and melancholy results followed. The convalescents relapsed, the furious became still more frantic from hunger; and the mortality increased to a frightful degree. Fifty-six patients died in one month in Salpêtrière; and in the space of two months, the mortality in Bicêtre exceeded that of the whole previous year, when the rations were liberal.

In smaller institutions, the evils arising from negligence or parsimony are probably still more aggravated. The dread of detection is there comparatively slight. Proprietor, servants, all may enter into an execrable league to gorge on the spoils of the poor and defenceless; and by whom can the conspiracy be traced or defeated? The lunatic who suffers, is not listened to; the barbarian who oppresses, is at once witness and jury. We hear of the wine and spirits which the exhausted maniac may be advised to take, being diluted or adulterated; we hear of patients being confined in outhouses which were formerly pig-sties, sleeping in cribs so small, as to cause permanent contraction of the limbs; we can scarcely picture to the mind three miserable, emaciated beings, huddled together in a bed intended for one person, without any straw or covering, save a single rug, or coarse hop sack: we can scarcely believe, that, in a climate such as this, a number of weak and diseased men should be compelled to sleep in a damp cellar containing a well. But if we once admit and believe these atrocities as possible, we can then understand the details of suffering and death from mortification and typhus fever, which are given as the consequence, and the peculation and fraud which are given as the cause. This applies chiefly to the want of proper clothing. An exposé of the system pursued, adds another and

G

darker shade to the picture I have drawn.   The patients are represented as furious and destructive, to their friends and guardians.   It is declared to be impossible to restrain them from tearing their clothes, and new supplies are frequently demanded : and the articles thus accumulated are sold, while those for whom they were intended sit naked and shivering in the cold, without even the solace of heat to mitigate their melancholy.*

The nature of the medical treatment which prevailed in this disease previous to 1815, which may he styled the era of the reformation, may be judged of from the following statements.   In a large asylum in England, the superintendent, who was intrusted with the moral management, as well as the direction of the internal economy, sometimes absented himself for two months ; in another, containing about four hundred patients, no attempt whatever was at any time made to restore mental health ; in a third, and that a metropolitan one, where an immense number of individuals are confined, and where the character of the various species of lunacy, is as different as the dispositions and temperament of these patients, and where every case may be accompanied with a different bodily disease, it was an established rule, that all, without any reservation, should be bled in June, and receive four emetics per annum.†   When the physician paid his regular visits, which were "few and far between," the patients were arranged in two rows, between which he passed rapidly, receiving reports of their complaints at second-hand from the apothecary ; prescribing, guided clearly by some intuitive knowledge, in this fashion.—"Number one, a purge ; number two, an emetic ; number ten, bleeding." We are assured by certain high authorities, that insanity is

* First Report of Minutes, 1816, *passim.*

† First Report of Minutes, &c., 1816 ; and First Report by Committee, 1815, p. 37.

the most easily cured of all serious maladies ; and I have attempted to show, that, under favourable circumstances, it is
much more easily cured than what was formerly supposed ;
but such conduct as that now described would force us to
conclude that the cures are spontaneous, and that Nature,
in her prodigality of power and affection, rejects altogether
the assistance of art. In those days, even experienced and
humane physicians gave their sanction to such an opinion,
by declaring that medicine was of little importance ; and
in compliance with these views, there were no baths, no de-
pletion, no regulation of diet, no interference in fact, further
than what was demanded for the ailments which sprung
from this neglect.

Moral treatment there was none. The mind was left to
recover its native strength and buoyancy spontaneously.
All classes of patients were crowded together without occupation, " without means," remarks one of their benefactors
and champions, " being thought of to lead their attention
from the disturbed objects with which a diseased mind is
pervaded ; indeed, it struck me that the hospital was much
more like a lock-up house to confine persons in, than an
hospital for the cure of disease."*

Classification was never thought of : criminals, lunatics,
the furious and the gentle were compelled to live promiscu-
ously ; nay, the doctrine was gravely promulgated, that it
ought to be refrained from on principle : the principle being,
so far as I can understand it, to convince one set of lunatics
of their insanity, by exposing before them the fury and
follies of another set. The following quotation may serve as
a commentary on this text : " In one of these rooms I found
four and twenty individuals, lying, some old, some infirm,
one or two dying, some insane, and in the centre of the

* Evidence of Mr. Ed. Wakefield, First Report, 1816.

room was left the corpse of one who died a few hours before."*

If the burden of disease was removed, it was not through the instrumentality of any process instituted for the purpose ; if it remained, and the mind sunk debilitated and worn out under the pressure, no active interference could be blamed for accelerating the event. In many instances there existed an obvious interest and unequivocal design to protract the duration of the disease. The curability of cases at that time depended, in many instances, less on the nature of the derangement, than the amount of board. Accordingly, we find, that where patients were not literally abandoned to their fate, whatever curative measures were adopted, have more the appearance of being obstacles and impediments to the restoration of reason, than of being dictated by common humanity, or common sense. The whole superintendence was committed to keepers, uneducated, coarse in manners, dissolute in morals, often cruel, and always irresponsible. It was their duty to administer, nay more, to prescribe baths, medicines, restraint, punishment. That which they might have done with safety and benefit, and without much in-struction, bathing, they neglected ; that, punishment, which, if resorted to, requires the nicest discrimination and the ealmest judgment to prescribe, and to apportion to the of-fence, and which almost all men now agree can be entirely dispensed with, they inflicted constantly, ignorantly, indis-criminately, and in retaliation. The lash, they conceived, was ever ready, of easy application, and of instantaneous effi-cacy. It is curious, that even the humane Pinel, biassed by the opinions and timidity of his coadjutors, and by the spirit of the age in which he lived, seemed inclined to admit the

* Report, Lunatic Poor in Ireland, p. 15. Evidence of Thomas Rice, Esq.

propriety of trying the " excitement of terror" as a remedy.
You must have heard of individuals being frightened *out* of
their senses ; but will not readily credit the statement, that
attempts have been gravely made to frighten a man *into* his
senses. This was evidently the principle and object of those
who covered the walls of the lunatic's cell with sketches in
phosphorus, of hobgoblins and hideous figures, so that his
eye might be arrested by the glare whenever he awoke. But
in justice to the memory of those who suggested or advocated this practice, I am bound to state, that it is still persevered in, even by men whose motives cannot be suspected,
and who declare that benefit has accrued from the application of what is obviously but a modification of the same
principle. It appears that in the Senavretta at Milan, they
have constructed an apartment, which can be placed in
darkness or light, into which the rain can be made to de-
scend, and around which the thunder can be made to peal
at pleasure.* These sources of terror are directed against
furious mania. I cannot conceive that much benefit should
accrue from such a plan. That insanity has been cured by
means of sudden, and powerful, and sometimes by depressing
impressions produced by external circumstances, may be admitted. But instances of this kind are of rare occurrence,
have generally been accidental, and of so dubious a character, that it is difficult to determine, whether the joy, or sorrow, or other vivid emotion excited, be the *cause* of the subsequent recovery, or merely an indication of returning health
and the last of a series of stages of improvement. If such a
measure succeed in rousing the fear or superstition of the
patient, as it fairly may be expected to do, but fail in removing the disease, it is highly probable that the mind may be
totally unhinged, or so deeply injured, as to sink into fatuity,

* Brierre de Boismont—Annales de Hygiéne, tom. xvi. p. 56.

or to baffle all other treatment. This risk is confessedly so imminent, that even the surprise bath, the mildest and most justifiable mode in which sudden and disagreeable impressions could be communicated, has fallen into disrepute, and has been in many places altogether abandoned. From these statements it is clear, that although this practice may be condemned as hazardous and unphilosophical, it cannot, in every case, be stigmatized as cruel.

That you may not imagine that I have made assertions of the prevalence of corporal punishment rashly, or that I have merely concluded that such a result was likely to follow conduct so irreconcilable with justice and humanity, two brief but striking narratives may be presented to you. A surgeon stated in evidence before a Committee of the House of Commons, that in visiting a private asylum, he saw a keeper beating in a most brutal manner a captain in the navy, who was confined by means of a chain on his legs, and hand-cuffs, so that he could neither escape nor defend himself. Mark the import of the concluding sentence : " He died shortly afterwards." The same keeper beat another patient so violently with a pair of boots that, mark again the consequence, " he died shortly afterwards." Now, I most fervently hope that although death unquestionably followed the infliction of this horrible cruelty, it was rather in the order of time than of causation. Yet what limits can be assigned, or can exist, to passion which would give rise to such an accusation as the following : " I have seen her, a keeper, lock her, a harmless maniac, down in her crib with wrist-locks and leg-locks, and horse-whip her: I have seen the blood follow the strokes."* This occurred in 1812, and was the result neither of indifference nor inhumanity on the part of the conductor of the establishment, but of the vicious system then prevalent, and especially of that most reprehensible part of it, which

---

* First Report of Minutes, &c. 1816, pp. 2, and 84.

consigned the care of the insane to the uneducated and brutal, to deputies and servants whose chief recommendation was a want of delicacy and refinement, and whose only object was aggrandisement.

I would be loath, indeed it would be unfair, to take the following relation, for the truth of which I can vouch, as illustrative of the moral treatment formerly pursued in public institutions. A patient affected with satyriasis was enabled, either from the relaxed state of morality or discipline existing in the asylum in which he was confined, to gratify his desires when he pleased. His gallantries were again and again discovered, and punished by blows and lashes so efficacious, that he was obliged to return to chastity, in order to preserve his life. This fact, although not adduced to prove that a universal corruption of morals pervaded our asylums, does prove two things, first, that the constitution of these was so utterly inefficient, so faulty, that such corruption *might* have existed ; and secondly, that the means taken to correct this corruption, while characteristic of the time and mode of thinking on the subject, were as much worthy the title of moral treatment as the whipping of negroes to promote subordination and industry. But while I have every disposition to avoid establishing the above case as a standard, it cannot be denied that gross immorality of a similar description existed, or rather was sanctioned by the absence of all enlightened management, by the selection of improper keepers, and by that secrecy and irresponsibility which characterised every proceeding within the walls of a madhouse. Thus, for example, a female of unimpeachable character became insane, and exposed, by the nature of her malady, to the designs of all around, whether they aimed at the destruction of her body or of her virtue, fell a victim to the demoniac passion of one of the keepers to whom she was intrusted for protection. In the asylum where this occurred the male servants had keys which admitted them to the sleeping rooms of the female patients.* This is unfortunately not a solitary·instance.†

Some individuals carry their horror of innovation so far as to contemplate with suspicion even .the partial overthrow of the ancient usages of madhouses.   Yet, within the space of a few years, and under the very eyes of these persons, so total was the disregard of decency, that in some institutions every thing was conducted as if there had been no distinction of sex.   Perhaps the sapient rulers of these imagined that the lunatic, in consequence of his or her affliction, lost all knowledge of such distinction, or all the shame, or modesty, or delicacy·which attends such a knowledge.   Be this as it may, the male and female patients were allowed to mingle indiscriminately, and to sleep in the same division of the house : indeed, it is somewhat doubtful that even now a separation has every where been carried into effect, for in 1818 no attempt of this kind had been made at Montpellier.‡ The unscrupulous liberality which saw no impropriety in such an arrangement could scarcely be expected to regulate the tone or scrutinize narrowly the decorum and purity of the intercourse which ensued.   If it be remembered that the beings thus having uninterrupted access to each other were irrational, acting under the impulse of ungovernable passions, and unrestrained, perhaps, by the sacred obligations of religion, and certainly unmindful of the conventional check of public opinion, the extent of the corruption of morals, at all events of the deterioration of manners, must have been appalling.   In an asylum, with the private history of which I am somewhat acquainted, long after parlours and sleeping wards had been provided, a woman continued to sleep in the division of the house appropriated to the men, and to be attended

* First Report from Committee, &c. 1815, p. 2.
† First Report of Minutes, &c. 1816, p. 28.
‡ Dict. des Sciences Méd. art. " Maison d'Aliénés."   First Report of Committee, &c. 1815, p. 46.

by the male keepers at all times and under all circumstances.*
The pretext for conduct so revolting was, that the individual
was so violent and powerful as to be unmanageable by
females. But the pretext was utterly false, and a betrayal
of the ignorance and brutality under which those who dared
to urge it acted. The customs of the present day prove its
falsity and folly. I have examined many thousands of maniacs, but I have yet to see one who could not be governed
or guided by one of her own sex.

Perhaps the most appalling example of negligence on the
part of the proprietors of asylums, I do not affirm which has
occurred, but which has been made public, was detected at
Fonthill in Wiltshire, by the Parliamentary Commissioners.
On opening the cells in which the patients lived, they were
found to be so dirty, and the smell so offensive, as to prevent
further inspection. Disgusting as I feel the task to be, duty
compels me to extract the description of one of the victims of
this savage tyranny:—" He was confined in one of the ob-
long troughs, chained down; he had evidently not been in
the open air for a considerable time, for when I made them
bring him out, the man could not endure the light; he was
like an Albino blinking; and they acknowledged that he had
not. Upon asking him how often he had been allowed to get
out of the trough, he said, ' perhaps once in a week, and
sometimes not for a fortnight.' He was not in the least violent,—he was perfectly calm, and answered the questions
put to him rationally; his breathing was so difficult that I
thought his life likely to be affected by it."† This man was
confined in an unwholesome cell, measuring nine feet by five.
Some idea may be formed of the mental capacity, if not of
the humanity, of the former governors of asylums in this

* Report from Committee, &c. 1815, p. 93, contains a case somewhat similar.

† First Report from Committee, &c., 1815, p. 46. Evidence of Dr.
Richard Fowler.

country, from the statement made by one of them to a Parliamentary Committee, that sleeping cells of 8 feet by 7 are as good as those measuring 10 feet 6 inches by 8.

But it is not merely accusations of unjustifiable confinement, unhealthy cells or arrangements, which threaten life, or deprive it of even physical enjoyment, of which I have to speak; charges are on record of systematic cruelty so extreme, that death was the consequence. The Inquisition never told the names or numbers of those who sunk under its tortures, or died exhausted under the pestilential atmosphere of its dungeons. The policy of certain asylums appears to have been the same. In the report given to the public by the superintendents of the York institution, it at one time appeared that 221 patients had died. On investigation, the actual number was discovered to be 365. What possible motive, or rather, what good motive, could suggest such a falsification ? Or to put the question in a different form : In what way can the deaths of 144 persons thus, for some interested purpose, consigned to oblivion, be explained? But this is not all,—the accusation was more explicit; to quote the words of Mr. Higgins :—" A patient disappears, and is never more heard of; he is said to be removed. A patient is killed, the body is hurried away, to prevent a coroner's inquest."* The human sacrifices of old served as the auguries of succeeding generations, and from the blood of the unfortunate man here alluded to may be traced that generous movement which was made by men of all creeds and parties simultaneously, by all those who acknowledged a sympathy in the sufferings of their fellow-men, for the purpose of destroying every remnant of this judicial torture, this legalised murder, and of extending protection and aid to the most helpless and miserable members of our race. It is not here insinuated that all the individuals whose deaths were con-

* First Report from Committee, &c., 1815, p. 4.

cealed, perished by unfair means, or in any way discreditable
to their ordinary or medical attendants ; but even after making this admission, and after supposing that this investigation
was prompted by malicious motives, of which there is not a
shadow of evidence, will it be believed that grounds could
exist for accusing the responsible officers of a long established
asylum, of such crimes as the following ? First, That patients
were killed by the fury of the keepers, and then reported to
have died ; secondly, That the real amount of mortality was
concealed ; thirdly, That no less than 144 deaths took place,
which were not recorded; fourthly, That in order effectually
to bury these and other malpractices in oblivion, the books
of the establishment were burned, and false registers substituted ; and, lastly, That this attempt failing, the house was
set fire to and nearly consumed, to the imminent danger of
all its miserable inmates, and the destruction of at least
four.* For the honour of our country I would willingly
believe, that these atrocities may have been too deeply
coloured, too strongly stated. The charge, however, was
made by a respectable and benevolent magistrate of the
county where the circumstances are said to have occurred,
and is supported by proofs of so clear and convincing a
kind, that any doubt of the guilt of the parties accused cannot be entertained for a moment.

I have said, that a sweeping charge against all institutions, as scenes of impurity, profligacy, and cruelty, would
be unjust. The indictment is sufficiently grave, if it include
among its counts, total absence of all attempts to secure
moral, or any other treatment, a callous indifference to the
comforts, wants, and reasonable wishes of the patients, and
bigoted perseverance in a system at variance with common
sense and justice.

Experiment has shewn in America, that isolation, com-

* First Report of Committee, &c., 1815. Evidence of Godfrey
Higgins, Esq., *passim.*

plete solitary confinement, reduces the convict to madness. Had it been designed to secure the continuance of this disease in all those afflicted, no better mode could have been devised than that formerly pursued towards lunatics. The vulgar have an opinion, that those keepers and medical men, who have been long associated with lunatics ultimately sink under the same disease. So horrible was the system of which these persons were the agents, or spectators; so distressing the sufferings which they were condemned to witness, or inflict, and so incessant must have been the excitement of their own passions, that this opinion may have been founded in truth. Let us pass a few minutes in an asylum as formerly regulated, and from the impression made by so brief a visit, let us judge of the effects which years, or a life-time spent amid such scenes, was calculated to produce. The building was gloomy, placed in some low, confined situation, without windows to the front, every chink barred and grated—a perfect gaol. As you enter, the creak of bolts, and the clank of chains are scarcely distinguishable amid the wild chorus of shrieks and sobs which issue from every apartment. The passages are narrow, dark, damp, exhale a noxious effluvia, and are provided with a door at every two or three yards. Your conductor has the head and visage of a Charib; carries, fit accompaniment, a whip and a bunch of keys, and speaks in harsh monosyllables. The first common room you examine, measuring twelve feet long, by seven wide, with a window which does not open, is perhaps for females. Ten of them, with no other covering than a rag round the waist, are chained to the wall, loathsome and hideous; but, when addressed, evidently retaining some of the intelligence, and much of the feeling which in other days ennobled their nature.* In shame or sorrow, one of them perhaps utters a cry; a blow which

* Report from Committee, &c., 1815, p. 11.

brings the blood from the temple, the tear from the eye, an additional chain, a gag, an indecent or contemptuous expression, produces silence. And if you ask where these creatures sleep, you are led to a kennel eight feet square, with an unglazed air-hole eight inches in diameter; in this, you are told, five women sleep. The floor is covered, the walls bedaubed with filth and excrement; no bedding but wet decayed straw is allowed, and the stench is so insupportable, that you turn away and hasten from the scene. Each of the sombre colours of this picture is a fact. And those facts are but a fraction of the evils which have been brought home to asylums as they were.

Doubtless, although the result of these proceedings was in every instance inhumanity, they cannot all be traced to sheer, gratuitous cruelty—the Moloch propensity to enjoy suffering. The motives must have been various. There would be the indifference arising from a false hypothesis, from the conclusion, that neither benefit nor injury could accrue from whatever was done ; the ignorant belief that the insane do not and cannot feel the evils heaped upon them ; the timid carefulness to prevent escape, destruction of clothes, &c. ; the careless sacrifice of the interests and comfort of the patient to the temporary accommodation of his attendant ; nay, there might even be, for such folly is possible, an expectation that bolts and bars, terror and stripes, are necessary, and endowed with remedial virtues. The evil of such measures was not, however, the less grave, that the views upon which they were founded, would not have consigned the proposer to the common hangman, or to the milder fate of becoming the companion of his victims. No arraignment, I repeat, is made of the *intentions* of the curators of the insane, but I do arraign the whole *system* of error which they have sanctioned ; I call for a verdict of guilty, and a sentence of total subversion, on the pernicious absurdities which continue to be practised in their name and authority.

LECTURE IV.

WHAT ASYLUMS ARE.

The old system not altogether exploded—Commencement of the present system—Liberation of lunatics at Bicêtre by Pinel—The adoption of enlightened principles partial, but a desire for improvement prevalent—First recognition of humanity and occupation as means of treatment in remote times, in Egypt and Belgium—Present mode of treatment characterized by want of classification, want of employment, want of bodily exercise—Asylums insufficiently heated—Error of supposing lunatics impregnable to cold—Inattention to personal comfort of lunatics—Corporal punishment professedly abandoned; but cruelty in various forms still committed—Patients confined to bed to accommodate servants—Inadequate number of keepers—Coercion as a means of cure, of protection—Character and qualifications of attendants on Insane—Evils of indiscriminate association of insane—No wards for convalescents exist—Grounds for separating lunatics—Erroneous views of moral treatment—Night visits—Mental anxiety and disturbance produced by the oppressive, harsh, indelicate or derisive conduct of keepers—Substitution of convalescent patients for keepers—Important duties imposed on this class of servants—Difficulty of procuring well-educated persons to undertake such responsibility—Exclusion, desertion of friends of lunatics—Asylums ill-adapted for reception of rich—Luxurious diet—Indiscriminate diet—Solitary meals—Prejudices of public present obstacles to improvement—Examples—How are these to be removed?

GREAT improvements have, undoubtedly, been effected in the internal economy of asylums. This result has proceeded partly from selfish motives, partly from the prevalence of sounder views of the nature and treatment of mental disease, and chiefly, so far as the metropolitan establishments are concerned, from the dread of Parliamentary investigations, and the surveillance and remonstrances of the medical commissioners. But that we have not altogether escaped from the evils characteristic of what asylums were, appears from the fact that, so recently as 1828, the Lunatic Hospital at Vienna was, according to Burrows, a disgrace to that capital and to the era of the nineteenth century; and from the following recital, which inpinges more closely on our national honour: " In a close room," says Dr. Bright, " in the yard two men were shut by an external bolt, and the room was remarkably close and offensive. In an outhouse at the bottom of the yard, ventilated only by cracks in the wall, were enclosed three females—the door was padlocked; upon an open rail-bottomed crib herein, without straw, was chained a female by the wrists, arms, and legs, and fixed also by chains to the crib—her wrists were blistered by the handcuffs: she was covered only by a rug. The only attendant upon all the lunatics appeared to be one female servant, who stated she was helped by the patients." " The windows of the bedrooms in which the patients pass the night without any attendants, are not defended by bars, and the only entrance to the men's bedroom is through that occupied by the women; the commissioners went up a staircase said to be stopt, and found at the end of it a ruinous room prepared with staples for the confinement of any violent patient, &c., —an establishment which the commissioners regret they have not the power to suppress."* Glad, however, to escape from the disgraceful details which occupied the preceding Lecture, my present purpose is to describe what is peculiar, and especially what is objectionable, in the existing arrangements, omitting, as much as possible, every thing that appears to be and ought to be more characteristic of the system which has been unanimously condemned, than of that benevolent and rational policy which is now pursued.

* Report, Pauper Lunatics in Middlesex, &c. 1827, pp. 156-7.

Exaggerations have unquestionably crept in, and become amalgamated with the rigid bare truth of many of the statements which have been advanced, both as to the past and present condition of the insane. But has the apocryphal no parallel in the accredited history ? Ignorance,—ignorance alike of all that could and of all that did befall within an asylum lent its aid. Fear, inspired by the unlimited and irresponsible power either conferred by the law, or exercised in defiance of the law by interested friends : inspired by the jealous secrecy of every proceeding which took place subsequent to incarceration, by the little that was disclosed, or rather that could not be concealed, of the mysteries of the prison-house, tended powerfully to aggravate the suggestions of that ignorance. And superstition entered as an ingredient into the compound feeling of awe and detestation with which all that related to the treatment of the insane was regarded and interpreted. A similar combination of ill-directed curiosity and suspicion has converted the apothecary's shop into a den of mercenary murder, and the medicine there vended into the exuviæ, the pharmaceutically disguised relics of humanity.

The cry of the lunatic uttered in the exuberance of his own self-inflicted anguish, or while writhing under the terrors of some self-created misfortune, may often have been construed into expressions of bodily pain proceeding from castigation, or from some other device of that gratuitous cruelty which takes a delight in suffering. In like manner, as many lunatics, the cunning and suspicious for example, are as capable of telling, and are as much disposed to tell, falsehoods as their more responsible fellow-men, and as they are certainly more strongly tempted to make out as favourable a case in their own behalf as possible, many of the complaints of hard usage, of stripes, and chains, and starvation, which have reached and been received by the world, merit no other title than that of sheer fabrications. But after

ample allowance has been made for such cases, after deducting for the credulity of mankind, and for the fictions which
an occasional discovery of actual inhumanity might give
rise to, the question still remains to be answered, is there
any case which ignorance, or fear, or superstition has conjured up or blackened with their own sombre colouring,
one-half so gross and revolting as those which have been
proved by evidence which cannot be disputed ? Is there any
fiction, cunningly devised in the mind of the insane prisoner
panting for liberation, at all to be compared with those facts
which have been seen and recorded by men who had no
motive but mercy, no objects in view but justice ?

An affecting picture has been drawn of the exhumation,—
it deserves no other name, of the prisoners from the Bastile,
and of the liberation of the condemned from the Abbaye on
the death of Robespiérre. But the moral interest of these
events is equalled by the scene which signalized the appointment of Pinel as physician to Bicêtre. The gaols used to be
thrown open on the accession of a new sovereign ; the assumption of office by this friend to human nature was attended by
a similar triumph. It was a jubilee initiative of the reign of
mercy. Eighty lunatics who had long been galled by chains
were set at liberty. And it is mentioned that the very act
of liberation, affecting the mind as other powerful impressions, restored many of them to tranquillity, if not to sanity.
" The first man on whom the experiment was to be tried,"
says the narrator of the scene, " was an English captain,
whose history no one knows, as he had been in chains forty
years. He was thought to be one of the most furious
amongst them ; his keepers approached him with caution, as
he had in a fit of fury killed one of them on the spot with a
blow from his manacles. He was chained more rigorously
than any of the others. Pinel entered his cell unattended,
and calmly said to him, ' Captain, I will order your chains
to be taken off, and give you liberty to walk in the court, if

you will promise me to behave well and injure no one.'
' Yes,' I promise you,' said the maniac ; ' but you are laugh-
ing at me ; you are all too much afraid of me.'   ' I have six
men,' answered Pinel, ' ready to enforce my commands if
necessary.   Believe me then, on my word, I will give you
your liberty if you will put on this waistcoat.'   He submitted
to this willingly, without a word ; his chains were removed,
and the keepers retired, leaving the door of his cell open.
He raised himself many times from his seat, but fell again
on it, for he had been in a sitting posture so long that he had
lost the use of his legs ; in a quarter of an hour he succeeded
in maintaining his balance, and with tottering steps came to
the door of his dark cell.   His first look was at the sky, and
he cried out enthusiastically, ' How beautiful !'   During the
rest of the day he was constantly in motion, walking up and
down the stair-cases, and uttering short exclamations of delight.   In the evening he returned of his own accord into his
cell, where a better bed than he had been accustomed to had
been prepared for him, and he slept tranquilly.   During the
two succeeding years which he spent in the Bicêtre, he had
no return of his previous paroxysms, but even rendered
himself useful by exercising a kind of authority over the insane patients whom he ruled in his own fashion."*

From this period, 1792, may be dated a total revolution
in the opinions of medical men and legislators, respecting
the insane, and in the principles upon which houses of detention are professed to be conducted.   The application of
these views has been tardy ; but, from aiming merely at safe
custody, the ambition of the humane and philosophic, at
least, has extended to the employment of means which promise to restore a proportion of those confined, to their places
and duties in society, and to reconcile the remainder to their
captivity.   From a blind and hard-hearted policy, which

* The British and Foreign Medical Review, No. I. p. 286.   Traité
Complet du Régime Sanitaire des Aliénés, p. 57.

embraced only the prevention of one evil by the infliction
of another, and which, to accomplish this end—amounting
in plain terms, to nothing more than the preservation of the
public peace—sacrificed every tie of justice, charity, and
human fellowship; a sudden transition was made to a system, professing to be based on a knowledge of the human
mind, and on the common sympathies of our nature, and
to have for its object the eradication, or if that appeared
Utopian, the amelioration of the evil. From darkness they
passed into light—from savage ferocity into Christian benevolence. These terms are energetic; but the change which
they commemorate was so momentous, as to deserve to be
so characterized. Yet no one must conclude that the views
from which it proceeded, or the consequences to which it
led, either realized what subsequent experience has proved
to be sound and necessary, or completely harmonized with
what judgment and conscientiousness would dictate. The
promised land was in sight; it was not reached. Vast and
manifest improvements even now require to be made on the
very soil of which Pinel was the cultivator; and although a
kindred spirit has succeeded to rear if not to reap the har-
vest, many years must roll on, and many changes intervene,
before it arrive at maturity. Unfortunately, every country
has not possessed a Pinel. The impulse of the reformation
which he began has been felt, it is true, less or more, in
every civilized country; but it has succeeded at certain
points only, in shaking the strongholds of prejudice and
ignorance. The change is still one of degree; for no where
has it been radical and complete. Even in those favoured
spots where the greatest care, and the greatest treasure have
been lavished, there exist organic evils, which nothing but
a more extended acquaintance with the moral constitution
of man can remedy. It will not readily be believed, that
in the country which has produced such men as Guislain, a
man, supposed to be labouring under hydrophobia, should

be confined for two days in a cell, without assistance or treatment, and ultimately should be allowed, in the presence of the whole medical staff of the hospital, to beat out his brains by running against the stove apparently urged to such a desperate act, rather by the mania of fear, than by the agonies of canine madness. It may be said that the cause of the lunatic has been eloquently pleaded at the bar of public opinion, but that the court has not yet pronounced judgment.

There is this characteristic feature in the present condition of asylums :—Those to whose care they are entrusted, are completely aware of the errors formerly committed, and of the grievous injustice which they or their predecessors may have been unwittingly perpetrating. Universally a decided change is contemplated and desired, and the din of preparation is heard wherever isolation is attempted. Good must accrue from the opinions that prevail ; and the only ground for apprehension which exists, is, that from the want of a just estimate of the healthy and diseased states of the mind, all the good may not be secured which in other circumstances would be perfectly practicable. For example, in many modern institutions, where every anxiety is displayed to promote the happiness and comfort of the inmates, the same plan of moral treatment, the same enjoyments, the same diet, are prescribed for all indiscriminately. It would be as rational to treat common cold and consumption by the same means, because they both attack the same organ. The intention in this instance, is unquestionably to produce pleasure ; but it is benevolence acting without the guidance of reason, which, for a momentary gratification, forfeits the chances of recovery. Notwithstanding this, and many similar inconsistencies and errors, which future philosophers will perceive and correct, the movement which commenced at the era alluded to, has produced incalculable benefit, and tends towards still greater improvement.

The present system is imperfect, and falls short of a standard which is evidently attainable, chiefly because it is not founded on, or regulated by any broad or practical philosophical principle. Glimpses of truth occasionally break in upon the minds of those who are the guardians of the lunatic, and changes are effected in accordance with the discovery. But no grand attempt has been made to place every part of the treatment in harmony with his condition. We must not quarrel, however, with great ameliorations, although they flow from sources less exalted than what the sanguine might desire.

Two of the earliest and most striking departures from the time-sanctified system of force, are to be traced to the substitution of a system of imposture. So much evil has been inflicted on man by superstition, that it is difficult to suppose it contributing to his happiness. The same principle which struggles to keep the mind in ignorance, seems, in these instances, to have desired to keep it in peace, and to restore to it intelligence. The first example of the compatibility of these objects is found in Egypt, where the most enlightened views of modern science are recorded to have been engrafted upon the darkest and most degrading forms of ancient superstition. The temples dedicated to Saturn were literally asylums of the best description. The intention of the priest was to enhance the popularity of the deity of whom he was the servant; and his mode of effecting this was founded upon a profound insight into the mechanism of the being he designed to repair. He knew the boundless credulity of his patients; and to gratify this feeling, while he used it as a powerful agent in giving efficacy to all subsequent treatment, he declared that the cure about to be performed was miraculous, and by the direct intervention of his tutelar god. Having established this belief, recourse was next had to all those means which a knowledge of mind has shewn to be most conducive to restore its original tone

and strength. Every new moral prescription was not, however, exhibited as a medicine, but as a formula of worship,
revealed by the benevolent member of the polytheism who
directed his energies to renovate the melancholic and the madman. Under this guise, the crowds which frequented these
shrines were engaged in every healthful and amusing exercise ; they were required to walk in the beautiful gardens
which surrounded the temples, or to row on the majestic
Nile. Delightful excursions were planned for them under
the plea of pilgrimages. Dances, concerts, and comic representations, occupied a part of the day, as constituting
the symbolical worship of some divinity. In short, a series
of powerful, yet pleasing impressions were communicated at
a time, and under circumstances, when the feelings were inspired with the most extravagant hope, and with perfect reliance
upon the power whose pity every act was intended to pro-
pitiate. The priests triumphed, and deserved to triumph.
The disease was subdued, and their reputation rose in proportion. We cannot determine whether they trusted chiefly
to the mere will of Saturn, or to the discipline he had the
credit of suggesting ; or whether they believed at all in the
delusion which they propagated ; nor is it material to know.
The simple fact of the employment of such means is sufficient to shew that exercise, occupation, and feelings of
enjoyment, were considered essentially contributive to the
efficacy of the miraculous interposition, if such was believed
to exist.*

The second example is drawn from a more recent period,
and is even more open to the suspicion of deception. The
village of Gheel, now attached to the asylum in Antwerp,
has long been celebrated as a retreat for lunatics. The
patients are boarded with the peasants, who employ them
in their gardens or fields. When unengaged, they are

* Voisin, Des Causes Morales et Physiques des Maladies Mentales,
p. 411.

permitted to roam about at perfect liberty, and neither accidents nor escapes are ever heard of. The labour is compulsory, but is regulated according to the strength and condition of the workman. The benefits which generally accrue from air, exercise, and occupation, are considered as of little avail in removing the disease, unless the patients regularly once a-day pass under the tomb of a certain St. Dymph, to whose sanctity, relics, and good offices, the restoration is solely attributable.* The ashes of this holy personage constitute the riches of the place. The physicians of Belgium may be sceptical of the virtue of these relics, but they appear still to avail themselves of the respect and confidence with which they are regarded by the lower orders. Such a combination of work and penance is admirably suited to the character of a people in whom the religious are the predominating feelings, and with whose most ordinary and trivial transactions the ritual of the Romish church is constantly interwoven. The cause which produced these changes in a remote age, has led to the improvements which we claim as peculiar to the present.

From the absence of any common design in the alterations which have taken place in the mode of conducting asylums, and from the want of similarity in the alterations themselves, no description can be attempted which would prove generally applicable; so that my remarks must be classified into statements of the excellencies and of the evils which attach to the present condition of such establishments, particularizing such countries or individual asylums as afford illustrations of the one or of the other, but excluding from the investigation those cases in which a maximum degree of improvement has been attained, as properly belonging to the view of what asylums ought to be.

Much of the present system may be described by nega-

* Dict. des Sciences Méd. Carter, Short Account of Principal Hospitals, &c. p. 191.

tives. There is no classification, no employment, no exercise. If you pass through an establishment, all may be tranquil, orderly, and humane, but the inmates are lethargically slumbering on chairs, or endeavouring to devise occupation by tormenting their fellows, or circumventing their keeper. Men have been proved to have remained seated in the same spot, during the day, for a dozen years, without an attempt being made to rouse their muscular or mental energies. This species of negligence is often presented in a more hideous form. Patients who at first are perfectly able to walk, are allowed to remain in bed; their limbs waste, contract, are partially anchylosed, and they ultimately become unable to rise. A contagious disease broke out in a small asylum; one-half of the patients died; the bodies having been carried to a public hospital, were inspected. In doing this, numbers were found to have contracted limbs—a deformity which was traced to the practice to which I have alluded; the position being, in all probability, originally assumed and retained in order to obtain as great a degree of warmth as possible.

Where peculation no longer exists, and where the lunatic is comfortably lodged and sufficiently clothed, there is still great inattention to the mode in which the building where he sleeps is heated. In winter he is compelled to pass, as if in imitation of a Russian bath, from the temperature of a crowded and probably over-heated common hall, to that of a damp cell which has been cooled down by the indispensable process of ventilation, to the freezing point. The cruel fallacy that lunatics are insensible to cold and to other modifications of pain, has long been acted upon. This error is countenanced by three circumstances. First, In cases of acute mania, from the state of the circulation there actually is much heat developed at the surface; secondly, In another class of cases there does exist a degree of insensibility to external circumstances; and, thirdly, Lunatics rarely tell their sufferings. But in these as in all other cases the depressing influence of cold must and does produce its usual consequences.

Although we have passed the period when cruelty was avowed and defended, if not actually prescribed, the spirit characteristic of that period has, in some cases, been perpetuated by avarice. Acts of oppression have been perpetrated in defiance of a parliamentary commission, expressly appointed to detect and report such offences, which are worthy of a darker age. One of these will suffice. In 1820, the Commissioners found a patient in a private institution alone in an out-house, without a fire—the visit was paid in winter —the windows were broken, probably by his own act. He was without shoes, but was in other respects sufficiently clothed. After much prevarication and deception, it was proved that this patient did not sleep in the apartment said to be his, but in a miserable room up a private stair, concealed by a door, which was discovered with considerable difficulty. It was a single room, small and offensive, containing only a wet and dirty piece of sacking filled with straw, with one rug and a blanket. For this treatment the patient paid L.50 per annum.*

One great revolution has been consummated, as a concession to public opinion ; slowly and reluctantly, but universally : one which every man can appreciate and applaud who has a spark of benevolence in his composition, and whether he understands the detrimental tendency of the former practice or not. Corporeal punishment has been professedly abandoned. The lash is not openly seen, or recommended as a medical instrument. That no cruelty is inflicted under the ridiculous name of punishment, or the more specious pretext of preserving order, it would be vain to expect ; but the infliction is no longer acknowledged. The perpetrators

* Report, Pauper Lunatics in Middlesex, p. 158, 1827.

H

shrink from, repudiate and conceal those deeds, in which a
few years back, if they did not absolutely glory, they at least
perceived no evil. The first object, then, is gained ; cruelty
is denounced as iniquitous and unnecessary. The next step
is to shew that it is inconsistent with the personal interest of
those who are empowered to care for and cure the insane.
Were men generally actuated by pure and exalted motives,
it would be superfluous to advance further than an exposition of the anti-christian spirit of the system : but seeing
that they are not so actuated, the conviction must be impressed upon their minds, that it is inefficacious in eradica-
ting or alleviating mental disease, and that it is inimical,
even fatal, to the reputation of all institutions where it is
supposed to be resorted to. That acts of cruelty are still
committed does not admit of doubt. They are less frequent
and less severe, but they have not ceased. But although
physical suffering be no longer inflicted, or inflicted to the
same extent, there are other species of harshness, nay, of
positive inhumanity, as repugnant to common sense and
common benevolence. Coercion is employed unnecessarily.
Either from the savage philosophy of terrifying into obedience, and, it is to be presumed, into the possession of reason, or from the despicable economy of employing a small
corps of keepers ; chains, muffs, manacles, are in many places
the substitutes for mildness and prudence, or suitable attendance. Not only the violent and the destructive but the
perverse, even the restless and noisy maniac must be secured,
I presume for the preservation of order; but that the keeper
may have more time to dispose of for his own amusement,
the same horrible practice is adopted. In fact, that he may
have freedom, they must be deprived of it. " I once," says
Tuke, " visited a house for insane persons, in which security
was a *primary* object. Here I saw three of the keepers, in
the middle of the day earnestly employed in—playing cards."*

* Description of the Retreat at York, &c., p. 107.

A refinement upon the old mode of economizing the labours of keepers has been brought to light by the investigations of the Commissioners.. The patients were compelled to remain in bed, or, as the terms of the justification run, were allowed to remain in bed during the whole of Sunday, in order that the servants of the establishment might visit their friends.* It is possible that the wishes of the patients themselves suggested this practice; but the gratifications of such desires would convert every day into one of rest and sleep, and sacrifice the interests of ultimate restoration to lethargy or whim. One of the excuses for resorting to such expedients, and for keeping a number of miserable creatures in chains, darkness, and filth, for thirty-six hours, was the small number of keepers employed. The reason was, in one point of view, valid. Servants so engaged are often timid, although otherwise well-disposed, and seek for protection: or they become depressed and gloomy, contaminated by the atmosphere in which they move, and seek for intervals of liberty as a relief. And unless actuated by a high sense of duty, they will not hesitate to obtain these objects, if the attainment does not lead to a glaring dereliction of duty. They, more than any other class of servants, undoubtedly require periods of relaxation; and the way to remove all temptation to obtain these by compromising the interests of the patients, is to have a large body employed. It appears that in one instance three keepers were expected to guide, govern and soothe 250 patients. In another asylum, 164 patients were intrusted to two keepers. In a third, each servant was appointed to take charge of 50 patients. The proportion usually is one keeper for 30 lunatics. This means that one man or woman is to attend to all the wants and wishes, regulate the employments and amusements, counsel, tranquillize, walk and converse with, feed, clothe, and put to bed thirty persons, every

* Report, Pauper Lunatics in Middlesex, &c., pp. 22, 30, 37, 90, 169, &c. 1837.

one of whom displays a different form of insanity, is furious
or fatuous, malicious or melancholy. The proposal is altogether preposterous. Formerly every female keeper in
Bethlem had sixty patients under her care. This state of
things is strongly contrasted with the law on the subject in
France, which accords one keeper for every ten lunatics.

To return to the subject of restraint. That there are some
lunatics so completely stript of the attributes of intelligence
and moral feeling, as neither to perceive nor to suffer from
the galling thongs with which they are bound, is true. Such
are the fatuous and imbecile, in whom every power more
elevated than the impressions of hunger and thirst is obliterated, and where no restraint is demanded. But such cases,
even when including those of furious maniacs, who are so
pre-occupied by some engrossing emotion as to be insensible
to every external circumstance, are rare, when compared
with the numbers of timid maniacs whose energies are for
ever paralyzed ; of irascible maniacs whose feelings of anger
and opposition are roused to a whirlwind of passion ; and of
proud maniacs, whose innocent arrogance is needlessly
wounded by the badges of moral slavery. There is now no
ground for retaining this practice as a means of cure. As a
source of protection it is sometimes indispensable : on all
other pretexts it is cruel and oppressive. Even when unavoidable it may be deprived of some of its horrors : the
appearance of force may be concealed : the apparatus may
be of the least repulsive description, and for bodily coercion,
confinement to a private room, classification, or permanent
isolation may be substituted. The best and most humane
judge of the mutual rights and relations of madmen and
their keepers, Esquirol, has said that the only estimate which
can be formed of the character of a house of detention, must
be founded on the number of individuals actually coerced.
And this estimate applies not merely to the general gentleness, but to the efficacy of the treatment pursued. But

although coercion is less resorted to, the adoption of the opposite method is slow, reluctant and partial. Not many years have elapsed since in one hall of an asylum, of very recent erection, not fewer than eighteen out of twenty-seven male patients were chained, muffed, or strapped to their seats. A keeper, when first intrusted with these men, was cautioned that his life would not be safe for an instant unless he adhered to the plan then existing. A brighter destiny has dawned upon these unfortunate beings. In the very same hall, containing the same number of persons and many of the same individuals, there is not now more than one requiring restraint.

The mere conviction that surveillance exists, that they are watched and distrusted, is sufficiently painful to the self-respect and sense of honour which many lunatics cherish, without the degradation,—for to minds so constituted it must appear degradation,—of personal thraldom. When violence or disobedience is displayed, it is never supposed that there are any other modes of controlling these than by brute force. A common axiom inculcates, that to obtain confidence it is necessary to confide. But all common axioms are set at nought in an asylum. No effort is made to act upon the sentiments of probity, or love of approbation, which are as strong, *cet. par.* in the insane as in the sane mind ; and what might be obtained by a promise, by an appeal to honour, or by some well-chosen expression of admiration, is extorted by a command or a chain.

The frequency with which restraint is even justifiably imposed, depends, in a great measure, upon the immediate attendants of the insane. And, unfortunately, this tremendous power is too often confided to men altogether unworthy of the trust. The labours of such a situation are great, varied, and of the most delicate nature. They are not, or ought not to be limited to the administration of food, attention to cleanliness, or the prevention of escape, but should

extend to the task of arousing and engaging such of the
faculties of the patients as still remain healthy, of amusing
or occupying all who are susceptible of such impressions—
of soothing the irritable and captious—of inspiring the desponding with hope—of presenting to all, such objects as are
calculated to communicate present enjoyment, and to restore the current of thought to its ordinary channels. Such
ministrations comprise a moral treatment of the most extended and exquisite form.   Yet to carry this into execution,
to set this complicated machinery in motion, who are the
persons, and what their standing and acquirements who are
employed ?   Do they possess natural talents or education
sufficient to perceive and to adapt their own behaviour to
the dispositions of those whom they are appointed to attend ?
Have they any knowledge of the human mind in its strength
or in its decay ; or are they even instructed in the routine
of duties which devolve upon those who have to superintend
the personal comforts of twenty or thirty men ?   Are they
in general distinguished for patience, kindness, or those
conciliating manners which secure the affections, and through
them the obedience or friendly co-operation of all who come
within their influence.   To not one of these qualifications
has the great majority of servants in asylums the slightest
pretension.   To shew the ideas entertained by such person-
ages of insanity, one fact may suffice.   The superintendent of
a public asylum, on paying his forenoon visit, found one of the
patients, and one subject to frequent fits of excitement, poised
upon his head.   The keeper was seated by the fire, reading ;
and on being questioned as to the meaning of the scene, re-
plied, " O, Mr. D. is perfectly quiet ; he has been standing
on his head for the last half hour !"   From the lowness of
the wages, and the difficult and sometimes dangerous duties
exacted, such servants are often of the very worst caste ; I
mean, of course, the worst adapted for such an office.   They
are hired for the express purpose of acting as spies or watch-

men, and they aspire to no higher sphere of utility. Coarse
and uneducated, their presence is offensive to all individuals,
either of polished mind or manners, or who have been accustomed to attendants of a better grade; and their society
can be of no use, even if it be agreeable, to those who might
be soothed by compassion and affability, or improved by
intercourse with a person who could understand, and could
direct to better objects, the distempered fancies under which
they labour. Keepers are the unemployed of other professions. If they possess physical strength, and a tolerable
reputation for sobriety, it is enough; and the latter quality
is frequently dispensed with. They enter upon their duties
altogether ignorant of what insanity is, fully impressed with
the idea that the creatures committed to their charge are no
longer men, that they are incapable of reasoning or feeling,
and that in order to rule or manage, it is necessary to terrify
and coerce them. They may not be devoid of good temper, or
active kindness; but from their inability to employ these
agents, and often from a belief that it is contrary to rule to
employ them, they will be found to punish, domineer, and
restrain, to the same degree as if actually cruel and tyrannical. The physician who has trained his powers for a life
time, in penetrating into the depths of the diseased mind,
and who, with all the assistance derived from such experience, from the views and observations of others, and from
the tranquillity and benevolence of manner which he has
learned to assume, should it not originally be his own;
often—how often, let the candid say—fails signally in de-
tecting the prevailing sentiments, in pacifying, in bending
to or from a certain purpose, in rendering happy. Yet, in
modern asylums, a similar course devolves upon the class of
persons of whom we have spoken; and who, if they do not
shrink from the responsibility which they incur, ought to
pursue it unflinchingly and unceasingly. From the individuals who, at present, occupy such situations, it would be

absurd to expect any co-operation of this kind. Until mankind perceive that it is as necessary that he who undertakes
to assist in improving the condition of the insane, should be
instructed in the mode of doing so, as he who professes to
improve the condition of the soil—all that can be expected
is a capability of securing the affections of the patients, and
a docility in promoting the plans suggested by others.
" Your first attempt," I was once told, " ought to be to cure
your keepers ; you need not proceed to your patients until
you have done so." Apart from the necessity of preserving
order, there is a necessity for the presence of a number of
this class of servants, arising out of the obvious evil of confining a lunatic among lunatics. This evil, which is, of
course, unavoidable, may be materially mitigated, first, by
the introduction of keepers of strong, healthy, well-constituted minds : secondly, by possessing ample means of
classification ; and, thirdly, by the exercise of sound discretion in the selection of those who are to associate together.
The disposition, rather than the rate of board, should be the
principle of this choice. The magnitude of the error committed, in banding together a crowd of lunatics in the same
hall, without any reference to the extent or form of their
malady, may be gathered from the feelings of horror and
distraction excited in a perfectly unimpaired mind, on coming into abrupt contact with the heterogeneous inmates of an
asylum ; or it may be more strikingly illustrated by the
pernicious consequences arising from the indiscriminate
intercourse permitted in prisons. How can the already
insecure and tottering intellect fail to be shaken by the
ribaldries, the ravings, the delusions which assail it from all
sides ?   Or how can healthy impressions be received in such
an infected region ? Besides the constant excitement, the
trepidation, the sentiment of disgrace or disgust which must
be produced, positively new delusions may be suggested by
this intercommunion, and so successfully engrafted, as to

supplant those originally characteristic of the disease. An example of this was recently under my care. A woman believed herself to be our Saviour; and so excellent a proselytizer was she, that she completely convinced one of her fellow-patients of the truth of her pretensions, and so far staggered another by relations of miracles, visions, and so forth, as to induce her, occasionally, to acknowledge the divinity claimed. Intercourse with. healthy minds is, in fact, indispensable; and at such stages of the disease as permit of the experiment, the greater the extent to which it is tried the better. The visits even of strangers is often beneficial, by interrupting the chain of morbid fancies, by arousing feelings long dead or dormant, and by re-establishing that bond of connection with the external world and its affairs, which lunatics often conceive, and often conceive with reason, is dissevered. Were a regular system, founded on such views, instituted and carried into operation by persons properly qualified, the benefit might be expected to be great and permanent. A practice somewhat similar to that here recommended, at one time received the sanction of the directors of the Retreat at York, but it does not appear to have been pursued to its legitimate extent.* Indeed, with its full application the timidity and prejudices of the public, from whom, under such circumstances, must arise the voluntary moral physicians, will, for a long period, it is to be feared, interfere with such outpourings of humanity, or direct them into channels widely different. Various expedients may be had recourse to in order to supply the deficiency. One of these is to take advantage of the different forms and degrees of alienation, and to employ him who is gentle and good-tempered to take charge of him who is habitually irritable and unruly, or to induce the partially insane, he who is irrational *ten* degrees, to associate with, and teach him who

* Tuke. Description of the Retreat, &c.

is irrational *twenty* degrees.   I have been informed that this
principle is acted upon in the excellent asylum at Perth. To
apply such a plan upon a grand scale would require great
delicacy in the analysis of character : but if this be stated as
an objection it equally attacks the very foundation of mental
medicine.

If it be true that the lunatic at the incursion of the disease
may be injured, his cure retarded or prevented, by injudiciously consigning him to the society of those whose deportment
must disturb or confuse, it will still less admit of question that
at the period of convalescence, the same danger must exist
and be felt in tenfold measure. The ease with which relapses
may be induced, the trifles which induce them are known to
all : but the knowledge has but in few instances led to any
provision by which the exciting causes, existing in hospitals,
may be removed.   No separation takes place of those who
are recovering from those who are lapsing, or have already
fallen into a state of confirmed insanity. Even subsequent to
the complete restoration to health, and during the interval of
probation, which is generally allowed to elapse between that
period and the dismissal of the patient, no new arrangement
is made. No one perceives the cruelty of thus compelling the
sane to mingle with, and to run all the risks of mingling with,
the insane. We remove the man recovering from fever from
the effects of the presence of individuals similarly affected,
and assist the progress of his convalescence by a change of
scene or society, cheerful occupations and moderate exercise;
but no such indulgence, no such precautions against a renewal
of the disease is extended to the lunatic ; he is left exposed
to the same influence as before. In France convalescent
wards exist in almost every asylum, and in our own country
the propriety of such an arrangement is generally admitted.
Where any efforts have been made to group lunatics together,
the principle adopted, that is the classification into noisy,
tranquil and convalescent, is too vague and too contracted.

It is not even enough that the idle shall be separated from the industrious, that the depressed and desponding be protected from the riotous bacchanal, the tyrannical and the deceitful. The slightest differences of disposition, and sympathies in pursuit or taste must be taken advantage of, and made the basis of separation and association. Dr. Abercrombie quotes a case from Pinel, exhibiting the evils of ignorance or negligence of such indications of treatment. A musician, confined at Bicêtre, as one of the first symptoms of returning reason, made some slight allusion to his favourite instrument. It was immediately procured for him : he occupied himself with music for several hours every day and his convalescence seemed to be advancing rapidly; but unfortunately he was then allowed to come frequently into contact with a furious maniac, by meeting him in the gardens. The musician's mind was unhinged—his violin was destroyed, and he fell back into a state of insanity which was considered as confirmed and hopeless.* Had his companions been selected from musicians, or those who delight in music, or even from the calm and amiable, his reason might have been saved.

There are certain glaring incompatabilities of character among lunatics which must strike, and ought to guide, the least observant physician in his practice.

1. Some lunatics enjoy a quarrel; one as a promoter, another as a spectator, a third as a participator.

2. The language of one is a mixed jargon of oaths, blasphemies and maledictions : the distempered fancy of another receives these as oracles from Heaven.

3. An oppressor soon discovers a slave; a sovereign, a subject; a fanatic, some self-deified maniac to worship.

4. The confiding are betrayed by the falsehoods and chicanery of the cunning : the timid are terrified by brutality and arrogance; the unsuspecting and unprotected are cheated and plundered.

* Inquiries concerning the Intellectual Powers, &c. p. 353.

All recent writers on insanity have spoken loudly in praise
of moral treatment. But they have spoken vaguely of its
nature. Each of them attaches a different meaning to the
word. Employment is the panacea of one ; amusement is
the specific of another; classification is advocated by a third.
Now, were every lunatic busily engaged in a suitable occupation : were recreations adapted to the dispositions or
previous predilections of all provided : was classification, even
on the broad basis which I would assign, universally adopted;
moral treatment, if confined to one or all of these, excellent
though they be, would be imperfect and comparatively inef-
ficatious. The authors to whom I have alluded have mistaken
parts, unexceptionable, it is true, but still merely parts of the
system for the whole. Every arrangement, beyond these for
the regulation of the animal functions, from the situation, the
architecture and furniture of the buildings intended for the
insane to the direct appeals made to the affections by means
of kindness, discipline, and social intercourse, ought to be
embraced by an effective system of moral treatment. Even
many of the details which affect personal comfort alone are
of greater importance, as moral, than as physical agents.
The denial of an article of dress, or an unanswered bell, has
produced a paroxysm of fury. It is not prudent nor conducive
to health to comply invariably with the frivolous demands or
unreasonable desires of lunatics ; neither is it prudent, nor
will it conduce to health, to act invariably upon the principle
of resisting these demands and desires, because they are
frivolous and unreasonable. Both of these errors are detectable in the existing system. The resistance or compliance
should be regulated not by the nature of the demand but by
the state of mind of the individual by whom it is urged.
Great use may be made of self-created wants. The partiality
for a piece of dress, or a cup of tea, is often found to be a
more powerful lever in acting upon the intractable, than sage
counsel or religious impressions. The rule formerly was,

and I suspect still is, to render an asylum as unlike the home
of which the patients had been deprived as possible. In
application, this was a partial and one-sided rule, however
specious and judicious it may appear. If the patient's home,
for instance, had been miserable, no attempt was seriously
and systematically made to reconcile him to the change by
increasing his comfort and happiness. The grand object was,
and perhaps is, to multiply impressions which would inspire
awe, submission, quiet, a wish to conceal, if not to correct,
the sallies of inordinate passion or misdirected intellect, and an
anxiety to escape from such restraint. This might be calculated to subdue the refractory and to weary out the perverse.
But while, in all probability, it would fail to cure even these,
what must its effects have been on the much more numerous
classes, the desponding, the suspicious, the timid, the vain?
Placing out of consideration the pernicious influence of such
a plan in relation to the particular feelings diseased, it obviously and unnecessarily diminishes the amount of enjoyment
in which persons so affected, could, without injury, participate.

In a bill recently submitted to Parliament as to the regulation of asylums, it was proposed to invest the commissioners,
to be appointed under it, with the power of visiting all houses
of the kind during the night.*   The proposal was, I believe,
negatived in consequence of the almost unanimous opposition of the medical men consulted on the subject: but it
indicates two things,—First, a total want of confidence in
the probity and competency of the managers of such institutions, and upon this ground it was approved of by some
medical men ; and, secondly, as total a want of knowledge
of the interests of the insane on the part of the legislator.
Such visits might disclose some of the evils which it is desir-

* Minutes of Evidence taken before the Select Committee, 1828,
passim.

able were corrected, but it would undo all that which quiet
and care had effected, by rousing every inmate to fear or
fury, and thus realizing the delusions which sleep so often
weakens or eradicates.

There exist a class of injuries connected with that discussed
above, which are as cruel and destructive of peace as the
laceration of the lash, or the deep degrading ulcer excavated
by the fetter, but which no medical or other commission,
however probing and penetrating its inquiries, could reach.
The inquisitors might be actuated by the best motives and
by the clearest views of the great duty which they had undertaken, and their visits might have been often repeated,
unannounced and inopportune, and yet nothing but the
most glaring errors and inconsistencies of the system which
they desired to investigate could be detected. They could
see the physical misery which it inflicted, the disease and
death which ensued, and they might believe that the sum of
its iniquities were numbered. But they could not see the
thousand moral impressions of pain and anxiety and offended
delicacy which daily and hourly embittered the existence of
the lunatic. They could not separate the suffering which
was the result of insanity, from that which arose out of the
situation in which the lunatic was placed, or from the various
sources of annoyance to which he was exposed. The interested and offending party would be the last to reveal the
insults, the ridicule, the disgusting expressions, or, where
no intentional culpability could be charged, the offensive or
irritating conversation with which he assailed his victim :
and, unfortunately, the testimony of that victim is not recognized as admissable. I hold this disqualification to be
not merely unfortunate but unjust. A wide distinction
ought to be drawn between the evidence of an insane person as to what he believes and as to what he feels. His
opinions may be delusions, his feelings cannot. Under a
system, the grand principle of which was fear, he might, if

unconscientious and desirous to deceive, complain of greater injuries than what he actually received: but still there would exist ground for his appeal. Under a rule of love, there is nothing real or imaginary of which to complain. From this distinction never having been acknowledged, and from constantly rejecting every statement made by a lunatic as unworthy of credit, the information on this part of the subject is necessarily defective. Enough, however, has been ascertained, and enough even now remains of that disregard to the feelings of insane patients, that some idea may be formed of the nature, although not of the extent of the moral torture to which they were necessarily subjected. It is to be hoped that this callous indifference proceeded, and is still manifested, in many cases at least, from the preposterous assumption that lunatics had no feelings, that they did not feel as other men. Their bodies were said to be unaffected by cold, and it was concluded to be analagous reasoning to hold that their minds could not be stung by shame, or dishonour, or injustice. But our business is less with the cause in which such conduct originated, than with its disgraceful inhumanity and its evil consequences. The exploded system has been well characterized as one in which "madmen were employed to torment madmen," and the following relations, applying although they do to the remains only of that system, appear to justify the force of the accusation. Keepers, the tormentors alluded to, rarely attempt to soothe or persuade: in addressing their charges they employ at best heartless or harsh terms, and often oaths and blasphemies, upon the principle of terrifying into obedience. I do not doubt the success of such an expedient. But if it be recollected what effect such expressions will produce on a well-constituted mind: upon the timid, or the virtuous : if it be recollected, that in the irritable and the passionate they will excite propensities corresponding to those from which they emanate, it may be imagined, that

they fall with tenfold force upon minds impaired and ener-
vated by disease, labouring under the monomania of fear,
viciously disposed, and, at the same time, furiously mad:
upon all, in fact, and there are ninety such in every hundred, retaining a sufficient degree of intelligence to understand the import, and a sufficient degree of feeling to be
disturbed and disgusted by the ribaldry and cruelty of what
is addressed to them. The mind in many cases of mania,
in place of becoming obtund or deadened, is endowed with
an unnatural sensitiveness, with an acuteness of perception,
upon which the insults and insinuations of the rude or the
indelicate, or the positively cruel must act in the same manner, and must produce pain upon the same principle that
harsh sounds and bright light grate upon the eye and ear
when excited by fever.

To females, whom nature has wisely made more keenly
alive to propriety of external deportment, and to the refinement and purity of language, it has been proved, that the
most gross obscenities have been addressed, the most offensive gesticulations exhibited, and this by individuals of their
own sex, by those very persons to whose tender mercies
they were intrusted. The maniacs may or may not have
been sensible of the treatment which they received, its brutality will not, however, be abated one jot by supposing that
it was expended in vain. Females who, from their original
situation in life, had been accustomed to all the luxuries of
dress, have been allowed to expose themselves in a state
bordering upon nudity, and then derided for the exposure.
If the unfortunate sufferers were at any time conscious of
their condition, how bitter the taunt: if reason ever returned, how bitter the recollection. The observation has often
been made by those who have paid but transient visits to
institutions for the insane, and is perfectly familiar to those
who have been domesticated in such abodes, that the impre-
cations, profane and indecent expressions, which are heard

even from the lips of those who, previous to the incursion of the disease, it is certain were respectable, chaste and virtuous, are horrible and altogether unaccountable. On making this remark to a physician who has spent a long lifetime in philanthropical attempts to uproot the prejudices and injustice which obtain wherever the insane are concerned; and adding my surprize as to where patients of superior rank and unblemished reputation could have learned such words, the rejoinder was emphatic and humiliating,—" Sir, they have been taught here : the wages of our servants are extremely low : we are accordingly compelled to receive whatever applicants may present themselves without much scrutiny as to character or previous conduct, and consequently the vile and abandoned flock to us because they will not be admitted elsewhere, and because we must have keepers. They inevitably bring with them their vices, and although under a certain degree of moral restraint, they cannot be prevented from propagating them, and thus corrupt all around, debasing still further those whom it is their duty to elevate." This happened in a country which boasts, and perhaps truly, of having taken the lead in the race of improvement, where paupers live in palaces, and a certain class of pensioners are served off plate. The blindness of Humanity is often singularly contrasted with that of Justice. The assertion, quoted above, must not be admitted without certain limitations, in as much as there are certain forms of mania which predispose, independently altogether of the influence of servants or any other secondary cause, to the use of the most gross and revolting language.

The practice of ill-disciplined school-boys has often been transferred to those places of refuge, where the imbecile or lunatic seeks, or at least ought to find protection from aggression ; and the very helplessness or delusion which it is the object of such places to remove, has been made the subject of merriment or derision. Conceive the poor idiot serving as

the butt for his protector or physician. Certain animals
destroy or persecute the weak and defenceless of their own
species ; man, without the guidance of the higher sentiments,
acts similarly. Sane and insane acts from the same impulses, and in the latter, as well as in the former, there exist
sore points, jarring strings, which, if touched, the whole soul
is roused under the infliction of pain to incontrollable fury,
or to that degree of excitement when its peculiarities become visible. This experiment was frequently tried, and
for a very obvious reason, especially when visitors were present. The very flame which it was essential to smother,
was thus fanned and kept perpetually burning. The proud
maniac was told that he was not a king, in order to witness
the extent of his royal rage : the desponding maniac was
confirmed in his forebodings and fears, that the wildness of
despair might be embodied ; and the incoherence of the
idiot was encouraged, that a laugh or a jest might not be
wanting. A still more systematic mode of aggravating
disease is on record, where two lunatics were induced to
quarrel—were inspired with mutual dislike and distrust—
where the strong was allowed to tyrannize over the weak,
or the fool set to mock the fool. It is somewhat difficult to
estimate either the motives or the effects of such conduct.
But this much may be affirmed, that as neither cure nor
alleviation could possibly be the object, neither could they
possibly be the result. Pinel acknowledges, that in his own
experience, lunatics, who were perfectly composed, and in
a fair way of recovery, have, in consequence of the silly
raillery and rude brutality of their attendants, relapsed into
the opposite condition of violent agitation and fury.* Tuke
gives an instance of the same kind.† These statements
may, and I hope will be received with loathing ; but it is
necessary for the accomplishment of the object now in view,

* Pinel. Treatise on Insanity, p. 67.
† Description of Retreat, &c. p. 144.

that the whole truth should be known. There is a difficulty in determining the amount of misery the human heart
can bear: there is equally a difficulty in determining the
amount it will inflict. The following description, however,
which is quoted verbatim, lest a particle of the effect should
be diminished or increased by a change of expression, approaches as nearly to the climax of human suffering and
human ferocity as can be imagined. "Another case which
I laid before the governors, was that of the Rev. Mr. ——
He was a clergyman reduced to indigence, I believe, in
consequence of his mental complaint. He had at times, and
for considerable periods, intervals of reason. In these intervals, when he was perfectly capable of understanding
every thing that was said or done to him, repeatedly in the
presence of his wife, he was exposed to personal indignity;
and on one occasion, he was inhumanly kicked down stairs
by the keepers, and told, in the presence of his wife, that
he was looked upon as no better than a dog. His person
swarmed with vermin; and to complete this poor man's
misery, the keepers insulted his wife with indecent ribaldry,
in order to deter her from visiting him in his unfortunate
situation. He had a gold watch which was lost there, and
which his wife could never recover."* This description belongs to the past; but unfortunately, all the features of which
it is composed, with the exception, perhaps, of personal violence, might be used to characterize the evils of the system
still prevailing. Within a very short period, an instance has
fallen under my own observation, of a superintendent re-
fusing to sit down at table with a lady, one of his own
patients, and a person of good birth, education and manners, because, and the reason was used in her presence, she
was a " mad creature." Surely it is a matter for regret,
that to men so ignorant and brutal, should be committed

* First Report from Committee on Madhouses, 1815. Evidence of
Godfrey Higgins, Esq.

the care of the "mind diseased." For weeks, and sometimes for months, they have the sole and irresponsible
control of hundreds of patients; they constitute at once the
legislative and the executive; they decree, and with their
own hands inflict punishment; or, should they feel disposed
to diminish their labours, they subsidize convalescent patients to perform the more menial duties, reserving for
themselves all the higher privileges of office.* The indiscriminate employment of lunatics who are partially recovered,
to wait upon their less rational companions, is certainly to
be condemned. Under proper regulation, the attachment
of one patient to another, either as a friend or a servant,
proves highly beneficial to both parties; but what is least
justifiable in the custom to which I have adverted, is the
substitution of patients for keepers, endowed with all the
tremendous power of coercing, confining, punishing, and
further, the detention of these useful convalescents, in order
to diminish the number of regular attendants.

The necessity for employing only well educated servants
in the care of the insane, has been so strongly felt in France,
that in many establishments the keepers are required to have
undergone a system of training previous to their appointment. They serve a sort of apprenticeship, if the expression
be allowable, attending some of the large public asylums as
assistants, where they have ample opportunities for observation, but are not intrusted with the charge of patients. This
laudable example has, in some few cases, been followed in
our own country. Tuke states, "several persons about to
engage in the superintendence of similar establishments,
have made a temporary residence at York, and have been
permitted to observe daily the economy of the house, and
the mode of managing the patients."† This is the true way
of grappling with the evils of the old system. We require

* Report. Pauper Lunatics in Middlesex, pp. 171, 33, &c. 1827.
† Description of Retreat. Preface, p. 12.

certificates of character from cooks and coachmen; we expect from them previous experience, probity, a knowledge
of the duties they have to perform. It is never dreamed,
that the rude hewer of wood, and drawer of water, can at
once be transformed into the compounder of the delicacies
of the table, or the guardian and guide of animals " of price."
A greater transformation, however, has hitherto been expected to take place, in those promoted from wielding the
shuttle, or erecting a dwelling-house, to wield the happiness
of men, and in great measure reconstruct the shattered mind.
It has never been considered that the keeper is the principal
agent in leading the mind back to its original condition.
Many difficulties exist in this country, which must be overcome before such training as that instituted in some parts
of France could ever be proposed. Our asylums are shut
against the medical student who pants and would pay ex-
orbitantly for the instruction to be gathered within ; and
it would be vain to hope that in this age of speculation
they will be opened to the domestic, whose only plea for
admission is poverty. But although it be highly desirable
that those undertaking so delicate and difficult a task should
be suitably prepared, sound objections may be urged against
the conversion of asylums into normal schools for this purpose. Unless such a suggestion could be carried into effect
in some of the large metropolitan institutions appropriated
exclusively to paupers, its success must be despaired of.
The reservation " exclusively to paupers" is used advisedly.
Wherever the rich lunatic is confined, a veto will at present
be placed upon such a plan. But on the same principle,
and I regard it as dictated by the most exalted humanity,
that the poor, labouring under disease of the body, when
admitted to an hospital, partly remunerate that public by
whose charity they are supported and treated, by contributing to the instruction of the surgeon and physician, in like
manner might nervous disease be studied, and the treatment,

moral and medical, of such of its victims as are placed in
public asylums, be observed by those who are ultimately to
be engaged in attempting to mitigate similar cases. In place
of the patients being injured by the admission of students,
they would in many cases be decidedly benefited: and
wherever the consequences of such a visitation would be
either dangerous or doubtful, no judicious physician would
allow it to take place. At Salpetrière this system of tuition
has been long in operation. Until this view be taken, or
until it be practicable, there is still another expedient by
which respectable and well-informed men might be secured as attendants. As these must be selected from the
mass of the community, their qualifications will, of course,
be more general and characteristic of the class to which
they belong. We must be content with kindness of heart
and intelligence. To these there need be no limit. But
how, it may be inquired, can individuals so endowed, be
drawn from their ordinary occupations? The answer is,
by raising the status in society assigned to them, and by
very largely increasing the remuneration they receive.
The cooks and coachmen, whose case has been before
quoted, are paid by enormous, but it may be adequate,
salaries; larger, or, at least, in many instances as large
as those given in situations requiring the exercise of talent
and a long preliminary education. To those, again, whose
care is the human mind,—for in no other light can the
office of an attendant upon the insane be viewed,—a pittance is given, not only far below the allowance to cooks
and coachmen, but which is even less than can be realized
by the common artizan, by thousands engaged in the most
servile employments. And if it be recollected, that the
labour of the conscientious keeper never terminates, that he
has neither nights nor days of rest, that anxieties, provocations, disappointments, and disgusts, follow each other in
constant succession, that his only respite is, or ought to be,

in the recovery of his patients, it will become matter for surprize that any one, however humble may be his pretensions,
can be induced to submit to such bondage.   There do exist
exceptions to the rate of payment now condemned, but they
are few and far between.

From the peculiar situation of a keeper, he is invested with
great and but ill defined power, and, as is ever the case, is
prone to abuse it.   If his disposition be kind, he is inclined
to favouritism : he grants unwarrantable indulgences ; he
deviates from the rules of the dietary, should there be one,
in order to gratify some capricious appetite : he commiserates
where he ought to repel, and soothes where he ought to
command.   If, as is more frequently the case, his temper be
irritable, malicious, or his conduct regulated by the current
opinions respecting madness, he will prove a despot, anxious
to exercise his functions, brooking no opposition or remonstrance, encouraging no confidence or affection : he will
annoy by petty grievances, excite by oppression or absolute
cruelty : he will employ restraint, prohibit all intercourse
among the patients, or between these and their friends ; he
will intercept and destroy all letters, petitions, &c., and be as
unscrupulous in his conversation as in his conduct.   These
are vices springing out of false views or bad management,
which are still uncorrected.   It is evident that they could
not exist were the servants of a more elevated and a better
educated class, or were the superintendents, by whom they
are directed and instructed, and under the sanction of whose
authority they at all times nominally act, either less assimilated to them in character and condition, or more rigidly
conscientious in the performance of their own duties.

Complaints are often made against the cruel separation of
relations consequent on the isolation of lunatics, and especially of the obstacles thrown in the way of subsequent communication to which I have referred.   The necessity for

excluding friends has unquestionably been exaggerated ; and the rule founded upon it, by being made applicable to all cases, has become injurious and oppressive. The presence of relatives, and the emotions they excite, are occasionally highly salutary. But although the accusation against super-intendents and servants of asylums of estranging those who might safely be allowed to meet, be perfectly just, a much graver and more startling accusation may be urged against the vast majority of the friends of the insane themselves. It is that of utterly forgetting or abandoning those to whom they are bound by ties of kindred and long companionship, if not of affection, and who might be improved, and who could not possibly be injured by their presence and counsel.* The difficulty of inducing friends to visit the insane is generally felt by superintendents to be much greater than that of pre-venting or regulating their visits. I have known the mother of a family, the members of which were moving in a respectable grade of society, remain in an asylum for thirty years, who was neither visited nor sought to be visited, save once, by husband, children, or friend. Children are consigned to this moral obli-vion by their parents; parents by their children. Remonstran-ces from medical advisers are often of no avail : the stroke of disease seems to have enfeebled affection in the one, because it has obliterated reason in the other ; and the death-bed is the only point at which reunion takes place, if even then. I have seen many individuals in the French asylums, whose name, origin, and country, are now altogether unknown, or conjec-tural. This has arisen partly from the imperfect manner in which the entries were formerly made in the books, but chiefly from these deserted beings having outlived the me-mories or the kindness of their friends. This humiliating description is particularly applicable to the condition of lu-natics supported by public charity. The rich cannot forget

* Report. Pauper Lunatics in Middlesex, 1827, p. 155.

their insane connexions, even when most disposed to do so, as they must dole out a yearly pittance for their support.

The very affluent, however, do not place their relations in asylums simply because there are no suitable provisions for their reception. And they act wisely. To strip a man suddenly, and for no reason that he can comprehend, of all the luxuries and elegancies to which he has been accustomed, and expose him to the bald simplicity or meagreness observed in establishments for the insane, would overthrow a tottering mind, and totally crush one that has been already weakened. Upon all men the transfer from a palace to a cell in Bedlam, would be a dangerous experiment, and upon such as are bowed down with misery, or rabid with passion, the effect cannot be salutary. More enlightened views are now adopted, and fitting preparations are made which will tempt the rich to have recourse to those measures from choice, which the poor have long pursued from necessity. In arranging and adorning suites of apartments, however, in laying out gardens and pleasure grounds, in providing sources of amusement, instruction and occupation, and in increasing the liberty, convenience and comfort of the patient of rank, it ought to be kept in view that no mere appetite is to be pampered, no idle whim humoured, that the only object in view is to avoid giving pain, where pain could be of no service. Occasionally a hermit's dinner and a dark room may be necessary to convince a lord that he is human, or to convince a commoner that he is no lord : but these deprivations are then employed upon the same principle as the shower-bath, not from any foolish notion that either the want of comfort, or the cold water will actually convince the distempered reason, but that they will act medicinally, quiet the excitemen upon which the delusion depends, and permit the functions of the nervous system to remain undisturbed by the process of digestion, or impressions from the external senses. No possible evil can accrue from a patient being clothed in the

I

same dress, surrounded by similar articles of furniture, or
in the enjoyment of the same pursuits, as when mingling
with the world, provided these are neither inimical to health,
nor inconsistent with virtue. Disadvantages do flow, however, from granting indulgences, to which the patient is
neither entitled nor accustomed. This occurs chiefly with
regard to diet. The irritable temper is soothed, the wayward disposition is coaxed, and the sickly or capricious
appetite is tempted by a profusion of delicacies which, while
they effect the object immediately in view, and restore order,
and subordination, and cheerfulness, poison the source of
future peace and ultimate recovery, by encouraging a renewal of irritability and waywardness, and by vitiating the
processes of digestion and nutrition. This practice of enabling patients to live well, as it is termed, can often boast
of no better origin than a desire to bestow kindness, to
afford a gratification of which all men are supposed to be
fond, and which is as generally supposed to be innocent.
This lamentable ignorance of the laws of the economy, has
given origin to another practice more generally adopted, and
even more pernicious. All the inmates of an asylum, although they may amount to many hundreds, will be found
to have the same diet prescribed for them; and not only
will their allowance consist of the same description of food,
but of the same quantity. The old, the young, the robust,
and the debilitated—those who are free from, and those who
are affected with bodily disease—the furious and the fatuous
—the confirmed and the convalescent lunatic, are one and
all condemned to the same regimen, which may be administered by a lavish hand, and dictated by a compassionating
heart, but which must be incompatible with the condition
of one half of those who receive it, precisely because it is
adapted to the condition of the other half. It would be as
reasonable to expect that five hundred men, all of them less
or more diseased should approach the same meal with the

same degree of appetite, as that they should all be endowed
with the same powers of digestion. I am perfectly aware
that certain difficulties exist in carrying a dietary, founded
upon sound physiological principles, and upon a consideration of every individual case, into execution. But no difficulties of whatever amount, should prevent the attempt
being made; and I am fully convinced, that under proper
management it will be completely successful. In many
asylums it is the custom to serve up the meals to the patients
belonging to the higher grades, in their own apartments, and
in solitude. This is to be condemned. The repast, presented in such a manner, is cheerless; it brings with it none
of the ideas of comfort and contentment which should invariably be superadded to the gratification of appetite. It
is eaten with a rapidity and voracity which put the powers
of deglutition and digestion to a severe test. It is so prepared as to do away with the necessity of sending in knives
and forks. Every circumstance bears the impress of degradation and suspicion. The patient has no inducement to
retain the observances of civilized life. There exists no
check to the substitution of negligent or filthy habits. All
which results, as they depend on the dominion of the in-
stinctive, or the extinction of the intellectual powers, are
obstacles to improvement. Convenience and economy will
most fortunately prove allies to humanity, in bringing about
a change in this respect. It is easier for the domestics, and
cheaper for the establishment, that the patients, when not
prevented by the nature of their malady, should eat in
society, and if practicable, at the same table with the superintendent or matron; or when paupers or poor, under the
eye of a keeper. The presence of those whom they respect, or of strangers whose applause they desire, will act as
a restraining force; ebullitions of passion or folly will be
controlled; the usages of society adhered to, and the restoration of sanity promoted.

Passing from these objections, it will long be difficult to convince the rich, who can purchase other, and, as they imagine, better modes of isolation, that the vicious condition brought home to certain asylums no longer continues, or to allay the horror inspired by the prospect of being exposed to the system supposed to be prevalent in all, because certainly prevailing in many. How deeply this opinion is rooted, is shewn by an application made a few years ago, to Dr. Fox of Brislington. A gentleman who was about to place his brother under Dr. Fox's care, said, " I hope you will be as gentle to my brother as you possibly can." " Certainly," said the Doctor. " I know," resumed the applicant, " It is very necessary you should exercise some severity on him ; but I hope it will be as gentle as possible." Dr. Fox asked him what he meant. " Sir," said the gentleman, " I understand it is necessary that you should let him go through a considerable degree of flagellation." " Sir," was Fox's indignant rejoinder, " You have brought him to the wrong place. I would never carry on a concern of the sort were I obliged to resort to such measures."* While the greatest proportion of the evils and errors chargeable against asylums as they are, can be proved to be inseparable from the plan upon which they are conducted ; many of the most praise-worthy attempts to enlarge the sphere of the lunatic's joys, and to increase the chances of his recovery, are frustrated or impeded by the prejudices and timidity of the public. We are told that in America a man's Christian privileges are abridged on account of the colour of his skin, and that the proscribed African cannot be permitted to worship in the same pew with the favoured pale-face, that God who is no respecter of persons. An objection which must have sprung from the same root, excluded the conval-

---

* Minutes of Evidence taken before the Select Committee, &c. 1828. p. 22.

escents belonging to the Hanwell Middlesex Asylum, from
the parish church. The knowledge of the fact, that certain
of their fellow-worshippers had at one time suffered under a
grievous malady, for a deliverance from which they had
come to testify their gratitude, disturbed the tranquillity
and devotion of these exclusive pietists. They would not
kneel down with those who had been stricken in spirit;
they would not mingle their voices in the thanksgivings of
those whose hearts overflowed with love and adoration;
they could not commune with their God in such society.
And yet may we not, are we not bound to hope that these
Pariahs in religion shall crowd the ranks, and swell the
hallelujahs around the throne of mercy? Here was the
promulgation of a ban against moral leprosy. The fiat was
respected, and the offending outcasts withdrawn. But the
persecution did not rest here; and although the next blow
was comparatively innocuous, it serves to show how steadily
and surely the spirit of improvement is met by the spirit of
resistance. A pony chaise had been procured by the superintendent of the same asylum, in order to present a
temptation to many of the patients to prolong their excursions to a distance, and to enable the weak or indolent to
diversify their walks within the grounds, by drives through
the neighbourhood.* But the inhabitants protested against
such an invasion of their rights, such a destruction of their
comfort. They could not, forsooth, so delicate was their
sensibility, bear the sight of mad people. The remonstrance
was again attended to, and the lunatic is again deprived of
his transient glimpses of happiness, of his visits to what is
literally to him another world.

There is little hope that any legislative interference could
finally arrest these abuses or eradicate these prejudices. It

* The Hanwell Lunatic Asylum, by Miss H. Martineau. Tait's
Edinburgh Magazine. June 1834. p. 309.

could do much; but the removal of ignorance is somewhat
beyond its power. So far, however, as an act of government
can be instrumental in offering a premium for knowledge, and
in discouraging quackery and speculation, some benefit might
result. Were men of enlightened minds, liberal education,
and kind dispositions, alone appointed or permitted to attend
the insane : in other words, were those who pretend to cure
required to understand the human mind, these abuses would
disappear. To accomplish this, it would become necessary
that all asylums should be public and under the control of
government, or of parties incorporated by charter for the
purpose. The great objects in such a change would be that
all the proceedings of those immediately intrusted with the
insane should be patent to the public and to the legal authorities, and under the management of a body whose sympathies
are all engaged in favour of the patient rather than of his
attendants. To bring about such a revolution as would place
all asylums in the class of public hospitals, there would be
required no act of suppression, no bill of pains and penalties
against private asylums, houses of detention, &c. Render
county asylums perfect, elevate all to the rank which a few now
occupy, give them the means and the reputation of curing
ninety in place of forty-two in a hundred, and increase their
opportunities of affording protection and happiness to those
who cannot be further benefited, and the number of private
institutions would speedily decrease, and if improvement was
pushed sufficiently far, they would, in all probability, cease
to exist : or, should this result not ensue, they must, in self-
defence, adopt the system pursued by their rivals, a step
which would effect all that is desired or desirable. The
difference between the interests of the proprietor of a private,
and the superintendent of a public establishment is very
obvious. It is the interest of the former to detain as long,
while it is the interest of the latter to dismiss patients as soon,
as possible. The man who is the servant of, and is paid by,

the public, is anxious for, and knows that his prosperity
depends upon, cures ; whereas, the man who is paid by the
patients or their friends, knows, or thinks that his prosperity
depends upon admissions and the duration of the complaint.
This may be a short-sighted but it is a common policy.   I
do not mean to insinuate that such motives generally actuate
the proprietors of such establishments.   Many of these are
models of the system which is here advocated.   But such
principles of action may be, as it is known that they have
been, the cause of protracting the cure of the convalescent
and of perpetuating the imprisonment of the sane. The merit
of the change now proposed would consist in preventing any
act to which a humane and intelligent body of the community
were not parties, and of divesting the care of the insane of
every occasion for the exercise of selfish and unworthy
motives.

LECTURE V.

WHAT ASYLUMS OUGHT TO BE.

A perfect asylum a Utopia—Belief of the inadequate provisions for the
cure of the insane in asylums, general—Character of the physician
—Benevolence, conscientiousness, courage—Intellectual qualifications—Site of an asylum—It may contribute to the cure of the
inmates—Construction of the building—Size of apartments—Night-
classification—Houses of one story—Dormitories—Night-keepers—
Portion of asylum fireproof—Padding of walls—Heating the apartments by the circulation of hot water—Clothing—Airing-grounds—
Shrubberies—Gardens—Farm-employment of patients—Payment for
labour—Classification—Religious worship and instruction—Fallacies
in moral treatment—Dancing—Voisin's and Esquirol's establishments—Asylum at Sonnenstein—Library—Asylums at Naples, at
Hartford, United States—Visit to an asylum as it ought to be.

A PERFECT asylum may appear to be a Utopia; "a sight to
dream of, not to see." It would be miserable policy to gratify
the ambition of the heart so far, or to pall the keen appetite
for doing good by admitting that any attempt had succeeded
in placing such retreats in complete accordance with the
necessities of the diseased mind. It would, in fact, be to
return to the old rule of "letting well alone." Unfortunately,
and, what is more to the purpose, it would be untrue. But
near approaches have been made to what reason and humanity point out as the standard of excellence. From these, and
from that standard itself, materials may be obtained for the
construction of a model which may serve to show how far
distant we still are from what must be the object of every
enlightened mind, and by what means that object is to be
arrived at.

The whole secret of the new system and of that moral treatment by which the number of cures has been doubled may be summed up in two words, kindness and occupation. To carry this system into effect, the first requisite is a mind which understands the wide meaning of these words. I have shewn that the grand objection to the present mode of conducting madhouses is rather that there is no system than that there is a bad one. The gross indecorums and neglect and inhumanity are abandoned, and the regulations which rendered mismanagement obligatory are cancelled, but there have been substituted no measures which shall render the recurrence of such errors impossible; at the same time securing the observance of those attempts at alleviation, of which every case of lunacy admits, and the application of those principles upon which the cure of so many depends. The opinion was, and perhaps still is, prevalent, that if a building of suitable dimensions and security was provided, and if medical advisers occasionally saw the inmates, all was done for the insane that could be expected or that could be useful. Every day, however, shews that these provisions are utterly inadequate to the end proposed, if that end be the recovery and not the confinement of the insane ; that they form the first but the smallest and most insignificant link of a mighty chain of merciful measures, which must lengthen with our increased acquaintance with the laws of the human mind and the privations of that mind, and can only terminate when the insane are out of the land. So indifferent is even now the repute of public asylums, that the physician in many instances recommends change of scene or of occupation, travelling, anything in fact rather than mere incarceration. And he gives this advice not from any preference of the step suggested, but from a conviction that mere isolation can do nothing, and that isolation, combined with treatment founded upon mistaken views of our moral nature, can do little to promote his object. Even when to isolation is added the

best treatment which the science of medicine indicates,
very little additional confidence is inspired, as however
useful the established routine of bleedings, blisters and
baths may prove to be as auxiliaries, the experience of a
thousand years has exposed their worthlessness when trusted
to alone.   A want of power or inclination to discriminate
between the inutility of medicine from its being inapplicable,
and from its being injudiciously applied, has led to the adoption of the absurd opinion that the insane ought not to be
committed to the charge of medical men.   A manager of a
large and excellent institution, entertaining this view, has
declared that the exhibition of medicine in insanity was
useless, and that the disease was to be cured by moral treatment only.   To the mere drug exhibiter, to the man who
conceives that he can combat mania by the lancet and tartar
emetic alone, or who believes that he can exorcise melancholia by a purge, it would certainly be unpardonable folly
to commit the insane ; although an authority of equal weight
to that quoted above has expressed the opinion, " that apothecaries must know much more about the practice of
medicine than physicians, because they are so much more
among drugs."*   But to whom, rather than the well-educated
physician, is such a sacred and momentous trust to be consigned.   The word well-educated is employed advisedly and
in its most comprehensive sense.   The combination of qualifications which it represents is assuredly rare, but it is as
assuredly indispensable.   The basis of such a character must
be dispositions truly Christian and catholic.   Coleridge has said
with great acumen, that, "in the treatment of nervous disease,
he is the best physician who is the most ingenious inspirer
of hope."†   There must exist a benevolent kindness which
shall be so deep and expansive as to feel sympathy for the

* Crowther, Observations respecting the Management of the Pauper Lunatic Asylum at Wakefield, p. 13.   1830.
† Table-Talk, p. 99.

lunatic, not merely because he is an alien to his kind, because he is visited with the heaviest and hardest affliction
which humanity can bear and live; but will feel an interest
in those unreal and artificial and self-created miseries with
which the distracted spirit is oppressed, and which will be
as solicitous to alleviate suffering, where it is absurd and
the result of violence and perversity of temper, as where it
flows from misfortune. There must be a benevolence which
will be prepared to make the lunatic a companion and a
friend in all the essential qualities of reciprocal confidence,
mutual forbearance, fellow-feeling, and rational counsel,
which will in all cases forget that an awful but not an
unpassable gulf of obliterated acquirements, numbed or lethargic emotions, and darkened reason can separate two
beings born of one family; and only hold before the mind's
eye the things that still remain in common. There must be
that benevolence, which will, at an immeasurable distance,
imitate the mercy of Him, who, in curing the broken and be-
wildered spirit of demonomania, "took him by the hand and
lifted him up." But this gentleness must be controlled; it
must be graduated. It may sink into a barren sympathy,
or, more fatally for the welfare of those towards whom it is
directed, it may be active in soothing momentary pangs at
the sacrifice of permanent peace; it may indulge vicious
propensities, it may give way to unreasonable demands, it
may rather than inflict uneasiness foster those very delusions
and irritability which are the root of the disease. The
purely benevolent physician can never be a good practitioner. There must be mingled with such a sentiment that
highly refined sense of duty, that keen perception of right
which guides even kindness and affection in their ministrations, and which holds the balance as scrupulously in deciding on the moral rights of lunatics as on the civil rights
of our fellow-citizens. That this quality is required, in
order to secure the discharge of the ordinary obligations of

regular attendance and the exertion of every means prescribed for the alleviation of insanity, every one must see
and admit. But it appears to be even more essential and
more important in indicating what the conduct of the physician and his subordinates ought to be towards their charges,
in enabling the former to feel what are the real interests of
the latter, and, aided by judgment, in distinguishing the
degree of responsibility attachable to each action ; but above
all, in conferring that impress of high integrity and honour
which is appreciated and reverenced and confided in almost as
generally among the insane as among the most shrewd and
intelligent of mankind. In this light, a disingenuous and
unconscientious, in other terms, a bad man, cannot be a good
physician. But even these noble attributes would be of
little avail in the trying situations in which the curator of
the insane is placed, without that moral and physical courage
and firmness which confer calmness and decision in the
midst of danger, and in dealing with the most furious and
unlistening madness, and imbues the whole character with
that controlling influence, which, tempered with mercy and
justice, governs the turbulent while it appears to guide, and
commands the most wild and ferocious by the sternness and
at the same time by the serenity of its orders,—by the absence
alike of timidity and anger. The intellectual qualifications
for such a trust are high and varied, but cannot easily be
specified. They must comprehend a familiarity with the
true and practical philosophy of the human mind, in order
that its diseases may be understood and controlled ; as general an acquaintance as is practicable with the usages and
workings of society, with the habits, the pursuits, and the
opinions and prejudices of different classes, with literature
and science so far as they contribute to the instruction,
happiness, or amusement of these classes, with every thing,
in short, which is or can be rendered influential in what
may be called adult education, in the management or modi-

fication of character, in order that as great a number of
moral means of cure, of restraining, persuading, engaging,
teaching the darkened and disordered mind may be created
as possible ; and finally, as liberal a professional education
as long preliminary study and equally long practical observation can accomplish, in order that the causes of alienation,
the physiological conditions by which its duration and
intensity may be increased or diminished, and the operation
of medicines or external agents in removing or modifying
either the one or the other, may be thoroughly mastered.
To acquire and apply this amount of knowledge and discrimination, it is not only necessary that he who devotes himself to the care of the insane should pass his noviciate in an
asylum ; or, in the active discharge of his duties, see his
patients, as has been recommended, once or twice a-week ;
he must live among them ; he must be their domestic associate ; he ought to join in their pursuits and pastimes ; he
ought to engage them in converse during the day, and listen
to their soliloquies in the retirement of their cells ; he must
watch, analyze, grapple with insanity among the insane, and
seek for his weapons of aggression in the constitution and
dispositions of each individual, and not in general rules or
universal specifics.

The next requisite is an establishment properly placed
and constructed. The site of an asylum is rarely considered
as of importance ; or, if any care be bestowed on the selection, it is in reference to salubrity. It certainly is indispensable that the situation chosen should be healthy, that it
should possess the advantage of a dry cultivated soil and
an ample supply of water, that it should be so far in the
country as to have an unpolluted atmosphere, a retired and
peaceful neighbourhood, and yet be so near to a town as to
enjoy all the comforts and privileges and intercourse which
can only be attained in large communities. The evils
arising from inattention to these and even to less obvious

considerations can scarcely escape observation, and have occasionally been proved by painful experience. The physicians in Paris have been forced to refuse baths, when clearly indicated, in consequence of the want of water. I am acquainted with asylums placed on ground so sandy and unproductive that common garden vegetables could not be raised from it, and the bare rock would have more liberally repaid the labours of the flower-gardener. I have likewise seen these institutions so surrounded by squares and streets and filthy densely inhabited lanes, that roofs and stone walls were the only objects visible from the windows, and all extension of gardens or airing grounds was out of the question.

But the locality in which the building is erected may be made to contribute to the cure of insanity, and to the enjoyment of those under treatment. If it occupy a dead insipid flat, the view is either bounded by walls, and if the structure be of one story only, according to the most approved plan, it must always be so, or should the longing eye be permitted to catch a glimpse beyond, the horizon is limited and the scenery tame. Patients are not, in such a situation, so easily induced to take exercise, nor so much benefited by it, as when the surface is irregular, the landscape varied, and the necessity for exertion and the exhilaration which attends it are greater. If the building be placed upon the summit or the slope of a rising ground, the advantages are incalculable. To many of those whose intellectual avenues to pleasure are for ever closed, the mere extent of country affords delight; to some the beauty of wood and water, hill and dale, convey grateful impressions; to some the inanimate objects, the changes of season, the activity of industry, the living and moving things which pass across the scene, form a strong and imperishable tie with the world and the friends to which the heart still clings; to others the same objects may remind of freedom, its value, and the price by which it may be purchased; to all a suc-

cession of new and varied and healthy impressions must be
imparted.

Wherever the institution is situate, it ought to be constructed with a direct reference to the comfort and the cure
of the inmates.   It would be preposterous to lay down rules
as to the precise plan to be adopted in the erection of an
asylum.   But there are certain principles applicable to every
case, which cannot properly be omitted.   Economy in space
is a sad extravagance in medicine and medical attendance
and human life.   It is not enough that the public rooms
should be large and lofty, the sleeping apartments should be
proportionally larger.   If it be desirable that the lunatic should
enjoy a quiet and refreshing sleep, it is indispensable that his
breathing be not disturbed by foul confined air, or by the
effluvia which is concentrated, as it were, in small ill-ventilated cells.   And putting out of view the classification
which ought to obtain in the daily pursuits and pleasures of
the inmates, there exist urgent reasons for building a retreat
for the insane in such a manner as to allow an extensive
system of night classification to be put in operation.   The
peculiarities and necessities of the furious, suicidal, and
fatuous must be provided for as carefully during the one
season as the other ; so that, although the external beauty of
the whole edifice ought not and need not to be sacrificed, it
is absolutely necessary that a large portion of it should be
built of one story only.   In this are to be placed all those
who might be injured or who might injure themselves, if
lodged in a house constructed in the ordinary way.   The
paralytic will not then be endangered in ascending or de-
scending stairs, the furious will have fewer opportunities of
wreaking their reckless violence or vengeance, and the
suicidal will be debarred from one of the most easily accessible means of gratifying their ruling propensity.   In the
older establishments, where stairs could not be dispensed
with, accidents were guarded against by the use of iron

screens or cages surrounding the exposed part of the ascent,
which answered the purpose in view very imperfectly, and
suggested the most gloomy and painful thoughts, alike in
those who meditated evil and in those who were innocent
of such designs. By placing individuals who cannot be
trusted elsewhere in a cottage, the windows of which are
only a few feet from the ground, all danger is obviated, the
presence of attendants and the employment of mechanical
precautions rendered unnecessary, while free egress to the
open air, to the grounds or gardens is enjoyed by the
patient.

While it is very clear that the arrangements for the different sexes must be varied according to their respective
wants, occupations, and recreations, it is likewise necessary
to be borne in mind, that in the case of a public asylum, a
larger portion of the building should be allotted to females,
as their numbers almost always preponderate. The continental establishments are all constructed on this principle.
" Mais," says Brierre de Boismont, in writing on the subject,
" au lieu de construire les sections pour vingt malades, on
les ferait pour trente, à cause du plus grand nombre des folles
aliénés." On the minute details of the internal economy, it
is not my purpose to enter: but two provisions for the
health and comfort of the inmates must be adverted to. The
first of these is an ample supply of baths. At certain seasons
they should be employed to secure the cleanliness of all the
patients: and during the whole year they are absolutely
required, in the treatment of particular cases. Leaving the
question of the propriety of using the plunge-bath, open for
discussion, I would strongly recommend, that in addition to
the customary complement of hot, and cold, and shower-baths,
every asylum should possess the means of directing a quantity of cold water upon the head, while the body is immersed
in a warm-bath. When moral treatment cannot, and bleeding and tartar emetic ought not to be resorted to, I have seen

the most frantic and ferocious maniac restored to tranquillity, by the discipline suggested. The second provision is the erection of what may be styled self-acting, or cleansing water-closets, in all convenient parts of the house and grounds. The water may be introduced in various ways, either by the valve being raised by the opening of the door, by the pressure of the feet on the floor, or of the hands on the seat ; but by whatever arrangement effected, the principle and the object are the same, to render the process of purification altogether independent of the habits or inclinations of the patient.*

It contributes greatly to the quiet of an asylum during the night, and to the remedial effects of sleep, if the noisy and furious can be placed at a distance from the other classes of patients. This is the first, and perhaps the most important step in classification. In the immense barracks which it was the fashion formerly to construct, it can only be accomplished by removing the turbulent patients to some remote and unoccupied wing, or by erecting cells distinct from the main body of the house. Modern establishments, instead of presenting an almost interminable succession of wards and corridors under one roof, generally consist of a number of separate houses, in which the patients are distributed according to their dispositions and the features and stage of their disease, and one of which is of course appropriated to that class of which we have spoken. This excellent arrangement exists at Ivry, at Mr. Warburton's asylum

* It is almost needless to add, that all suitable expedients should be had recourse to for the purpose of sufficiently ventilating every chamber, corridor, and corner of such an establishment. For copious directions of the best means of effecting this, I would recommend the perusal of Sylvester's Philosophy of Domestic Economy, and Dr. D. B. Reid's Brief Outlines Illustrative of the Alterations in the House of Commons.

near to London, and at Burlington asylum, under the super-intendence of Dr. Fox.*

When the patients sleep in separate apartments, it appears to be a great improvement on the old plan that these should open into a long and spacious gallery. This, besides sub-serving to ventilation, may be used as a common hall, as a work-room, as the place where the night keeper or nurse may watch, and for various other purposes equally useful. But where the interests of paupers, or of such individuals as cannot afford to provide a servant, are to be considered, dormitories appear to be in many respects preferable to cells. In giving this preference, it is, of course, supposed that the rooms set apart as common sleeping places are large, cheer-ful, well aired, that classification is rigidly attended to, that the beds of the patients are wide apart, and that a keeper either watches or sleeps beside them. The presence of this person is even of greater consequence than an unvitiated atmosphere, as it yields the pleasure of society and protection, as it prolongs the influence of moral training into the silent watches of the night. To many the step, the admonition, even the presence of such an attendant acts as a powerful restraint; some ebullition of ill temper, some wild fancy or horrible delusion is arrested : the timid and superstitious are inspired with confidence and courage, and sleep in peace, while the docile and affectionate derive absolute delight from the attentions of such a friend. The real or imaginary wants of all are thus supplied. How often may the bitter cry or earnest supplication, which is heard echoing through the corridors of an asylum during the night, be for a drop of water to appease the burning thirst of passion, or for some friendly voice to dispel the self-created horrors of a distem-

* Combe, Physiology applied to Health, &c., fifth edition, p. 427. Minutes of Evidence taken before the Select Committee, &c., 1828, p. 5.

pered or remorseful conscience. More than this, a paroxysm
of insanity or of some other disease is often developed during
the night, which, raging unnoticed and unresisted for hours,
either destroys life, or renders all previous and subsequent
treatment unavailing ; whereas had a keeper been present,
which, unless dormitories exist, he cannot be expected to
be, these evils might have been prevented or mitigated.
These wards, or at least such of them as are inhabited by
those who from their malice and recklessness are most likely
to attempt fire-raising, and who from their imbecility are
most likely to suffer from it, ought to be fire-proof.   This
plan has been adopted in Mr. Drury's excellent asylum,
Glasgow, and at once secures valuable property, and, what
is of infinitely more value, the lives of the patients from
danger. The French asylums are now principally built of
one story ; and this is done, as I have stated, to avoid the
possibility of accidents, or attempts at suicide being suggested by the height from the ground, and to prevent the
success of the attempt should it be made.   In these cases
the windows are likewise of the cottage fashion, and formed
of iron, which prevent escape without appearing to do so.
Among other precautions, and especially where solitary
cells are used for the furious, and no personal restraint is
resorted to, the walls should invariably be padded with
wool or cotton or some soft material, an expedient which
precludes the possibility of any injuries being inflicted by
running the head against the walls, which is a common
mode of mutilation.

Many of the old institutions were either wholly or in part
constructed without fire places, stoves, chimneys, or any means
of affording warmth to their inmates.   This proceeded from
a fear for the safety of the building.   The lunatic who could
scarcely be trusted with a fire during the day in the presence
of his companions and keeper, and even when guarded by an
ample grating, could not expect such a luxury in his cell or

bedroom during the night. It is not, however, to be regarded merely as a luxury. In consequence of a great fall in the temperature, aided probably by the lethargic habits and condition of the nervous system in lunatics, limbs and lives have been lost. The fear of conflagration has so far subsided, and the public halls and parlours are in almost every case sufficiently warmed. But the sleeping apartments are still as cold and injurious to health as ever. And the lunatic now passes suddenly from the common hall, where he has enjoyed a heat as high as 70° or 80° during the whole day, to his cell, where the thermometer indicates the freezing point. This partly explains the great mortality in some asylums, and is eminently unfavourable to the recovery of the tone of the nervous system. How is it to be remedied? It is quite clear that although it may be preposterous to conclude, as was formerly done, that any great number of lunatics are so destructive, suicidal, or idiotic, as to set fire to the house in which they live, their custodiers must act as if they were, and devise a plan which shall yield them sufficient warmth, and be compatible with the safety of all around. There are three modes of doing this: by heated air, by steam, and by the circulation of boiling water. Without commenting on the advantages of the two first it is enough to say that the third mode appears to be preferable. The apparatus by which this is effected consists of a furnace connected with a boiler or coil of pipes in which the water is heated, and two series of pipes, by one of which the hot water is conveyed to all parts of the building, whatever may be its dimensions, imparting its heat as it flows along: by the other the water is returned to the boiler to be again heated and again circulated. These pipes may be carried along passages, introduced into sitting and sleeping rooms, and in such a manner as neither to be seen nor to be accessible to the patients. This plan is completely adequate to the end in view. The degree of heat produced can be regulated, is equable, and does not

alter the qualities of the air.   The plan is likewise economical for, after deducting the first outlay for pipes, which,
although considerable, must greatly increase the value of the
house as property, the current expense of heating a large
building, capable of accommodating several hundred patients,
is said not to exceed that of a common fire.   It is, further,
perfectly safe, and affords a genial warmth to the body of
the lunatic without afflicting or irritating his mind by the
distrust implied by the iron-grating, and other provisions
employed to keep him at a distance from the fire-place.

As a means of attaining the same object, the clothing of
lunatics should be rigidly attended to.   One great difficulty
has generally to be contended with in arranging the details
of this part of the domestic economy of an asylum.   Whether
we have to act for the poor or the rich the supply of clothes
is inadequate : in the one case from the poverty or parsimony
of the parishes, public bodies or individuals by whose charity
they are supported : and in the other, from the supposition
very frequently entertained, even by compassionating friends,
that anything is good enough for a madman, who cares not
for cold, and attends neither to comfort nor decency.   I have
shewn that this supposition is directly at variance with the
truth.   There must accordingly be an attempt made to provide, not only warm and clean clothes, but changes of these
adapted to the different seasons and variations of temperature
and weather, and resembling, as closely as possible, those to
which the individual had been accustomed ; and, if practicable, there should be no uniformity of costume.   It may
have advantages, but it reminds of the workhouse, the prison,
the galley-slave.

Let us pass to the exterior.   We must not rest content with
airing-grounds.   However extensive the area of these may
be, and in certain establishments they are as ample as can
be expected, they are, in reality, nothing more than narrow
strips of sward or gravel surrounded by high walls.   They
present all the characteristics of imprisonment without one

of its alleviations. Within them a patient may walk his
weary round for half a century without obtaining a glimpse
of the world he has left, with no other objects to gaze upon
save his miserable companions in misfortune below, and the
interminable blue sky above. The expedients to relieve the
monotony of such a scene are interesting. A patient under
my own charge walked fifteen miles per day for a considerable length of time in making the circuit of one of these
courts ; another counts the stones in the wall ; a third watches
the appearance of faces at the windows by which the court is
overlooked. These places should be planted, have a foun-
tain ; a portion of ground prepared as a bowling green ; they
should be stocked with sheep, hares, a monkey, or some other
domestic or social animals. In the spirit of a bygone period,
it may be objected that the trees will be uprooted or used
for gallows, that the bowling-green will be destroyed, the
pets killed. But in any institution where such arrangements
exist the principles of classification would likewise be recognised, and no lunatics, whose dispositions or delusions prompt
them to commit such acts, would be admitted to this part of
the establishment, or, if admitted, would be under the eye
and guidance of the attendant : one of the most useful duties
of a keeper being to render many enjoyments accessible and
innocent by his presence and superintendence, which in his
absence might be dangerous. The courts and promenades
in Salpetrière, containing a thousand lunatics, have been
planted for twenty years, and no suicide by suspension has
taken place. The grounds at Charenton, Rouen, Sonnenstein, &c., are laid out in the same style, and have neither
been destroyed, nor have they proved inconsistent with the
safety of the patients. But, besides, or in default of these
minor attempts to enliven the aspect of these prison-yards,
the centre should be raised as a mound or terrace, so high
only as will give a wide and animated horizon but so low
as will prevent any intercourse taking place with the inhabitants in the immediate neighbourhood. The patients are

thus, in a certain sense, restored to the world while reaping all the benefits of seclusion. They have an immense number of new and pleasing and yet unexciting impressions conveyed to their minds, all calculated to suggest healthy trains of thought, all foreign to their morbid feelings, and furnishing some materials for reflection more allied to sanity than the ravings of their fellow-prisoners, or the glare of a dead wall. All these changes might be wrought without expense and with great moral benefit by the lunatics themselves. What lunatics can accomplish by mere manual exertion may be learned from the following quotation : " The supply of water for the establishment, Hanwell, having been principally derived from the canal, inconvenience was often experienced in dry weather from its insufficiency : a very powerful spring had been found upon the premises by boring to the depth of nearly three hundred feet. A large reservoir, to contain the daily overflow, which was sufficient for the consumption, was found to be the cheapest mode of rendering this spring available to the institution. At the sessions held last April, the court granted L.650 for that purpose, the sum at which the cost of it was estimated. Your committee have to state that it is now finished. The excavation is thirty feet deep, and forty-five feet in circumference. This work having in a great measure been accomplished by the labour of the patients, the cost has fallen considerably below the estimate, so that instead of L.650, the sum voted by the court, your committee have only to call upon the treasurer for the county for L.318, 2s. 10d. for that purpose."* There are labourers and gardeners and masons in every asylum, or should there not, there will always be found men with sinews sufficiently strong to carry earth and lay turf, and this is all that is wanted. And why, under such circumstances, should not lunatics be *taught* to do these and many other things ? There is besides

* Sixth Report of the resident Physician and Treasurer of the Hanwell Pauper Middlesex Asylum. 1837. P. 4.

in such an undertaking a definite object in view, and this
invariably facilitates all operations in which lunatics are
concerned. Intrust the most irreflective with a frivolous
commission, or with some piece of work which is evidently
prescribed as an occupation, and of no utility either to himself or others, his pride is offended, the task is performed
reluctantly and without interest, and the moral effect is lost.
But in employment, the object and the utility of which is
explained and understood, the great majority of patients
will, at a certain stage of the disease, cheerfully engage.
This is a strong argument for enabling each to pursue his
own profession, so far as is practicable. But care should be
taken in the selection of the kind of occupation, for an
egregious and irremediable error may be committed in
allowing madmen to engage in an employment about which
their mind is deranged.*

It must be confessed, however, that the airing grounds,
as at present laid out, are great improvements upon the
dark ill-ventilated halls which used to be the only places for
recreation and exercise. Light and air are no longer con-
traband, although they are still severely taxed. But in
addition to the changes of which mention has been made,
there ought to run along the walls of these courts, or through
their centre, covered galleries, which, while they in the
former case prevent escape, protect from heat or rain, and
allow of exercise being taken in defiance of either. Where
the situation of the asylum affords a commanding view, such
as at Charenton, these alleys are favourite places of resort,
and during summer are frequented not only by the idle
saunterer or sentimental gazer, but are crowded with read-
ing-desks and drawing and work tables, and by all those
who have the wisdom, or are instructed, to associate the
pleasures which the beauty of nature affords with the ordinary and obligatory occupations of life. But even were

* Spurzheim. Physiognomical System, p. 568.

these yards modified in the manner proposed, we must not rest content. A wider sphere for physical exertion and means for multiplying pleasureable sensations must be procured. Gardens, grounds, farms must be attached to each establishment, and must be cultivated by or under the direction of the lunatics. Many of the existing establishments have from thirty to forty acres in their own hands, and at Bicêtre the least productive part of the farm has been converted into a bleaching-green. In the same institution, now under the able superintendence of Ferrus, there are 150 patients constantly employed in levelling, masonry, digging, joiner's, blacksmith's, and even carpenter's work. I have before adverted to the benefits of engaging every patient in some suitable occupation, and shall now only allude to the principles which ought to regulate all attempts to induce them to take such a step. In many respects an asylum should be assimilated to an infant school. The mind has been reduced by disease to the state of childhood; it displays the same waywardness, the same impatience of control and of compulsory labour, the same capricious desire for the gratification of the most urgent motive, and sometimes the same stubbornness and ill-temper. But while there exist similar difficulties, other characteristics of youth are present, which may be employed in this instance as well as in education to communicate strength, or to awaken powers that perhaps require only a proper stimulus to assume their legitimate exercise. There is often docility, the gratitude inspired by habitual affection, the sense of justice which fair dealing will enlist on the side of health, and too frequently that simplicity, depending on diminished intelligence, which permits the patient to be cheated by amusement or active employment into health and serenity of mind, as the learner is cheated into a knowledge of important truths or practical facts by means of a game at

K

romps, or some merry carol. Place the undertaking of acquisition, in the one case of health, in the other of information, before the parties as a duty, a task, and as a duty which must be performed, a task which must be learned or punishment and disgrace will follow, and the probability is, that in a majority of cases the proposal would be spurned, or would excite disgust or insubordination, which even the infliction of the threatened punishment would fail to remove. Nor need we wonder at this result ; it is children of different ages that we treat. Certain individuals might be awed, or coaxed, or bribed into compliance: that is, the point is carried by an appeal to the sense of fear, to vanity, or to the wish to possess some desirable object, and not in virtue of the reasonableness of the request, or the convinced understanding of the party. These modes of carrying our plans extensively into operation are occasionally unavoidable. But let those who have tried to teach children by these methods, and who, departing from such a vicious discipline, have endeavoured to make what is valuable attractive, and what is attractive valuable, declare the comparative results, and their experience will be found to coincide exactly with the recorded effects of compelling the insane to do what is necessary and proper, and of inducing them voluntarily to do the same things, by connecting them with their comfort and happiness. No argument against the system pursued in infant schools is valid, because in some instances it fails to unfold the embryo mind ; nor should an objection to the proposition advanced be founded on the inapplicability of persuasion and moral training to certain lunatics, inasmuch as in the great majority of cases they bring peace and pleasure. If the infant school teacher be efficient, he discriminates not only the talents but the dispositions of his pupils, and metes out instruction of a nature and a quantity and in a manner suited to both : and if the superintendent

of the insane knows his duty, he likewise adapts the impressions he is desirous of conveying to the condition of the
mind which he is solicitous to restore.   No superintendent
or keeper would be so grossly ignorant as to force a man to
dig who was disposed to weave, and none ought to be so
ignorant as to overtax the weakened or already burdened
mind by long sustained attention to either.   The comparison
between the enlightened treatment of lunatics and the principles of infant teaching proceeds no farther.   In the infant
school one invariable mode of tuition is applied to all, whether judicious or not is not here the question ; in an asylum,
while general principles are held in view, a different plan
must be pursued in leading every individual, or at least
every class of individuals, to the point at which we desire
to arrive.   We may be justified in giving the stern tones
of command to our voice, when it is necessary to govern
the proud or venerative maniac, but it would be absurd and
cruel to do so in order to guide the timid, the affectionate,
or the irascible.

The deception is virtuous, when by an imagined pursuit
of pleasure we lead on the mind unwittingly in the pursuit
of sanity ; but if a higher motive can be used, if reason can
be made to assist in its own restoration, no deception, however pure and praiseworthy the intention, should be resorted
to.   Even in intercourse with the insane, honesty is the best
policy.

There is a rule in many asylums, that when we have
succeeded, when the pauper lunatic, in obedience to our
injunctions, has engaged in some useful occupation, he shall
receive no wages for his labour.   I think the rule in every
way a bad one.   It says, in other words, he shall have no
interest in what he does.   " Mais," says a kind and judicious
friend to the lunatic, "nous le répétons, il faut rémunérer
l'activité par une récompense quelconque, par un léger
salaire, une plus grande liberté, de plus beaux habits.   La

plupart des aliénés aiment le tabac. On fera ce besoin au
profit du travail."* There can exist no doubt but that an
establishment is fully entitled to the proceeds of the labour
of all those supported upon charity, and even of those who
pay board. In many places these proceeds are considerable,
and constitute a part of the annual income of the house,
one of the means, in fact, whereby its beneficence is maintained, and its benefits extended. In 1836, the proceeds of
work done by lunatics amounted in the Dundee Asylum to
L.200, and in that at Armagh to L.250. It would be indis-
creet to sacrifice this, it may be argued, and preposterous
to stipendize those who can want for nothing, and who very
often neither know the value of money, nor how it can be
converted into gratification. But this is not the principle at
stake, this is not the bearing of the question upon which we
would stamp the stigma of error. Every one will admit
that the lunatic has no *claim* on the asylum, where he is
cherished and supported, to a compensation for his earnings;
that the amount of these are as nothing in liquidation of the
debt he owes for the peace and protection and chance of
recovery which he enjoys; and that it would be ridiculous,
and might be dangerous, to inculcate upon him that he has
any such claim. The gravamen lies in the declaration,
that he has, and can have, no interest in, or reward for, his
daily occupations. To tell the madman, as an encouragement, that although he can expect no reward or indulgence
for what he does, still the inducement of being improved by
labour ought to be to him a consideration paramount to all
others, is to describe colours to the blind, sounds to the deaf.
He cannot appreciate the temptation, for he will not acknowledge that he is ill, or stands in need of improvement.
It will scarcely be denied that a man will do that best and
most cheerfully, in which he has some real or fancied in-

* Briere de Boismont, Annales d'Hygiène, tom. xvi.

terest; that if he expect honour, or ease, or remuneration,
or the satisfaction of any desire, he will exert his powers
more continuously and energetically than if he expects no
results whatever.   It is because the enforcement of such a
rule divests labour of all those attractions, that I conceive
it to be bad.   Could we act upon all lunatics through higher
motives than by wages or bribes or commands, it would be
well, but the great majority of the worst cases, at least, are
ceasing to be lunatics, becoming convalescent, before you
can do so.   As the minds of the lower orders are at present
constituted, the most powerful stimulus is gain, and if by
addressing ourselves to the propensity to acquire, we can
subdue more violent propensities, or still the agitation of
disease, it would be imprudent and unphilosophical to reject
the aid of such an agent.   Payments in money are not advocated, although in certain cases they are found to be
strongly desired, and more desired and more irresistible
than any other temptation ; but it is generally more convenient, and equally acceptable to the other contracting party,
to pay in another manner.   First, either better diet and
clothing are given, certain coveted luxuries are awarded to
the industrious patient, to which as a pauper he has no right,
and which his board, if in a higher class, could not purchase ;
or secondly, a portion of his earnings is set apart for his
behoof, to be accumulated until restoration of reason take
place, and to be then delivered to him to meet the exigencies
of his dismissal.   The first of these plans is chiefly applicable to the incurable and the most debased lunatics ; the
second to those who are curable, or who retain sufficient
intelligence and feeling to cherish the hope of reunion with
their friends, who are gladdened by the sympathies and
cheerful prospects which such a hope creates, and will
struggle to co-operate in your designs for their welfare in
order to gratify that hope.   In both cases it would be wise
to allow so much per cent. on all labour, the rate to increase

both according to the amount of work done and the spirit
in which it is executed. Certain tasks and working hours
should be appointed, otherwise the anxiety to win may frustrate the whole scheme, by first exciting and then fatiguing
all the powers. The patient must, of course, be acquainted
with the conditions upon which he is solicited to engage in
active employment, and a certain degree of choice permitted
as to the kind of compensation most acceptable, and the
period at which it shall be made. The discretion of the
employer must decide whether compliance is justifiable, but
after the bargain is concluded, the terms, although they
refer to nothing more than an ounce of tobacco or a cup of
tea, should be observed as sacred. Violations of such
agreements have often led to serious consequences.

The kindness and expediency of the proposal to accumu-
late part of the earnings of the curable insane, until their
health be completely restored, can best be understood by
considering the situation of such individuals when liberated.
Supported by their parishes or by public benevolence while
insane and confined, they lose all claim upon such resources
by their dismissal, they pass from a quiet home, are thrown
upon society pennyless, it may be without friends or a single
being who will shelter or sustain them, incapable of engaging
in their ordinary trade, and unable to obtain employment
were they capable of undertaking it. This cannot fail to
inflict misery, to threaten the still delicate tenure of health,
and undoing all that care and kindness had accomplished
to bring about a relapse. The remedy is self-evident. Let
all institutions, where occupation is extensively carried on,
tax the revenue derived from the articles manufactured, or
saved by the services performed ; the amount of the tax to
be expended in providing for the safety and support of
patients after they have left the house ; the funds to be confided to themselves if trustworthy, or, what would be better,
to responsible guardians. This is just continuing the sur-

veillance and treatment for a longer time, and spreading the benefits of such institutions over a period and scenes more critical as to the permanence of health, than even the first weeks of convalescence. These suggestions are founded upon experience, and are sufficiently justified by what has long been the practice at Salpetrière, although there the distinct right of the lunatic to wages is recognized. The "Samaritan" societies proposed by Sir W. Blizard and, I believe, organized in London about forty years ago, had a similar object in view. The benevolent intentions of their founders were, however, confined to the support of the poor when discharged from the public hospitals. The necessity for such a provision is very urgent, and obvious to all familiar with the class of individuals received into these establishments, or with their fate subsequent to their recovery and dismissal. But the case of the recovered but destitute lunatic is ten times more clamant; he is not only without work, but the malady from which he has been relieved proves all but an insurmountable obstacle to his obtaining any, however well established his character for honesty and industry may be.

Classification may proceed on various principles. There is first the very obvious ground for separation, the rates of board. The accommodation, the fare, the attendance required for the rich, cannot be extended to the poor, nor is it necessary that it should. The pauper could not appreciate, nor prize, nor derive benefit from the refinement and delicacies essential to the comfort, and instrumental in the recovery of the affluent. Most fortunately this arrangement, which is called for by the usages of society, is found to correspond with those higher and less artificial distinctions which are dictated by philosophy. The second principle to be recognised, is the stage of the disease. Common sense would indicate ; but common sense has not yet effected a separation of the curable from the incurable, and both of these from the

convalescent, that class of patients who may be said to have
recommenced their existence, and to require the gentle and
strengthening treatment bestowed on infancy. For the incurable, little active interference is required : but much may be
done to render them happy and contented, to reconcile them
with captivity, and to enable them to pass the close of their
dreamy existence in tranquillity. As a class, they are isolated for the behoof of others, that they may not prove
injurious to those who are still capable of being influenced
by moral impressions, and liable according to the nature of
these impressions, to be confirmed in their alienation, to be
afflicted with a still more intense form of mental disease, or
to be restored to health. That evil has been done, and this
is the principal point at issue, by ignorance of this fact may
be gathered from Pinel. To the curable and convalescent,
then, our greatest care ought to be consecrated. The object
is to place them in the most favourable circumstances for
the re-development of impaired, impoverished, or imperfect
power. Unless classification be pushed farther than has
hitherto been suggested, this object can never be attained.
The third principle, and that next in importance, is, that
these classes should be subdivided according to the character
of the malady and of the dispositions of each individual. It
is not enough that the furious should be separated from the
docile, or the imaginative from the fatuous ; the mind of
every individual should be carefully studied, its healthy as
well as its insane bearings analyzed, and the relations which
these may have with, or the influence they may acquire upon
the minds of others calculated, and groups formed in reference to the result. The violent or malicious may often be
confided with perfect safety to the acquisitive, or vain, or
religious monomaniac. The affectionate and happy may be
associated with the desponding and despairing, and the helpless idiot may become the adopted child of some mother
whose only delusion is weeping for infants which she never

bore. A system somewhat similar to that here described is, I believe, pursued in the excellent asylum at Perth. But it may be carried farther; and whole families may be formed. A vain idler may be intrusted to the tutelage or example of three or four industrious knitters or oakum teasers; and being encircled by temptations to exertion, and stimulated by the desire of rivalry, abstraction from the dominant idea is often the consequence. A contented, self-satisfied, and active minded maniac is joined to a timid, a lethargic, and a gloomy maniac, and seldom fails to communicate some portion of those qualities which it is our object to infuse. In a great majority of cases, the members of these small communities contract lasting attachments. The first step in giving efficacy to the principle under discussion, is a short and an easy one. The great affinities of gentleness, of docility, of despondency, of vehemence, &c., are readily perceived. But the nearer approaches to the complete working of the plan are more difficult, because generally impeded by the structure of asylums, the small number of attendants, and the inefficient assistance afforded by them, and above all, by the prevailing ignorance of the laws of the human mind, and consequently of those differences of disposition, upon a knowledge of which the successful application of such a principle must depend. Notwithstanding these obstacles, a little tact and management will bring together those who are fitted for each other's society. The fourth principle is a corollary to the last. It is based, however, rather upon the amount of cultivation which the mental powers and dispositions have received, than upon their nature. Our confederacies must often be constructed with a reference to the degree of education, the tastes, and pursuits, and manners of the parties. The unhappiness which would flow from bringing the ignorant and brutal into constant and compulsory contact with the enlightened and refined may be imagined. In acting upon this principle we are sometimes forced to violate a rule pre-

viously laid down. Wherever the poor lunatic has been
well educated, accustomed to the courtesies and amenities
of good society, and retains amid his hallucinations, the feelings and tastes which characterize that condition, he should
be raised from the grade of paupers, and placed among those
who still cherish similar feelings and tastes. His degradation,
his loss of caste may be fatal, while his elevation may prove
curative, and is in perfect conformity with the spirit and aim
of the principle now insisted. Wherever practicable, that is
wherever the acquirements and deportment of the superintendent admits of such an arrangement, the well-educated
and well-bred convalescent lunatic should reside and associate with their physician and governor. The advantages
of this have been before adverted to; but it may be stated
here, that besides many examples of the partial success of
the plan, which might be quoted from the reports of asylums
in this country, there is at present an excellent private establishment in Paris, where about thirty patients take all their
meals, spend their time, and pursue their occupations and
pleasures in the company of their medical attendant.

Much may be done in certain classes by an appeal to
honour, to that conventional integrity and faithfulness which
is more frequently the offspring of a dread of the world's
censure, than a dread of the culpability of disingenuousness.
Men who have long lived and acted under such a motive,
may often, even during the access of frenzy, be guided by
it. To a man of the world with confused notions of duty
and virtue, but with a clear conception of the code of chi-
valry, and an elevated opinion of the character which it
becomes him to support, all doubt, all suspicion of the possibility of his breaking his word, of his doing that which he
has promised not to do, will communicate intense pain, destroy all reciprocity of sentiment, confirm his delusions, and
increase his malady. Whatever the supposed intentions of
such a patient, personal restraint would be improper. Es-

quirol acting on this rule, trusted a military man who was determined on suicide with the means of destruction on his pledging his honour that he would make no attempt to use them. He passed through the ordeal in safety, but not without a struggle. This was venturing far, perhaps too far, but when well assured of the strength and influence of this feeling, it would be wise and prudent to appeal to it in preference to resorting to harsh or compulsory measures. It may be turned to good account in classifying patients of the higher ranks, but the dangerous error should be carefully avoided of attributing a greater strength and influence to this feeling in lunatics than in sane individuals.

The association of lunatics requires to be skilfully managed. But when classes have been formed in conformance to the mutual wants, and wishes, and dispositions of the parties, the system is at once beautiful and self-operating. There is no need of keepers to direct, and chide, and caution. Their presence is required to regulate the machine, but its motions are spontaneous. The little kindnesses of co-operation and assistance go forward, the weaver plies his shuttle as vigorously, and the dance and song conclude the day as regularly as if a whip or a comfit were displayed. It is a mistake to suppose that, as a general rule, these bands should consist of patients of similar dispositions.

When once associated, there ought to be as much liberty as is consistent with the safety of the whole community, and just as much restraint as is consistent with the happiness and recovery of each of the members. By liberty I do not mean independence of authority, idleness, or even a mere exemption from strait jackets and fetters. There must be laws vigorously enforced, and industry, and rewards, and punishments, in an asylum, as in every other body. I would here, however, make a distinction, confining punishments to moral delinquencies exclusively, exonerating the offender from all penal consequences where the offence is

clearly the result, the manifestation of his derangement.
But by liberty I mean the power of gratifying every innocent propensity, every justifiable desire, of pursuing every
object which is calculated to inspire present pleasure, or
conduce to the ultimate re-establishment of reason. Be nig-
gard of mere indulgence; but you cannot be too extravagant of enlightened humanity. Many establishments have
been condemned and ruined, by the occurrence of a case of
suicide within their walls, or an attempt to escape proving
successful. I never heard of one suffering any penalty for
undue severity or restraint, if these fell short of absolute
cruelty. Self-destruction under such circumstances, is peculiarly distressing; but it cannot be construed as a proof of
laxity of discipline, or of too great indulgence in the particular case, nor as an argument against general lenity and
humanity. The lunatic turns some of the very means
employed to protect him against himself, to his own destruction. This, however, cannot be prevented under the
best management, unless chains and unfurnished cells be
resorted to; and even then the security is not complete.
Every object may be converted into a deadly weapon.
Pieces of glass, rusted nails, worsted thread taken from the
carpet, medicine, the very walls, may be so employed.
Escapes, while every precaution should be taken to prevent
them, in general prove nothing more than that great freedom is enjoyed by the inmates of the asylum—greater by
one degree only, than what they ought to enjoy. There
sometimes, however, arises danger from patients being too
kindly treated. From being obliging, useful, amusing, and it
may happen from the very nature of their malady, individuals
become favourites. Out of this favouritism grow indulgences, exemptions from medicines, duties, or punishments, and
the encouragement of delusions, lest contradiction should
annoy or render refractory. It is certainly very difficult to
avoid forming and practically shewing a stronger attachment

for those who trust, serve, and it may be, love you, than for those who bend every thought to irritate or destroy you, or circumvent your plans. The preventive or remedy for such partialities, is to be found in the judicious selection of servants—in the employment of those only who perceive and feel, that the fewer the endearing qualities of the patient, and the farther he is removed from participating in the sympathies of the healthy mind, the greater are his claims upon those around; or who in the administration of justice, or the distribution of favours, recognize a perfect equality between the patient with one sound feeling, and the patient with many. An easier, and perhaps safer mode of interrupting such ties, is the frequent change of servants from ward to ward. This is practicable in large establishments only. The same expedient is strongly recommended in cases of relapse. Celebrated authors go so far as to say, that patients should never be attended during two attacks, by the same servant. No vestige, it is argued, of their former illness, should be allowed to appear; and accordingly, every object calculated to recall the impressions existing during its continuance should be excluded. Almost every one has heard of the unfortunate victim of the blue devils, who was first hunted from London, and ultimately from his native country, by the reappearance of these persecutors, whenever he was surrounded by certain pieces of furniture. The visual deception was here associated with, and constantly excited by a real visual impression. Upon a similar principle is the change of attendants proposed. But it is doubtful how far it ought to be pushed, as the recollections of the state of convalescence which took place under the care of the servant, must be more vivid than the recollections of the state of insanity, and in proportion to the vividness and agreeableness of an impression, will it prove beneficial or injurious. But this change is advocated upon still another ground; that of the dislike which is supposed to arise in the mind of those who have recovered from insanity, towards those who have been instrumental in the cure. This supposition is altogether erroneous and libellous to human nature. When the hand of the curator of the insane was armed with the lash, and when insult and the bastinado were prescribed as specifics, it is highly probable that the re-covered lunatic did regard his oppressors with loathing and detestation. But now when the insane are treated as human beings, there exists evidence that gratitude and esteem as frequently reward the kindness and care of their attend-ants, as in any other of the relations of life where such sentiments are likely to be called forth. Upon this ground then, a change of attendants cannot be justified. Indeed where kindly feelings are known to exist, or to have existed, they should be received as indications of the propriety of resorting to the original attendant.

Many profound sophisms have been delivered as to the introduction of religious worship among lunatics. It has been argued that such exercises are addressed to the highest feelings of our nature, and bring before the attention the most awful truths—that they are eminently exciting, and consequently prejudicial ; and the aphorism has been quot-ed, that it is necessary to avoid all excitement ; that as no opportunity should be given for the irritation of the furious, or for the intimidation of the timid, neither should any plan be adopted which may tend to foster religious impressions in the superstitious. This opinion has been controverted by the assertion, that such an appeal is tranquillizing and con-solatory, and leads the enfeebled mind to the only source of strength and succour. One authority adduces examples of the efficacy, another of the evils of such an attempt. It is prohibited, because it sometimes causes insanity, or aggra-vates a predisposition to the disease : it is recommended, because it brings hope and peace to those who, although sane, are miserable. I regard the grounds of opposition

and advocacy as equally invalid. Upon certain forms of
mental disease, religious teaching or ceremonies would act
as a direct irritant ; upon others they would fall powerless ;
upon a third class, such ministrations would operate as any
other novel scene or occupation which assisted in relieving
the monotony of their mode of life ; while upon a fourth,
their influence would be altogether benign, affording a legitimate gratification to healthy feelings, directing the mind
from depressing, or agitating, *to* soothing associations, and
tending to inspire with brighter and nobler hopes, which
disease can neither darken nor quench, which will beam in
on the troubled spirit amidst its gloomiest delusions, as clear
and certain points of guidance, like shore-lights to the storm-
bound sailor. Upon the discrimination of the patients to
whom religious instruction is adapted, the whole question of
its utility rests. To prescribe it as applicable to all cases,
would be as wise as to seek for the *elixir vitæ ;* and to exclude it because sometimes injurious, betrays a deplorable
ignorance of the constitution and the wants of the human
mind. I may, with all reverence, compare the employment
to that of any other medicine. It must be regulated by
the idiosyncracies of the patients, by the symptoms, the
duration and the complications of the disease. No man
entertaining this view, will establish public worship as an
hospital routine duty, in which all must or may participate.
It should be reserved for the few who can understand its
meaning, who may be quieted by its solemnity, cheered by
the prospects which it affords, attracted by the beauty of
the service, or roused by the recollections which it calls up
—the condition of each of these classes having been previously examined and tested as to the extent to which such
impressions may be borne, and may prove beneficial. It
will be observed, that many are here proposed to be admitted to these rites, who cannot be expected to regard them,
or be influenced by them as religious duty. The imagina-

tive, the musical, the lethargic lunatic, are thus all included,
because pleasure would be communicated, and a new and
healthly direction may be given to their thoughts by the
aspect and accessory circumstances of the assembly, independently altogether of its sacred character.   Many
exceptions, however, must be made, and the pleasure derivable must not be chosen as the ground of admission.
Those, in fact, who most ardently desire to join such meet-
ings, and who pant for spiritual communion, are often those
who are least fitted for it.   They doubt or despair of their
salvation, or their whole soul is in wild exultation at the
prospect of the bliss which awaits them: or they have seen
visions, or they prostrate every power before the conviction
that they are incarnations of Deity, or of the angelic host.
In such states as these, any act connected with religion,
must generally contribute to promote and perpetuate the
activity of the diseased feeling.   I say generally, for where
the reason remains intact, and the dominant emotions are
terror, despondency, penitence for imaginary crimes, and so
forth, a clear exposition of the promises of Christianity made
to the understanding, in a clear and conciliating manner,
sometimes acts as if miraculously.   Such cases must be selected, and not experimented on.   Under such circumstances,
private religious instruction would be infinitely preferable
to any public devotional service.   It is somewhat singular,
that this mode of conveying powerful impressions is scarcely
at all resorted to in our establishments.   Apart from all
other considerations, it enables the clergyman to study and
probe the wound he desires to heal, to know the dispositions
he has to contend with, and to frame his exhortations, and
to regulate his intercourse accordingly.   In a promiscuous
congregation this cannot be attempted.   The propriety of
such a mode of communication is strongly insisted upon by
the English physicians, and even by some of those who
express doubts as to the salutariness of public worship, or

entertain a decided opinion against its employment. This practice was at a very remote period, 1677, introduced at Bethlem, but for reasons which cannot now be ascertained, has fallen into disuetude. In order to take advantage of every impression which public worship is calculated to excite, it appears to be highly expedient that it should be performed on Sunday, in the manner to which the patients have been accustomed in health, and in some apartment consecrated to the purpose. Many objects are hereby gained : the regular passage of time is marked, I have two patients under my care, who lost all conception of this, apparently from the want of a calendar : the nature of the institution is recalled, and with that fact many of the thoughts of other years, which, as connected with an unimpaired state of mind, and the performance of a sacred duty, are generally serene and salutary ; sentiments of reverence and humility are engendered, and the hope of the return of the day is excited, and an anticipation of the same calm thoughts and recollections. " They all look forward to it with pleasure," says Dr. Fox. I am disposed to urge the propriety of Sunday being observed in the same manner within as without an asylum for another, and what may be condemned as too much of a secular, reason. It is there a day of idleness and lethargy ; it is shortened as much as possible by indulgence in sleep, or prolonged by the uninterrupted sufferings of self-tormenting spirits : in short, all moral treatment is suspended. This monotony is very hurtful. To continue that regimen by which occupation is provided, and by which unhappiness is combated, by calling healthy feelings into play, some act of public worship would be essential.

There are certain descriptions of madness in the treatment of which religion is indispensable. But in the employment of such an agent, great difficulties occur, so great indeed, as to discourage the most zealous of its advocates. These consist in determining the modes in which its effects

may be best obtained. If its doctrines are taught to weak
or perverted intellects, they may add to the confusion already
existing; if its mysteries are brought prominently forward,
they are apt to mingle with superstitious fears and delusions;
if its duties alone are commented on, the doubting and ignorant may be left unsatisfied ; if preaching is the vehicle, the
attention may be fatigued and exhausted ; if prayer, the sentiments may be strongly affected. These suppositions are
all obviously founded upon the injudicious use of such an
agent. Men are surely to be found with discretion sufficient
to avoid the extremes here indicated, and to select these really
catholic truths upon which men of all sects and shades of
opinion, and even men of all degrees of intellectual enlight-
enment and moral excitement, may agree, and from which
the insane as well as the sane may derive comfort. Prayer
and praise certainly appear to be the least susceptible of
abuse. They are placed by their nature beyond the control
of the pastor. Either as if dubious how far even an educated
mind can be trusted in dealing with these for the behoof of
lunatics, or in the spirit of their peculiar views, the philosophical and humane governors of the Retreat at York, have
confined the religious service performed there to the reading
of certain portions of Scripture. But that, under proper
management, this department of mental medicine may be
carried much farther, is proved by the statements contained
in the Annual Reports of various asylums. " When they do
attend," says Mr. Ricketts, " they are attentive generally,
and well conducted; so much so, that I have known when
a paroxysm was likely to come on ; five or six minutes before
prayers, the patient has been brought in, and he has had such
command over himself, that the paroxysm has been checked."*   " It was only about the beginning of 1833," I quote
now the experience of the medical officers of the Dundee

* Minutes of Evidence taken before the Select Committee, &c.
1828, p. 45.

Asylum on the subject, "that a regular chaplain was appointed ; and who ever has witnessed the preparation made by the patients for their appearance at chapel—the solemn demeanour and strict decorum observed during the whole of the service—the close attention paid to the words of the preacher—and one of the patients occasionally officiating as precentor with becoming propriety and tasteful execution—will contemplate the picture with feelings of the deepest interest, and fondly hope that the swelling notes that delight the ear have proceeded from lips which God has touched : and the words listened to with such attention, have been embraced by those whose heart has felt the power of divine truth." " No class is excluded : and though there must necessarily be some whose state of health does not admit of attendance, and some who are without the inclination—and, in this case compulsion is out of the question—yet upwards of three-fourths of the whole number regularly assemble in chapel ; and it is found that, in regard to those whose temper is the most restless, and who are the most easily excited, the solemn nature of the religious service has a wonderful effect in subduing their irritation, in calming their minds and composing their spirits, not only during the time of the service, but during the remaining hours of the day of rest."*
The following is the result of my own observations :—" The effects in each individual are probably as different as in the members of an ordinary congregation, but the general impression produced is that of reverence and order. In whatever spirit the simple truths announced to them may be received, the meeting is almost invariably distinguished by perfect decorum and propriety. The stocking and book are laid aside —the involuntary and incoherent exclamation is no longer uttered, or subdued into a whisper, and one of those who usually spurns the authority and rejects the entreaties of

* Fourteenth Report of the Directors of the Dundee Lunatic Asylum, 1834, p. 7.

those around, kneels calmly and reverently down as if perfectly conscious of the majesty of the Being whom her more rational companions are uniting to worship. Where convalescence has advanced to a certain stage, or where observation has shown that a patient is trust-worthy, permission is given to attend church, of course under proper superintendence. This is done partly that the idea of imprisonment may be eradicated, partly that reunion with society may be gradual, but chiefly that the mind may be strongly directed to those principles and duties, a knowledge of which renders mental exertion and the cultivation of internal peace and harmony alike an obligation, a reward, and a blessing. No violation of the promises given previous to the grant of such permission as to the deportment and return has occurred. One individual, after a seclusion of *thirteen* years, during which she had never been permitted to go to church, was deeply affected, and wept on again joining in the service, but otherwise her behaviour was irreproachable. It would have been extraordinary and unnatural had no feeling been manifested, and this conduct was accordingly regarded rather as an indication of sound mind than of alienation."* The practice of allowing patients to attend the parish church has, I perceive, been adopted in other places. "Prayers," says Mr. Ricketts," are read in my establishment every Sunday, to every patient capable of receiving religious instruction. The convalescents go to church ; some of the highest classes with my own family." " But in other cases," is the statement of Dr. Finch, " I have been so convinced of the utility of religious services, that many of my patients go regularly to the village church, &c."†

* Report of the Directors of the Montrose Lunatic Asylum, &c. 1835, p. 16.

† Minutes of Evidence, &c. 1828.   Evidence of Mr. W. H. Ricketts of Droitwitch, Worcestershire, and of Dr. W. Finch of Salisbury, pp. 42–49.

Similar efforts have been made at Sonnenstein and other places on the Continent, and have been attended with similar success. But these attempts to administer consolation by means of religious ordinances, have been pushed much farther, and the results have been supposed to be proportionally great. Patients have been permitted to participate in the sacrament of the Lord's Supper, and have been recommended to direct their thoughts constantly to the contemplation of their moral condition as the only course by which health and happiness can be secured. How far any physician is justified in countenancing such measures as these, appear to be very doubtful. The first of them presupposes, I presume, a state of convalescence in the communicant, such a state at least as admits of a clear conception of the nature of the rite and of the obligations which its celebration imposes. The great objection to which it appears open, is the excitement to which the mind is exposed by the imposing aspect and duration of the ceremony, and the mingled feelings of awe, and penitence, and hope to which it gives rise. The determination of the question whether the probable amount of good to be obtained counterbalances the certain amount of danger to be encountered, must rest in each case on the discretion and judgment of the medical adviser: for to establish a general rule on the subject would be most unphilosophical and pernicious. I am, however, inclined to think that when patients have advanced so far towards restoration as to be intrusted with such high and holy privileges, that they should not longer be detained in an asylum, but should be reinstated in society, and in the possession of rights, and the discharge of duties of an important but less exciting character. The second measure, although sanctioned by a few practical observers, is in direct opposition to every rule laid down for the regulation and tranquillization of the unhealthy mind. To occupy the attention in a sustained manner, with any powerfully affecting topic, is prejudicial; but when the object is the ultimate des-

tiny of the troubled soul itself, the disturbance, the despondency, the exultation necessarily ensuing from the particular
view taken by the unstable intellect, or waiving this position,
even the anxiety, the tumultuous struggle of hope and fear,
roused in the coolest, and strongest, and purest mind by such
a train of thought, must inevitably overthrow that equanimity which it is the aim of all rational treatment to establish ;
and create that internal conflict, and agitation, and intense
feeling which it is equally the aim of all rational treatment
to prevent or remove. Many, if not all the cases where individuals incurably lunatic have expressed apparently clear
ideas on religious subjects, and satisfaction that they had
been led to the consideration of these, have terminated
almost immediately afterwards in death, and cannot accordingly be admitted as evidence, either of the permanency or
of the remedial efficacy of the impressions produced. If
great caution ought to be exercised in dealing with the insane
mind, still greater care is required in drawing conclusions as
to the effects of such interference.

It would be foreign to my present object to delineate the
detailed application of the principles of moral treatment in a
well conducted asylum ; but it is of some importance to
point out certain fallacies which have misled the public as to
the nature of the system pursued, and give to it an appearance of empiricism which it actually does not possess. They
farther countenance the prejudice that the management of
the insane depends upon a peculiar and mysterious tact, and
is not founded upon a knowledge of human character. Thus,
for example, the idea that an unanswerable argument or piece
of pleasantry can eradicate a delusion, is altogether erroneous. The most plausible case of this kind is that of the
mechanician mentioned by Pinel. This person was haunted
by the imagination that he was one of the victims of the Revolution ; that he had been guillotined ; but the sentence
having been reversed just at the moment the execution had

been completed, the judges in order to remedy, so far as
possible, what had been done, commanded that the heads
should be replaced on the respective bodies.   In the confusion, two heads were transposed: the mechanician lost his own,
but was provided with another, which he very much disliked,
and which he attempted to prove was not his own property by
saying, " look at these teeth ; mine were exceedingly handsome, these are rotten and decayed. What a difference between
this hair and that of my own head !" He likewise imagined that he had discovered the perpetual motion, and
worked night and day in the construction of a machine on
this principle.   He often quarrelled with his companions on
the subject of his head ; and one of them being instructed
how to act, led the conversation to the miracle of St. Denis,
who, it is said, walked about with his head under his arm,
and kissed his own lips.   The mechanician maintained the
possibility of this : his opponent retorted, " madman that
thou art, how could St. Denis kiss his own head—was it
with his heels ?"   This discomfiture is said to have restored
him to reason.   But here it is quite evident, that the six
months' course of vigorous application to his business was
more instrumental in the cure than the biting repartee.
Equally undeserving of confidence is the belief in the efficacy of an acquiescence in the whim of the maniac, and the
institution of some process to remove the evil complained of,
it being acknowledged to be real.   Esquirol advises this to
be tried as a last resource.   It is especially applicable to
hypochondriacal maniacs, who imagine that they labour
under disease, are devoured by animals, &c.   The following
examples are not intended to justify the practice, but will
show to what cases it is applicable, and in what cases it has
been supposed to prove successful.   A woman suffered
from pain on the top of the head, and believed that it was
caused by an animal burrowing beneath the skin.   She was
for a time restored to sanity by an incision made in the

spot, and the pretended extraction of an earth worm. A hypochondriac who believed that he had frogs in his stomach, is said to have been cured by a purgative, and the introduction of one or two frogs in the night stool. But admitting that such instances are worthy of consideration, is it not more likely that the incision and the purgative were the remedial agents than the deception practised? But without insisting upon such a construction, the plan is objectionable from its tending to foster the delusion, by suggesting, as often happens, under somewhat similar circumstances, that although one worm had been removed, others more deeply imbedded remained behind : and in the case of the hypochondriac, that before the expulsion of his full-grown enemies they had spawned, and that his malady was renewed by their growing progeny.

Quackeries of a more marked character, and of a less innocent description, have at all periods in the history of mental medicine, obtained celebrity, shrunk from the test of experience, and ultimately been rejected. Any mode which is reputed to cure insanity instantaneously, or in the course of a few hours, may be looked upon with suspicion, when the nature of the remedy is concealed, and the mystery thus created employed as a means of enriching the discoverer. In our own country, in former times, lunatics were supposed to be cured in a single night, by sleeping in churches of great sanctity, or by a bath in particular springs. A Milanese physician cured all cases of mania in a given time, by chaining his patients in a well. The water was allowed gradually to ascend to the mouth, and when the maniac was in terror of being drowned his disease ceased. He was thus terrified into his senses. In our own country, and in our own day, a medical man has declared, that he has in his possession a remedy, which, when properly administered, will cure the most incurable maniac, and that in a few days. Mr. Lucett's method has received high sanction. In one instance he received L.200 from the Board of Treasury, for the cure of a servant of the Duke of Kent. He professes to perform the cures attributed to him—miracles they deserve to be named—by the aid of kindness, a lotion applied to the head and the secret nostrum, before alluded to. A committee of medical men was appointed to enquire into the facts of the case; and their report shows, that mitigation of symptoms, and not cure, was the amount of Mr. Lucett's success—a mitigation which is within the reach of every practitioner, if he chooses to push the exhibition of a powerful and unmanageable drug to a great extent—a mitigation which, although occasionally desirable, has not been proved to facilitate the cure of the patient, while it places his life in jeopardy. Mr. Lucett's success may be contrasted with his pretensions, as narrated by one of his patrons. "The third experiment was upon an idiot, without the powers of speech, or the use of his limbs, and blind from pressure on the optic nerve. Within seven weeks he was restored to reason, speech, sight, and the use of his limbs." The only commentary which such a relation requires, is that all other physicians would find it nearly as easy a task to imbue the dead with life, as to raise such a being as that described to intelligence.

It may be laid down as a general rule, that all mystery is foolish and hurtful. It creates a suspicion that there is something which requires to be concealed. It inspires dread —the very opposite of the feeling which it is desirable should be entertained both by the public and the patients. It is allied to quackery, as founded upon the pretence of superior or secret knowledge, or upon the existence of proceedings, the nature of which it would be unsafe or imprudent to disclose. For a long period English practitioners arrogated to themselves the possession of some specific which enabled them to cure a greater number of lunatics than their continental rivals. This secret and all powerful remedy, in

order to bolster up their own reputation they had the selfishness and cruelty to conceal. There was in fact nothing
to reveal. Pinel exposes this compound, fraud and folly by
detailing his own benevolent views as to the moral treatment of the insane, and by proving that the boasted secret
consisted in nothing more than the judicious application of
these.

On the continent, a very powerful movement has been
made to place the treatment of lunatics upon a true basis;
and were we to believe some of our periodical writers, the
improvements already effected, infinitely exceed any thing
which has been attempted or thought of in this country.
For instance, a writer in the Medical Gazette favours the
public with the following relation and remarks: "The
French certainly carry their treatment of the insane to a far
higher pitch of refinement than we do. The idea of giving
a ball in a lunatic asylum, may startle some of our mad
doctors; but what think they of the following precedent.
On the 7th instant, May 1835, the females of Salpetrière
were treated to a grand ball. The insane ladies themselves
were entrusted with the getting up of the entertainment.
They adorned the ball-room with festoons, garlands, and
devices; and in the midst they crowned with *immortelles*,
the bust of Pinel, the liberator of the insane from the old
system of cruelty and terror. The dancing, it is said, went
off with charming effect; the students, intern and extern,
did the honours; and the festivity was kept up to an hour
sufficiently advanced to satisfy all parties, who, to do them
justice, were indefatigable in their efforts to please and to be
pleased. It should be added, that the gay scene, (which
was appointed and arranged with the most serious object)
has been generally attended with good results: it served
admirably to fix and amuse the minds of the patients; and
several who laboured under melancholia were much diverted for the time from their imaginary woes. M. Esquirol

some years ago tried this method with success ; but it is to
M. Pariset, the physician to Salpetrière, that the credit is
due of having so happily ventured on its repetition in the
present instance."*   Now, in place of this statement creating
any astonishment in the minds of those intrusted with the
care of the insane in Britain, they will experience regret and
surprise, that what they have done for the behoof of their
charges should be so little known even to their professional
brethren.   Dancing, both as a physical exercise, and as a
recreation, has been introduced, and with excellent effects,
into many well-regulated British asylums ; and to speak
from personal experience, were the foregoing account di-
vested of some of the embellishments—the festoons and
immortelles—it would very correctly describe what takes
place, and has for years taken place, once every week in the
establishment under my care.   So that while I would speak
with veneration and gratitude of all that Esquirol and
Pariset have advised or accomplished, it is but justice to
our national discernment to say, that we have already
reduced to a system what they have only tried as an experiment.   I cannot speak so decidedly as to the introduction
of dramatic representations as a means of cure.   The attempt
has been made at Charenton unsuccessfully, at Copenhagen
without injury ; but the inhabitants of this country manifest during health so little taste for such spectacles, and
depend so little upon them as sources of amusement, that it
would be injudicious to resort to them in order to arouse,
or attract, or amuse the insane, while we have so many better modes of abstraction at our disposal.

   In front of the philanthropical enterprize in favour of the
insane in France, may be placed, Drs. Falret and Voisin.
They have long studied mental disease in the best school ;
they have long cherished the desire of putting the prin-

* London Medical Gazette, May 23, 1835. p. 288.

ciples dictated by humanity and philosophy to the treatment
of the insane, to a fair and full test, and they have now embarked their whole fortune and hopes of prosperity in the
experiment. They possess a large domain of about sixty
acres, partly farm, party ornamental garden, situate in one
of the many picturesque villages in the vicinity of Paris.
From many points in their enclosure, the whole of the
surrounding country is visible, while the bustle and annoy-
ances of the metropolis are shut out. The banks of the
Seine being undulated, every walk and turn presents a new
aspect of the natural panorama. Fertility and beauty are
constantly before the eye; the luxuriance of a rich soil, the
products of human skill. Within, the resources are equally
great. The extensive grounds afford constant employment
in the open air. Detached buildings render a scientific and
rigid classification easy; spacious apartments contain all the
ordinary means of amusement, music, billiards, &c., and no
appendage of which reminds the inmate that he is mad or
not trust-worthy. In addition to these excellent arrangements, there is the constant superintendence of two humane
and enlightened physicians, the society of their families,
accommodation for the patients' friends, should their presence be deemed expedient, the active administration of
every moral agent, and the main spring of all, gentleness and
affection.

As an additional instance of the progress of sound principles in France, and as an example of what an asylum for the
upper ranks ought to be, I make the following quotation
from the valuable work of Dr. Combe on "Physiology
applied to Health and Education." "The celebrated and
benevolent Esquirol has been loud and eloquent in enforcing
regard to the feelings, and attention to the real welfare of
the insane; and in his private establishment at Ivry, near
Paris, which I had the gratification of visiting along with
him in September 1831, he exemplifies almost every prin-

ciple upon which an asylum ought to be conducted. The asylum is placed in a beautiful and airy situation, with a pleasant exposure; and its general aspect is that of an inhabited and well kept villa. Four distinct buildings, of ample size and elegant appearance, are conveniently distributed through a well laid out and ornamented park of twenty-five acres, part in garden, part in grass, and part in plantation, with neat walks bordered with flowers, running in every direction; which, it will be observed, is a very handsome provision for thirty or thirty-five patients, to which number he restricts himself. For the troublesome or excited patients, there are two neat one-story buildings, one for males, and the other for females, separate from each other, and far removed from those appropriated to the convalescent and tranquil. These one-story tenements open upon, and look into spacious grass plots, surrounded on two sides by high walls, along which covered galleries are made for shelter from the rain and sun; so that the height of the walls seems as if intended to admit of galleries being made, rather than for the purpose of preventing escape. The third side is occupied by a plain, neat, high railing, like that of Tuilleries Garden. To these plots and galleries the patients have access at pleasure; and most of them prefer coming out at the window, from which they can easily step, no restraint being visible, and nothing of the prison being apparent. This degree of harmless freedom tranquillizes them amazingly. Each room (neatly and plainly furnished) has beside it a room for a servant, each patient having one, so that ample surveillance is exercised. When a little confirmed in tranquillity, they are allowed to go out by a back door to a large ornamental walk, shrubbery and garden, with a fine view over a lower wall, apparently opening upon the public fields, but in reality perfectly retired. The attendants are more refined and gentle in their manners, and better educated, as well as naturally more humane and intelligent,

than the corresponding class of persons in this country.
Their number, intelligence, and amiable dispositions, are a
great advantage both to themselves and to the patients.
Being less exclusively confined to the society of the insane,
they have not that peculiar expression of eye, and general
appearance, which our keepers so often acquire, and which
indicate a state in some degree allied to insanity. Esquirol
says that his English visitors complain of the difficulty of getting any but coarse and ignorant men for keepers, and wonder
how he succeeds ; but the French, of all classes, are naturally more observant of the kindnesses of ordinary intercourse,
especially with their inferiors, than we are, and are habitually more tolerant of the caprices and weaknesses of others.
The different classes of society thus stand at all times in a
more favourable position than with us for acquiring an interest in each other, and for becoming friends, or, in other
words, for effecting a cure. The importance of this confidence was well illustrated by an expression of Esquirol's, in
speaking of a patient. ' At last,' he said, ' I succeeded in
gaining his confidence, and after that,' he added with a significant look, ' on va vite à la guerison.' This, of course,
must be received as a general proposition only, but it shows
the force of the principle. When tranquillity is secured, the
patient is removed to another building, and from that to a
third, each bringing him nearer and nearer to ordinary life,
till, in a third, convalescents meet, in the character of ladies
and gentlemen, at meals, music, billiards, reading, &c., along
with the family of Dr. Metivier, a nephew of Esquirol, who
resides there with his wife and children. There the patients
receive their friends, and with them make excursions to the
environs, or to go to the theatre,—or if from the provinces,
they go and see the wonders of the capital. They are thus
gradually prepared to resume their station in society, and
from being treated throughout with most considerate kindness, they become attached to the family, and cease to repine

at their temporary separation from friends and home. But
not to dwell too long on this most interesting subject, I shall
conclude at once by remarking, that it is necessary only to
see the different appearance and conduct of the patients in a
well contrived and properly regulated asylum, as contrasted
with one of an opposite character, to perceive at once how
influential active moral treatment is in promoting recovery,
and how necessary it is to devote more attention than hitherto
to this and the other conditions of health in our treatment
of the insane."*

In some parts of America, there appears to be a complete
realization of all that I have wished to inculcate as necessary
to place the lunatic in that condition which is most conducive
to his happiness and recovery. " In respect to the moral
and intellectual treatment," remark the Visiting Physicians
of the Retreat at Hartford, " the first business of the physician, on the admission of a patient, is to gain his entire
confidence. With this view he is treated with the greatest
kindness, however violent his conduct may be—is allowed
all the liberty which his case admits of, and is made to understand, if he is still capable of reflection, that so far from
having arrived at a madhouse, where he is to be confined,
he has come to a pleasant and cheerful residence, where all
kindness and attention will be shown him, and where every
means will be employed for the recovery of his health. In
case coercion and confinement become necessary, it is impressed upon his mind, that this is not done for the purpose
of punishment, but for his own safety and that of the keepers.
In no case is deception on the patient employed or allowed :

* The Principles of Physiology applied to the preservation of health,
and to the improvement of Physical and Mental Education. By Andrew Combe, M.D. Fifth Edition, pp. 425—428.

A very interesting account of this institution has just appeared in
the New Monthly Magazine. May 1837.

on the contrary, the greatest frankness, as well as kindness, forms a part of the moral treatment. His case is explained to him, and he is made to understand, as far as possible, the reasons why the treatment to which he is subjected has become necessary."[*] A plan commenced on principles so rational and benign, could not fail to effect all that is in the power of art : we accordingly find towards the conclusion of the Report, that in one year there had been admitted twenty-three recent cases, of which twenty-one recovered, a number equivalent to $91\frac{5}{10}$ per cent.

Dr. Burrows gives the following description of a justly celebrated asylum at Pirna in Saxony. To some of the arrangements, however, I entertain strong objections. "This lunatic establishment was formerly the castle of Sonnenstein, and is situated on an almost perpendicular rock, two hundred feet above the river Elbe, over which it projects. The ascent has now been rendered less abrupt; and the castle, gardens, courts, and out-buildings, have been converted into the best lunatic asylum I have seen out of England. The number of patients which it contains is about 120, and twenty more in the private house of Dr. Pienetz, the head physician. We first visited a court-yard, where numbers of patients were employed in sawing and chopping wood, others drawing water from a deep well, and in fact all were occupied. The bath-room is of a good size, containing eight metal baths, in which the patient may be fixed if necessary. There is an excellent apparatus for directing a powerful stream of water upon any part of the bath-room. In an adjoining room is the bath of surprise. Here the patient is seated in a metal slipper bath, sunk in the ground, the attendant then comes to a window about fourteen feet above the patient, and throws a large bucketfull of water upon the head. This is often made use of both as a remedy and as a

* Hall's Travels in North America, vol. ii. p. 195.

punishment, and the patients complain of pain as if the lateral lobes of the cerebrum were split asunder. We next went into a large billiard room, to which the patients have constant access of an evening, especially during winter. The evening winter-room is extremely well-fitted up with pianofortes, violins, flutes, three or four backgammon and draftboards, and a very good book-case, which is at all times open to the patients. They are allowed to remain here until ten o'clock, and music and these games are encouraged as much as possible. The patients, in respect to their living, are divided into three classes, according to the money that is paid for their maintenance. The first class have two small rooms for two patients, with one attendant, and they eat their meals separate from the others. The second class have also two rooms for two patients, with one attendant, but their accommodations and fare are not so good. The third class dine together, and are six, seven, or eight in one room. There is a Protestant church and clergyman in the building, and they find that the most noisy patients are quiet during divine service. The women's house is quite separate from the men's, and is conducted upon the same plan. The gardens around the building are immense, and are almost entirely cultivated by the patients. There are various summer amusements in the gardens. Separate from these houses is a new house, calculated for sixteen patients and the clergyman, situated upon a beautiful slope, with an excellent garden, and most delightful prospects. This is the convalescent house, and here the ladies and gentlemen dine with the clergyman altogether. They are allowed to take walks in the environs, and divert themselves as they please."*

It is here stated that books are placed within the reach of the patients. Dr. Abercrombie recommends a regular course of historical reading as a part of the moral discipline in cer-

---

* Burrow's Commentaries, pp. 528, 529.

tain species of derangement.* I am inclined to think that a course of reading of any kind adapted to the powers, previous tastes and acquirements regularly pursued, will prove beneficial. But it is not enough that there should be a well selected and easily accessible library in an asylum ; nor that books, and maps, and attractive drawings be placed before the convalescent patient; there must be inducements to read and examine. And these must be suggested and supplied, principally by a study of the dispositions of those whom it is our object to interest. We may inflict punishment where it is our wish to communicate pleasure, by condemning a man who abhors fiction to the perusal of the last new novel ; and disgust for every description of reading may be inspired by the injudicious choice of such works as offend a prejudice or reanimate a delusion. Religious authors are most frequently resorted to. No error can be more natural or more pernicious. It is a noble and beautiful conception that the reinvigorated mind should turn in adoration and gratitude to the power from whence these new-born energies have been derived ; but the effort often proves fatal to the worshipper by whom it is made. The attempt is akin to that which is made by the weak, worn-out, partially restored victim of bodily disease to try his strength, that is, to task his nerves and muscles, as if they were endowed with their original power and activity, and no longer predisposed to lapse into that condition from which they have so recently recovered. The general practice is alone condemned. For that cases every day occur where it is not only safe but expedient, that religious impressions should be encouraged by reading as well as by preaching, is as evident as that in a country where so large a number of persons become insane, either from the inherent intensity, or the cultivation of religious feelings, or, rendered insane by some other cause, are affected with reli-

---

* Inquiries concerning the Intellectual Powers, &c. p. 355.

gious mania, it would be eminently hazardous to place works on religious subjects within the reach of all those who have scarcely yet ceased to be lunatics. But not only are such works objectionable because they are religious, but because, in common with every matter which is of great importance, and involves our interest and happiness, they are powerfully exciting. When the lungs, or heart, or stomach, have been diseased, we avoid stimuli, whether they are ardent spirits or violent passions, whether they affect the weakened part merely, or the whole system. The brain is not exempt from the necessity of this precaution. And the instances must be extremely rare in which fears or intense desires can be made instruments of cure. Indeed, the selection of books, as every other arrangement for the behoof of the insane, should be regulated by the maxim, dictated as evidently by prudence as by philosophy, that the mind should be led back to its original and healthy condition, by appealing to those powers, the exercise of which is attended with the least possible degree of excitement.

The most recent accounts of the Italian asylums which have reached this country, are contained in Willis' "Pencillings by the Way." This author has been said to eulogize where he ought to describe, and to give hyperbole, where statistics are required. There are, it is true, some men of so happy a temperament, as to see every thing as through a kaleidoscope. The most trivial and hideous objects arrange themselves to such minds in forms of beauty and novelty, and the medium by means of which the images are created is forgotten. But so far as the very interesting picture of the visit to the asylum is concerned, this remark does not apply to it. It bears truth and fidelity in every line, and although the announcement, that in Naples exist "two of the best conducted asylums in the world," may startle those who are accustomed to look upon the distant south as the land of

sunshine and mental darkness: this opinion is fully borne
out by the facts adduced. When we are informed, that
" the secret of his, the governor's, whole system, was employment and constant kindness," we can readily credit all the
marvels which ensue.   An eccentric old nobleman is the
wizard who performed these, or, as he is pleased to style
himself, " the first fool."   In moving through a kitchen
where culinary preparations, extensive enough to occupy
eight or ten people, are going on, and on encountering
peaceful and cheerful individuals engaged in painting or
reading, it is with considerable difficulty that Mr. Willis
could be convinced that they were all mad.   And his
scepticism must have been still more excited, when he inspected curiously paved courts ornamented with Chinese
grottoes, trees, artificial rocks, &c., the walls painted as the
perspective of such a scene, with fountains gushing up in
the centre, the whole opening upon a large and lovely garden,
and is told that every thing around is the work of the
patients.   The great charm, the spell which gives the colouring of happiness to the whole community is, that its members
are ruled by love, that their sympathies, and not their fears,
are employed as the ground work of subordination and cure.
Several exacerbations of fury took place during Mr. Willis'
visit : they were all, save one, hushed, and tranquillity
immediately restored by the voice of kind expostulation or
commiseration.   In the stubborn case, which occurred in a
female,—and I may mention, that the governor has arrived
at the conclusion, that his most rebellious subjects are
females, a swing in a hammock was prescribed with the
desired effect.   Had punishment or restraint been substituted,
the paroxysm would in all probability have been exasper-
ated, and continued until sleep or exhaustion soothed the
passion or obliterated the insult.   This system has been
suitably rewarded.   Two thirds of the patients are stated

2

to be discharged cured.   This proposition refers, I presume, although the information is not supplied, to the recent cases. If it does not, it is the most signal success on record.

In place of multiplying individual examples of excellence, let me conclude by describing the aspect of an asylum as it ought to be.   Conceive a spacious building resembling the palace of a peer, airy, and elevated, and elegant, surrounded by extensive and swelling grounds and gardens.   The interior is fitted up with galleries, and workshops, and music-rooms.   The sun and the air are allowed to enter at every window, the view of the shrubberies and fields, and groups of labourers, is unobstructed by shutters or bars ; all is clean, quiet, and attractive.   The inmates all seem to be actuated by the common impulse of enjoyment, all are busy, and delighted by being so.   The house and all around appears a hive of industry.   When you pass the lodge, it is as if you had entered the precincts of some vast emporium of manufacture ; labour is divided, so that it may be easy and well performed, and so apportioned, that it may suit the tastes and powers of each labourer.   You meet the gardener, the common agriculturist, the mower, the weeder, all intent on their several occupations, and loud in their merriment.   The flowers are tended, and trained, and watered by one, the humbler task of preparing the vegetables for table, is committed to another.   Some of the inhabitants act as domestic servants, some as artizans, some rise to the rank of overseers. The bakehouse, the laundry, the kitchen, are all well supplied with indefatigable workers.   In one part of the edifice are companies of straw-plaiters, basket-makers, knitters, spinners, among the women; in another, weavers, tailors, saddlers, and shoemakers, among the men.   For those who are ignorant of these gentle crafts, but are strong and steady, there are loads to carry, water to draw, wood to cut, and for those who are both ignorant and weakly, there is oakum to tease and yarn to wind.   The curious thing is, that all

M

are anxious to be engaged, toil incessantly, and in general
without any other recompense than being kept from disagreeable thoughts and the pains of illness. They literally
work in order to please themselves, and having once experienced the possibility of doing this, and of earning peace,
self-applause, and the approbation of all around, sound sleep,
and it may be some small remuneration, a difficulty is found
in restraining their eagerness, and moderating their exertions.
There is in this community no compulsion, no chains, no
whips, no corporal chastisement, simply because these are
proved to be less effectual means of carrying any point than
persuasion, emulation, and the desire of obtaining gratification. But there are gradations of employment. You may
visit rooms where there are ladies reading, or at the harp or
piano, or flowering muslin, or engaged in some of those thousand ornamental productions in which female taste and ingenuity are displayed. You will encounter them going to church
or to market, or returning from walking, riding, and driving
in the country. You will see them ministering at the bed-
side of some sick companion. Another wing contains those
gentlemen who can engage in intellectual pursuits, or in the
amusements and accomplishments of the station to which
they belong. The billiard-room will, in all probability,
present an animated scene. Adjoining apartments are used
as news-rooms, the politicians will be there. You will pass
those who are fond of reading, drawing, music, scattered
through handsome suits of rooms, furnished chastely, but
beautifully, and looking down upon such fair and fertile
scenes as harmonize with the tranquillity which reigns within,
and tend to conjure up images of beauty and serenity in the
mind which are akin to happiness. But these persons have
pursuits, their time is not wholly occupied in the agreeable
trifling of conning a debate, or gaining so many points.
One acts as an amanuensis, another is engaged in landscape
painting, a third devolves to himself a course of historical
l

reading, and submits to examination on the subject of his studies, a fourth seeks consolation from binding the books which he does not read.*   In short, all are so busy as to overlook, or all are so contented as to forget their misery.

Such is a faithful picture of what may be seen in many institutions, and of what might be seen in all, were asylums conducted as they ought to be.

* To exemplify the various modes of engaging the attention of lunatics, it may be mentioned that the manuscripts of these pages were transcribed, and the proofs corrected by individuals in the asylum under my charge.

Edinburgh : Balfour & Jack, Printers, Niddry Street.

INDEX.

N